,00

D0045042

WITHDRAWN

Also by Cristina Rathbone

On the Outside Looking In:
A Year in an Inner-City High School

A World
Apart

Random House • New York

A World

Women, Prison, and Life Behind Bars

Apart

Cristina Rathbone

There are no composite characters in this book. For the sake of the women's privacy, and that of their families, all inmates' names and some personal characteristics have been changed—except those of women who took their lives in prison and whose deaths are a matter of public record. I also changed the names of all correctional officers—save two whose names are also part of the public record. In order to remind readers of this, I refer to the COs simply with initials. It should be noted, however, that these initials do not represent real names. Any resemblance to any persons, living or dead, resulting from these changes is entirely coincidental.

Copyright © 2005 by Cristina Rathbone

All rights reserved.

Published in the United States by Random House, an imprint of
The Random House Publishing Group, a division of Random House, Inc.,
New York.

RANDOM HOUSE and colophon are registered trademarks of
Random House, Inc.

Grateful acknowledgment is made to the following for permission to reprint
previously published material:

Boston Herald: Excerpt from "Records Reveal Light Sentencing" by Karen E.
Crummy from the January 12, 2001, edition of the *Boston Herald.* Reprinted with
permission of the *Boston Herald.*

New Directions Publishing Corporation: Excerpt from "To a Poor Old Woman" by
William Carlos Williams, from *Collected Poems: 1909–1939, Volume 1,* copyright
© 1938 by New Directions Publishing Corp. Reprinted by permission of New
Directions Publishing Corp.

Perseus Books Group: Excerpt from *The Leaf and the Cloud: A Poem* by Mary Oliver,
copyright © 2000 by Mary Oliver, published by Da Capo Press. Reprinted by
permission of Perseus Books Group.

Library of Congress Cataloging-in-Publication Data

Rathbone, Cristina.
A world apart: women, prison, and life behind bars / Cristina Rathbone.
p.   cm.
ISBN 1-4000-6166-0
1. Women prisoners—Massachusetts.   2. Reformatories for women—
Massachusetts.   3. MCI-Framingham (Correctional facility)
I. Title: A world apart.   II. Title: Women, prison, and life behind bars.
III. Title.
HV9475.M42M357 2005
365'.43'097444—dc22   2004058378

Printed in the United States of America on acid-free paper

Random House website address: www.atrandom.com

987654321

First U.S. Edition

Book design by Mercedes Everett

For Jack and Lucas

(the greatest boys in the world)

(Oh heart, I would not dangle you down into
    the sorry places,
but there are things there as well
    to see, to imagine.)
                    —Mary Oliver, *The Leaf and the Cloud*

Prologue

It's important that you know this: except for the visiting room, which I still go to occasionally, I have seen little of the prison I write about in this book. Despite nearly five years of research, two successful lawsuits, and countless trips to court, the Massachusetts Department of Correction continues to deny me access.

My long fight for access to MCI-Framingham began in January 2000. I felt hopeful about my chances back then. The department's book of regulations acknowledged that "conditions in a state correctional institution are a matter of interest to the general public." It further stated that "the department has a proactive posture when communicating with the news media" and listed only five conditions under which media access to its facilities could be denied—none of which applied to my case.

In the end, however, the DOC came up with a reason entirely unrelated to those published in its book of regulations. After months of consideration, it concluded that my work might upset the victims of the women I write about, and it was on these grounds that they finally denied access. Perhaps because the state had long been under a court order for failing to take care of even the most basic of crime victims' rights, the sudden concern was hard to take seriously. Nonetheless, its position stood. This project had effectively been killed.

Almost every major periodical in the country has had to shelve prison stories because access was denied. Despite attempts by press organizations to rally against such restrictions, the trend to exclude media from prisons continues to grow apace with the system itself. In 1998, for example, California, which has the nation's third-largest prison system, banned all face-to-face interviews with, as well as confidential correspondence to, every inmate in its system. Arizona followed suit. Pennsylvania maintains a blanket ban on all news-media contact with inmates, as does South Carolina, whose regulations state that "news media interviews with any inmate . . . will be strictly prohibited." Alaska insists on officials monitoring interviews. Connecticut instructs journalists to include in their requests "a statement of any perceived benefit to law enforcement agencies," and Mississippi states that consideration will be given only to media requests to develop stories "portraying rehabilitative efforts."

Most states are less severe in their restrictions, at least on paper. Alabama, North Carolina, Indiana, Kansas, Louisiana, Nevada, and Massachusetts all officially allow media access to their prisons as long as interviews pose no threat to security. But this often means little in practice. Idaho's written policy, for example, allows interviews in all of its facilities, but the state's corrections director did not approve a single interview request for five years. As he told a reporter: "We look for compelling reasons why the interview should take place. How will the interview benefit the department?"

The same is true for Massachusetts. Despite an annual budget of close to $860 million, its Department of Correction operates with an almost complete lack of oversight and a level of fiscal opacity that would be unacceptable in any other government agency. On matters of policy, the commissioner of corrections (herself a political appointee) answers only to the governor. There are currently no legislative checks to discourage the abuses of power that such a closed system can so readily promote.

Even the Department of Correction has to operate within the law, however, and when the American Civil Liberties Union concluded that its grounds for denying me access were unconstitutional, another avenue of approach opened up. With their help, and that of an energetic young partner at one of Boston's leading corporate law firms who did the work pro bono, I brought suit. Ten minutes before the case was due to be heard, and a full nine months after I had first requested access, the Department of Correction finally reversed its decision. On paper at least, it gave me the access I had been asking for: the ability to meet with any woman at MCI-Framingham who agreed to meet with me.

Another month passed, however, before I was actually able to enter the visiting room at MCI-Framingham. To begin with, the DOC insisted I sign a gag order surrendering my rights to write or even speak about the case. When it lost that legal skirmish, it used administrative procedure to delay my entry. For the first couple of months, correctional officers routinely kept me waiting for hours before allowing me into the visiting room. Sometimes they wouldn't let me in at all, citing failure on my part to provide this or that piece of previously unnecessary paperwork. The first few times I went in, they selected me for a "random" full-body pat-down. And though for the most part they seemed finally to come to terms with my being around, a year later I found myself back in court suing for access to a mother-child program at the prison.

I had understood, by then, that people at the DOC were determined to do all they could to keep me from discovering the worst of their practices. I was surprised, however, by the vehemence with which they tried to keep me from seeing even this most shining example of success. The Girl Scouts Beyond Bars program was small, tiny if you looked at it statistically, but it was uniquely successful at maintaining relationships between incarcerated mothers and their daughters. Such relationships have been proven not only to help the child but to reduce the risk of the mother returning to prison after being released. Yet the DOC seemed determined to keep me away. This time it didn't back down from the lawsuit. Before the case was finally resolved, it had wound its way through the courtrooms of three consecutive superior court judges.

The book that follows could not have been written without the legal victories that ensued. But the DOC didn't lose out entirely either. The constraints of the prison system, as well as those placed on a journalist attempting to write about what she herself has never seen, have taken their toll. Even after four and a half years, my view of prison life remains circumscribed. There can be no omniscient view.

Most journalists respond to these restrictions by forcing their way in only when confronted with extreme examples of abuse. Scandalous revelation, however, though necessary and morally just, tends to reduce those involved to their roles in the particular scandal revealed. I have tried here to do the reverse: to render the lives of women in prison as fully and humanly as possible—with all their varied, often maddening complexities intact. There is horror in prison for sure, but there is also humor and vigor and downright bloody-mindedness—just as there is every place human beings gather. Ironically, this life stuff is, in the end, precisely what the DOC's posture toward the media prevents you from seeing.

Contents

PART

BEGINNINGS

ONE

FLOSS

FLUFFY WAS A surprise. An aging seventies throwback with piles of teased blond hair and too much makeup, she was older than Denise Russell, past her prime perhaps, and sad, but not frightening, not threatening at all. Denise had never been in prison before. Thirty-two years old, with long dark hair, high cheekbones, and the kind of body that only rigorous exercise can maintain, she'd expected to be confronted by the kind of crazed and violent criminals she had always seen portrayed on TV. But Fluffy had been helpful when Denise first moved into her cell. Motherly almost. She had explained, if in a sometimes showy, desperate way, how Denise should store her papers and valuable canteen snacks in the lockable one-foot cubby, and how to climb up onto the top bunk by straddling the pull-out chair and then leaping onto the corner of their shared metal desk. Originally designed for one, the ninety-square-foot cells had long served as doubles. There wasn't enough room for a ladder.

Every once in a while Fluffy did manage to startle Denise with a sudden burst of frantic exuberance. She sang hippie love tunes off-key and belly-danced around their cell and out onto the unit itself, down the corridor to the officer's glass-walled office, or "bubble" as it was known, and around the airless dayroom. Most of Fluffy's time, though, was spent lying around on her bunk, watching soap operas and dreaming of her triumphant return to Han Lan's, the divey Chinese restaurant where she'd ruled the roost before being sent away on a three-year mandatory for drugs. Her stories about the place were long and often dull, but as long as Denise indulged them the two managed to share their cell with relative ease. Fluffy was kind, that was the thing. Open-hearted. Denise had known women like her all her life.

LIFE IN A women's prison was full of surprises like this. Not that MCI-Framingham was a pleasant place to be. The housing units were crowded, dark, and noisy, and the aimless vacuum of daily life there often made you want to curl into yourself on your thin little bunk up close to the ceiling and cry. But it was nothing, *nothing* like Denise thought it would be. There were the locks, of course—including, most impressively, the one to her own cell—to which she would never hold a key. And there were the guards and continually blaring intercoms, which controlled the smallest minutiae of her everyday life. There were full, bend-over-and-cough strip searches both before and after a visit, and random urine checks, and cell searches, called raids, which left her prison-approved personal items (mostly letters and drawings from her son, Patrick) scattered all over the floor. She'd heard there were punishment cells too. Dismal, solitary cages with nothing but a concrete bed and a seatless toilet, to which women sometimes disappeared for months.

Despite all this, Framingham seemed more like a high school than a prison. Some of the guards were rougher than teachers would ever be, of course. Dressed in quasi-military uniforms and calf-length black leather boots, a few also flaunted their power, making irrational demands simply because they could. For the most part, though, Denise found it easy to keep out of their way. No, it was the inmates, not the guards, who reminded her of her days at Wecausset High—as did the unfamiliar experience of being with so many women. Framingham girls were older, and so lacked the freshness that graced even the plainest girls back at Wecausset. They were tougher too. Some had scars stretching across cheeks, jagging up from lips, or curved around their necks. Others, when they smiled, revealed the telltale toothlessness of crack addiction. But the overwhelming majority were mothers, as well, their walls decorated not, as she'd imagined, with images of muscle-bound men but with photos of their kids and sheets of construction paper scrawled over with crayon—valentines and birthday and Christmas cards saved year after year.

There were some unsavory types, and a smattering of women who seemed plausibly threatening. But even the handful in for murder looked more defeated than frightening. Most were long-term victims of domestic abuse who had killed their spouses, and though one or two of them did have an unnerving deadness to their eyes, they pretty much kept to themselves. Lifers, like everyone else at Framingham, were a cliquey lot, by turns supportive and undermining in the manner of, well, high school girls. As a group, they sat firmly at the top of the hierarchy—no matter how meek they appeared, they were, after all, in for murder—while the real social maneuvering took place in an ever-shifting universe of less powerful cliques beneath them.

There were the popular girls, who tended to be prettier than the rest and confidently rule-abiding at Framingham; the repeat offenders; the "intellectual" college crowd; the rabble-rousers; the hard workers; the butches; the femmes; and the group of untouchables—baby beaters mostly—whom nobody wanted anything much to do with. Most of these groups were self-segregated along racial lines, but those in parallel ranks often intermingled. Popular black women like Charlene

Williams, a mother serving fifteen years for her first (nonviolent) drug offense, spent a lot of time with Marsha Pigett, a striking redhead and longtime victim of domestic abuse who was also in for drugs and who pretty much ran, for a time, the popular white set. The language barrier often made things more difficult for what everyone called "the Spanish women," but they too were measured and graded and sorted into type, and a handful of Dominicans, Central Americans, and, separately, Puerto Ricans shared the ability to break free from stereotype and mix it up with the in crowd.

At first, none of this was clear to Denise. For months she could not tell the difference between a potential ally and a troublemaker when they stood next to her in line for meals, or for count, or for what they called "movement," which were the only times in the day inmates were allowed to walk from one area of the prison to another. Besides, she wasn't that interested. She didn't belong there, she still believed. It was just as good to subsist quietly in the small shadow cast by Fluffy and to cradle there as much of her old life as possible.

But roommates are just one of the myriad things over which inmates have no control. While violence is the main concern in a male prison, at Framingham it is the creation of intimacy that most worries the authorities. For this reason, the population is kept fluid. Women are not allowed, officially, to hold the same job for more than six months, and roommates are routinely moved around.

So it was that one day Fluffy was gone, replaced by an elderly, drug-addled woman, the kind who steals extra chicken from the dining hall by hiding it in her bra, and who then pulls it out sometime later in the day to eat in her cell. Her name was Sonia, and like so many women in Framingham, she was a heroin addict serving time for drugs. Sonia's age made her seem more damaged than most—she was old and worn both inside and out. Denise tried hard to be nice at first, leaping to her feet to help like the obedient grandchild she had, in fact, always been. But after a couple of weeks Sonia's fragility began to wear her down and the reality of her own powerlessness in prison began, at last, to congeal.

IT HAD TAKEN a surprisingly long time for this to happen. The first few weeks had been terrible, of course, frightening and degrading and completely unnerving. "Just try to imagine it," she told me. "Everything was gone. My son, my home, my family, my car, my friends, my cigarettes, my alcohol, my drugs, my clothes, my makeup, my dishes, my paintings, my socks, my glasses, my bills, my *life*—not to mention my dignity and my self-esteem (which wasn't much anyways) . . . everything."

She could see, however, that in a way the shock and anxiety of it all had protected her back then too. One minute she'd been at home, packing her son Pat's brand-new Nintendo and his smart new clothes into the case he'd bring with him to her mother-in-law's house, the next she was inmate number F24447, being stripped naked, checked for STDs, and asked if she felt depressed by someone in a uniform on the other side of a desk. This last question seemed the cruelest of all because it wasn't as if she cared, the nurse or whoever she was. She didn't even look up from the checklist in front of her when she asked. And how was Denise supposed to feel anyway, facing five years and a day in this place?

She cried all night, every night, that first week. She didn't know, yet, how expensive collect-call rates were from prison, so she spent hours on the phone with her mother and her son, and endlessly marched around the yard, the headphones of her prison-bought Walkman tuned to heavy metal because she knew enough, even then, to stay away from anything in the least bit emotional. It only made her cry.

Then, two weeks after she'd arrived in August, just as her fixed

daily routine had begun to numb her, three correctional officers unlocked the door to her room in the middle of the night. "Denise Russell? Denise Russell?" they asked, shining their flashlights in her face, so
that even before she was fully awake, she knew something terrible had
happened.

Silently the officers escorted her down linoleum-tiled corridors
and through clanking metal doors to the Health Services Unit. There a
nurse asked her to sit down, then told her that her son had just threatened to kill himself. He'd walked into her mother-in-law's living room
with a knife, she said. They needed her permission to have him admitted to a psychiatric hospital.

Pat was her little just-nine-year-old boy, and right then he was in
the admitting room of a state-run psychiatric hospital up in Maine
someplace, while she, his mother, was in the Health Services Unit of
MCI-Framingham, flanked by guards, and hundreds of miles away.
Someone passed her a phone, and she found herself speaking to a
nurse up in Maine who tried to assure her that Pat would be well taken
care of. Denise felt that she had no choice. She gave her permission for
him to be admitted, handed the receiver back to the prison nurse, who
had a few words with her counterpart in Maine, and then hung it back
in its cradle. After that there was nothing to do. It was hard to fully con-
ceive of, but there was nothing in the world Denise could do then to
help her son. She felt like throwing up.

Time slowed after that. She no longer marched around the yard—
even that much activity threw her impotence into glaring relief. Sometimes she held her breath. She called her mother. She called her father.
Then she called her mother again, over and over, because it was a terrible place where they had Pat, she was discovering. The prison wouldn't
let her visit, of course, but they did allow her to call once a week, and
Pat almost always came to the phone sobbing. He missed her. That was

all, he said. And he worried about her and he'd even tried to come and find her, but they put him in restraints when he did that—in four-point restraints, he said.

The messages she got from her own parents didn't help. Her mother went to visit and came back horrified; her father told her he thought it looked like a fine place. Neither was able to take Patrick in. They had both remarried and had their own lives to lead. Patrick's father, Alan, was willing to have him, but Denise couldn't even begin to think about the consequences of that. Alan was a lunatic—a self-styled Christian with a history of violence and manic depression. And besides, he'd moved to Hawaii the year before, and Denise would lose all contact with Patrick if he moved out there.

She took the pills that Psychiatric Services had prescribed and tried to sleep. But she'd known something like this would happen, that was the thing. She'd done her best to avert it. She'd set up her mother-in-law's house as best she could with a TV, a VCR, and a brand-new Super Nintendo she'd bought for Pat with some of the proceeds of the furniture sale she'd held before "going away." She'd even arranged his Beanie Baby collection, creature by creature, so he'd feel more or less at home in his new room. But what, really, could she do to make up for her sudden and disastrous absence? Pat was nine. His mother was in prison. His father was in Hawaii. He was, suddenly, unprotected. She took more pills.

THIS WAS THE nature of life in prison, Denise knew now, having to shut down whole parts of yourself, to compartmentalize. Over 60 percent of the women at Framingham were on some kind of psychotropic drug to help with this process. And though this internal division of the self into a series of solitary, isolated cells seemed like a further incarceration, it was, for some, the only way they could begin to tolerate their complete impotence in the world.

Most, it has to be said, had spent their lives reaching for medication at the first sign of discomfort. Across the nation more than nine out of ten incarcerated women are drug addicts, and a full half are actually drunk or high at the time of their arrest. The addicts in Framingham divide into two main camps, the crackheads and the smackheads, and there is very little difference in the way they detox in prison. Unless you're pregnant, when the stress to the baby is deemed too dangerous, you go cold turkey. Framingham has two entire wards for women who come in high. Each year, nine hundred women use these twenty-nine beds to get clean. The rooms reek of the vomit and the green liquid feces they release in all-night convulsions, along with the last traces of drugs from their bodies. Residence in these wards is so dreaded, in fact, that women in the know do everything they can to avoid being placed in them, and there are often one or two inmates in the mainstream residential units detoxing on their own. Sometimes there are illegal drugs in Framingham too, but very rarely, nowhere near enough to sustain an addiction, and mostly the women are forced to make do with fermented Jell-O juice when they want to get high. Wine, they called it. Jell-O wine.

FOR THE FIRST few weeks Denise allowed herself to believe that the outside world was still her realm. Frantic in confinement, she somehow managed to stand for inmate count four times a day, to march through corridors at the appointed times for breakfast, lunch, and dinner, and to sit down quietly on her bed as she was locked into her room every night. But somewhere deep down, she persisted in believing that this mindlessly repetitive and passive routine was only some kind of dream, or mistake, or bizarre experiment even, that would end soon, prompting everyone to step out of their roles and smile, perhaps just a little bit abashed by all they had subjected her to, before sending her on her way.

How could all the accumulated weight of adult life, the rent and the food-on-the-table, the work, the men—fending them off while keeping them keen—and the bills, mostly the bills, how could all that so suddenly disappear? Denise was the first to admit that she hadn't been your typical Suzy Homemaker, of course. She'd been a crack addict, for a start, a relatively functioning, suburban one, unlike many of the women in Framingham who'd spent years living on the streets of Boston and Worcester, but a crack addict nonetheless. When she finally left Alan, she'd become a stripper too.

It hadn't been an ideal life. No one's in prison had. But she'd learned to enjoy dancing. Had been proud of the independence four hundred dollars a day so instantly brought her—the car she'd bought and the new furniture for the apartment she and Pat shared. She'd done okay by him, overall. Kept him fed and clothed and well taken care of the way a mother should. And now, suddenly, here she was, a child again herself, being fed huge, unappetizing meals three times a day, and locked into what she'd quickly learned to call her room, never her cell, at nine o'clock every night with nothing more pressing to do than watch bad TV, or stare, inanely, out the window.

THE PRISON SITS at the edge of town, and when it is dark out and the lights are on in the women's rooms there is no place to undress in private. There are no window coverings of any kind at Framingham. The new director of security had demanded their removal recently, and most of the women complained bitterly about this. But Denise found a measure of relief in the space the clear window provided. She could see a residential street from her bunk, houses and cars and people coming home from work. For a time she'd enjoyed letting her mind drift through all that life to thoughts of her future and memories of her past. Now that Patrick was in the hospital, though, she was increasingly interrupted from these soft-focus reveries by images so sharp that they felt almost physical. She'd see him fishing on the beach, or playing soccer, or, once, staring calmly at her from across the emergency room, covered with bruises sustained at age three, at the hands of his father.

Alan had been abusive for years by then, hitting Denise and throwing things and leaving her and Pat for days at a time with no money at all. But that was the first time he'd ever hit Pat. The boy had marks from Alan's hand imprinted on his neck in black and blue. Denise panicked. The bruises were identical to the ones Alan had left around her own neck when she'd first tried to leave him. She was determined to press charges, but the police persuaded her not to. She was a what? An exotic dancer? She'd be dragged through the courts herself, they told her. They'd take her son away for sure. So she took out a restraining order instead, and when Patrick's bruises finally disappeared, she put the incident out of her mind and went back to work.

She felt pretty much fine, she thought, when she started dancing again for the daytime crowd at the club where she worked. When, on her second day back, an okay-looking guy with a lot of cash came in and asked her to sit with him, she did. He bought a bottle of Mumm's for two hundred dollars, which meant a forty-dollar commission for Denise, for her "gracious company" they used to say, but this didn't cheer her the way it normally would. Even when he ordered a bottle of Dom Pérignon (a sixty-dollar commission!) her mood didn't lift. Next thing she knew, she was sitting there with this guy who called himself Bill and his half-empty bottle of Dom Pérignon, all dressed up in her thigh-length boots and her see-through black robe, sobbing. She felt terrible for that poor guy Bill—they wouldn't even give him a refund, she remembered—but there was nothing she could do to stop crying. Even after her boss yelled for her to "get over here!" and then sent her home in a cab with five hundred dollars and strict instructions not to come back for a week, she couldn't calm down. All she could think about was Pat (and Alan—she would never be free of him!).

Denise was usually good at controlling her emotions. But she had never felt so sad and angry and upset as she did those days after Alan first turned on Patrick. She wanted to die. There was nothing vague or hazy about the desire. She longed to stop existing, to disappear. Back in her apartment, she locked herself in her bedroom, sobbing. Pat grew scared and started banging on her door—all two and a half feet of him screaming and pushing and kicking. When she finally opened it he came rushing over to her, getting in her face with tissues and worry and questions until she screamed at him—my God, it was hard, remembering this—screamed at him really loud: "Get away! I hate you!" She would never forget the look on his face. Her three-year-old boy, beautiful and innocent and so hurt already, crumpling then into silence.

Denise didn't sleep on nights like that. Even with the pills. Like most mothers at Framingham, she hadn't seen her son once since coming to prison. Even if he weren't locked up in the hospital, his grandmother would have found it impossible to make the long trek down to the prison from Maine. Surprisingly, though, she'd almost grown used to his physical absence. It was the spectral visitations she couldn't handle, the memories. Night after night she'd force herself to stare out the window and see them (Pat running to her, laughing. Pat helping cut coupons. Pat losing it in the kitchen when Denise told him she'd be going away) until she began to suspect that torturing herself like this was foolish and masochistic, even selfish in a way.

BY THE MIDDLE of November, three months after she first arrived at Framingham, it seemed clear that Patrick would move out to Hawaii to live with his father. His insurance had run out, so the hospital couldn't keep him, and Denise's parents continued to insist that they couldn't take him in. This left Alan or foster care, and from what everyone told Denise, anything was better than the foster-care system. At least Alan was family. And he'd been in a program, she kept telling herself. He was involved with the church again too, and he must be working because he had his own apartment, apparently, in a fancy condo complex called Gentle Bay. It was still tempting to dwell on the dangers that might lurk for Patrick there: on Alan's mood swings, his drinking, his obsession with paid sex. But after a while Denise began to see that it did her son no good to drive herself crazy that way. Five years of it and she'd end up embittered and enraged and even less capable of caring for Patrick than she'd been when she was high on coke and taking her clothes off for a living.

She was beginning to see, all around her, examples of what happened if you allowed these strands of your old life to get tangled into knots of rage and despair. Some women would explode in rebellion, call a CO a woman-hating faggot who couldn't make it in a men's prison, or spit at him, or throw a fit and get themselves hauled off to solitary confinement in the Hole for a week or a month or more. Others turned the pain inward and mutilated themselves with blades extracted from razors. It was an old story. And a predictable one. When all else failed, when connections with family were severed, or when parents died, or children were adopted away, there was always the visible and finite certainty of a razor's deep incursion into flesh. Wrists, arms, necks, legs. Over and over they cut themselves, until even Denise began to respond more with irritation than with sympathy: "Oh God, not again, not another interruption, another mess to clean up."

No. In order to survive in prison you had to give way to it, Denise began to see, you had to engage. The trouble was that there was so little, in prison, to engage with. College-level courses weren't available to women who didn't already have sixteen credits, which Denise didn't. She'd married before she'd even thought about college. She had graduated high school, so there was no point enrolling in GED classes. The manicuring course had a waiting list that stretched on for months, as did the computer class. There was a place available in construction arts, the prison's only other job-training program, so Denise wound up keeping her mornings busy by climbing up and down ladders with a hard hat on, hammering and painting and fixing things up. She started going to church again too. It didn't much matter which denomination—she found a measure of redemption in them all. And she spent hours reading the fashion magazines her mother sent her from home and compiling a collection of low-fat, high-nutrition recipes that she arranged in perfect alphabetical order in her room.

With the help of a check bouncer named Teresa who lived on her unit, Denise also learned how to prepare relatively wholesome, nutritionally balanced meals for herself out of ingredients available from Canteen, the prison store: tuna-and-peanut salad for protein, chicken broth for ease, anything to avoid the dining-hall meals, which consisted of rice and potatoes mostly, and were designed to subdue, she was convinced. All you had to do was look at the women who ate in the dining hall every day—at their slow, lumbering progress down the corridors, and their shortness of breath.

Later, Denise made a deal with the diabetic woman in the room next door who qualified for a special diet. For $1.80 a week—about half a weekly wage in prison—Denise gave her three Diet Cokes in exchange for her extra mini cereal box, her small carton of milk, and her piece of fresh fruit every morning. Like everyone else, she still binged every now and then, Twix bars mostly, on the days Canteen items were delivered, but with the help of the regular power-walk routine she'd established for herself in the yard, she managed to keep in pretty good shape.

Except for her teeth. There was one small rectangle of polished stainless steel in her room that served as a mirror, and when she checked her appearance there each morning she couldn't help noticing that her gums were beginning to recede. Trips to the dentist were not generally recommended, however. Like many prison employees, he was said to find women most interesting around the chest area, and dental-hygiene products were strangely unavailable at Framingham, even through Canteen.

Floss, for example, was strictly prohibited, though even after six months Denise still found it hard to discern exactly why. A kind of floss did circulate around the prison. It was made of nylon, which workers in the flag factory smuggled out for the purpose. Unlike almost every-thing else at Framingham, the smugglers gave it out, free, to anyone who wanted it. But the thread was harsh and unsanitary, and the one time Denise tried it, it had cut her gums and made them bleed. For a while she was so desperate that she thought about asking someone to smuggle some in to her through the mail, threaded through the page of a letter perhaps, or stuck in a book. But then she heard that Wendy, the upscale and rather beautiful brothel madam from Laurel Unit, had been caught, recently, doing the exact same thing and sent down to the Hole. Denise dropped the idea. The last place she ever wanted to be was the Hole.

Besides, she tried to console herself, what good was even the best kind of waxed floss when the only toothbrushes available were ridicu-lously small and so soft-bristled that they left your teeth feeling as furry and ridged as if they'd never been brushed at all? She went to her construction-arts classes and tried not to think about it. She prayed. She power-walked around the yard with a woman named Carol, a DWI who made her laugh, and started hanging out a little with Fly, a crazy Puerto Rican butch, who'd stood up for her one day when she'd wanted to watch *Private Homes* instead of *Divorce Court* on the day-room TV.

Of course she still worried about Pat, sometimes to the point of hysteria. But with the telephone system the way it was—collect calls only and absolutely no connection to Hawaii, collect or otherwise— there was no way on earth she could speak to him. She did everything she could to change this: talked to her unit manager and wrote letters to her lawyers. She even submitted formal requests for a phone-system pass to the superintendent and to the newly arrived director of security (a small, fractious man who everyone said had been transferred to Framingham after being intimidated by his own officers in a medium-security men's facility nearby), but nothing had come of any of it. So now, aside from writing to Pat all the time, and sending a video of her-self reading to him through a program sponsored by the Catholic chap-lain, she had trained herself to live with that gaping vortex of fear and guilt and was managing, pretty much, to keep focused on her much re-duced present instead. Which is to say that she'd finally constructed a box around Pat too—everyone had to do it sooner or later, she under-stood now. If they didn't, the pain drove them crazy, and every year one or two tried to kill themselves as a result, by hanging themselves with strips of twisted sheet in their rooms.

THEN CAME CHRISTMAS. Everything pales beside the agonies of Christmas in prison. All the holidays are bad: birthdays, New Year's, Thanksgiving, and Easter, but Christmas is the worst. The administra-tion did allow a party for the handful of kids who could make it, but for some reason it was held in November. Half-torn decorations remained up on the visiting-room walls for several weeks after that, but no deco-rations were allowed elsewhere in the facility. Women who received cards stuck them up with dabs of toothpaste, which froze like glue against the section of painted frieze block where such things were allowed, and that felt nice and new and hopeful. But there were no other concessions to the holidays, none. The guards, who always seemed so distant and unapproachable to Denise, were sullen, worse than usual. Even the food was unchanged—chicken burrito this year, and beans.

Denise brushed her teeth. She pulled her hair back and then dabbed illegal foundation on her cheeks, fresh from a free sample pouch in *Glamour* magazine. Some of the women had made presents for one another, packages of Twinkies and Hershey's kisses from Canteen. They'd even wrapped them, Martha Stewart–style, with holiday images from old magazines and had made cards, or bought them from Louise, a wheeler-dealer with artistic talent, who sold individualized drawings for two dollars. Denise had prepared five or six of these gifts herself. Some moisturizing cream for Julia, who always complained of dry skin. Salami and crackers for Fly, Pepsis for Charlene, who never had any money and who longed, always, for the cans of cold soda. She could hear some of them exchanging their presents out in the dayroom now, but this only made her feel worse. It was Christmas outside.

At home she and Patrick had had a crèche that they put up every year and a collection of miniature houses too, the kind that light up inside. They were expensive, those little houses, but Denise bought two new ones every year, and they spent hours laying them out with tiny people, benches, streetlights, and trees, before spreading white cotton all around to look like snow. They'd had a good-sized town by the time Denise left—almost like the real town of New Bedford, they used to think. But there'd be no snow for Pat this year. Not in Hawaii. Denise pulled out the photos his father had sent. Patrick was grinning hugely in most of them, straddling the seat of Alan's new, golden motorbike. He'd grown. The day she was arrested, he'd been small enough to bury his head in her chest when he sat on her lap. Police had forced her onto the floor in handcuffs, and when Patrick came back home and saw her he screamed so desperately that an officer unlocked Denise's handcuffs and let him sit on her lap. There he sat wiping her tears. This was another one of those memories she never wanted to have: Pat wiping her tears away as she wiped his.

Denise gathered up the few gifts she had prepared for her friends and headed for the dayroom. Just then, out of nowhere, the Catholic chaplain and a group of volunteers burst into the unit. Dressed in red felt hats and bright red scarves, they danced around the place like goofballs, Denise thought, adorable and generous goofballs. And they handed out gifts, delicately wrapped packages containing hand lotions and sweet-smelling soap and, miraculously, tucked into a corner, real, medium-bristled, full-sized toothbrushes.

Denise couldn't believe it. A real, adult toothbrush! Her new roommate had just shown her how to twist strips of garbage bag into smooth, flosslike strings, and now this! For a moment the wonder of it completely overwhelmed her. Then she rushed back into her room, ignoring the photographs of Patrick spread out on her bunk now, and got to work quickly assembling things to trade: the Twix bars she'd been keeping and her tuna and beans and peanuts—even the sodas she'd put aside for the diabetic woman. Then she went to the dayroom, where everyone was still gathered, and let it be known that she was trading for toothbrushes—not the Canteen kind, but the ones Sister Maureen had just given out. She could make the next year bearable, she thought, if she just traded right.

WITCHES

MCI-FRAMINGHAM'S MODERN entrance area is generic and faceless. Its red brick walls, neatly cropped grass, and huge flag atop a tall white pole make it look like American government buildings everywhere. There is no reference to the history that pervades the plot on which the prison has stood for 128 years. There is, however, another entrance, though it is no longer in use. Before I was allowed into the prison itself, I used to circle its perimeter occasionally, and once discovered a way to sneak right up next to it. Pretending I was lost, I entered the prison grounds through an open and untended side gate and drove right up to the old superintendent's house, which stood directly in front of it. I could peer into the ancient conservatory and see the shadowy outlines of wilting plants behind algae-smeared glass. I even got close enough to the front of the building to see flecks of just-peeled paint scattered on the ground beneath the arch of the abandoned old entranceway. I spent a lot of time in the state archives reading up on Framingham's history back then, so it wasn't difficult to imagine horse-drawn carriages pulling up to the grand old portico in the late 1880s, whole groups of them clattering together on the stone path, and troupes of women in crinolines stepping out, being welcomed as speakers, volunteers, and friends of the prison and of prisoners alike. Despite the current department's determination to seal everything off, the history of the prison remains more or less available to anyone who goes looking for it.

MCI-Framingham is the oldest running women's prison in America. Its history both parallels and defines the story of women in prison in this country. Just thirty years after first opening its doors, Framingham was regarded as the most successful female reformatory in the country. By the 1930s people traveled from all over the world to learn about its progressive, gender-specific policies firsthand. Eleanor Roosevelt was a frequent visitor, as well as an avid supporter of the institution.

No fences surrounded the then-thirty-acre parcel. With education and reform at a premium, the women had the use of a children's cottage and nursery, a theater, a gymnasium, and a women-run, on-site hospital. There were also four theater troupes, two orchestras, seven singing groups, numerous literary and art clubs, a poetry magazine, a playwriting group, philosophy and foreign-language classes, and a lecture series featuring some of the greatest speakers in the country. In addition, the prison's farm provided produce for the entire state correctional system and afforded inmates the opportunity to grow their own vegetables and also flowers with which to decorate their rooms.

Today, staring up at the huge red-brick smokestack and at the acres of looped, razor-wire fence, it's hard to believe all that ever existed. In line with the prevailing trends of the past twenty years, MCI-Framingham has become an arid, isolated place—one of seven state facilities run by the centralized Massachusetts Department of Correction, which has spent the better part of the last decade trying to bring the women's institution in line with the "real" prisons in the state, which is to say, the prisons for men.

Despite the fact that escape is rare among female prisoners, extra barbed-wire fences have been added to the perimeter. The children's nursery has been closed. The farm no longer exists. There is no theater or orchestra or literary group, no inmate-run clubs at all, in fact, aside from constitutionally protected religious ones, because prisoners are forbidden to meet in groups of any kind. Both Alcoholics and Narcotics Anonymous groups do meet here still, but most other volunteer-run programs from the outside, programs that frequently operate in men's prisons and that cost the department nothing, such as job training and entry-level college classes, are unavailable to the women of MCI-Framingham.

This is particularly sad, as women behind bars are startlingly unlike their more violent male counterparts. Predominantly incarcerated for nonviolent, drug-related offenses, they are frequently mere accessories to their crimes: girlfriends, wives, or lovers of drug dealers, even leaseholders of apartments in which drugs are stashed. Almost all have serious drug problems themselves, and about half are victims of domestic abuse.

To be statistical: a full 72.8 percent of women in prison today are serving time for nonviolent offenses. Of the almost 28 percent who are deemed violent, three quarters are incarcerated for "simple assault"— the lowest rung on the ladder of violent crimes. Eighty-four percent of all incarcerated women have histories of drug addiction, and 57.2 percent have been victims of sustained physical and sexual abuse. An astonishing 68 percent of incarcerated women are found to be clinically depressed when they are examined in prison—a statistic probably exacerbated by the fact that approximately two thirds are mothers and were the primary caretakers of children before being sent away. As a result, there are currently more than 1.3 million children in this country whose mothers are under what official reports call "correctional sanction." And the numbers continue to grow. In fact, while the male prison population in the United States has doubled since the 1980s, there are currently five times the number of women in prison than there were just twenty years ago. As I write this more than 950,000 women are under some kind of correctional supervision in the United States. That's one in a hundred.

I thought of this figure one afternoon while walking to the train. Hurrying through the rush-hour crowds, pressing against both the rain and the expressions of strangers fixed hard against yet another day of unnatural frostiness, I began to wonder just who the women were who were pushing through the turnstiles and boarding the train with me. Had that woman sitting in the corner, the one hunched in a coat too small with the open-toed sandals, so incongruous on a day like today, ever been in prison? Or that one, the large, older woman there, with the fixed, vacant expression? What about the woman in front of me, the very picture of the young professional in her nicely tied London Fog and sensible shoes? If one woman in a hundred was under correctional supervision, I must have encountered many of them in my day-to-day travels through the city. I must see them all the time.

BACK IN 1877, when the prison at Framingham first opened its doors, women were a smaller percentage of the prison population than they are today. But as I started to spend more time in the library, I began to see that, even back then, women were incarcerated for mostly nonviolent, behavioral crimes. In fact, tracing the slightly browned and curved script of some neatnik administrator in an old prison logbook, I found that Framingham's first inmate was sentenced not for murder or assault or theft, but for being homeless.

Her name was Hannah Sullivan. She is listed as prisoner number one, having arrived at Framingham on its first day of operation: November 7, 1877. The notes about her were concise: born in Ireland,

Hannah Sullivan was "in bad drinking habits" before she arrived, but she "worked well at the prison," and administrators noted that she left, just under a year later, for a domestic situation in a small Massachusetts town named Holliston. Other than that, there was nothing—no references to her in either the punishment or the deprivation-of-privileges logbooks.

Despite the prison's noble ambitions, more than half the 246 women incarcerated at Framingham that first year were sentenced, simply, for being drunk. A third were prostitutes. Seventy-six were petty thieves or shoplifters, and, including Hannah, thirty-one were vagrants. Six, that first year alone, were convicted for "being stubborn." Ten for being lewd and for "cohabitation." Three were in for something called "simple fornication" and only two for assault. Just one woman was there for attempting murder; one, also, for breaking glass. One for being idle, one for begging, and one for "committing" an abortion.

Here are some of the logbook entries:

Ann Amsock, Adultery. 2 years. Does not know her age. Born in Ireland. Married 21 years ago. Husband went back to Ireland. Has been intemperate 9 years. Was convicted of adultery with Daniel Greyson, husband of Maggie Greyson—a one eyed, lame colored man. Says she is innocent.

Anne Mahoney. Born in Ireland. Married 1862. Deserted by husband 1870. Since then in house of correction, house of industry or common jail a great deal of the time—common drunkard for 6 years—came broken down and rum sick.

Mary Smith, real name Delanty. Born in England. Operative in mills. Lost her liberation through lewd and drinking habits.

Criminally intimate with men—usually when drunk. Came in wretched condition.

Mary Maguire. Larceny. 6 months. Does not know her age. Never went to school. Lived out in families. Intemperate. 8 children. 5 living. James 18, John 10. Jasmine, Katie and Eddie here with her. Husband was crazy before she married him. First sentence.

Mary O'Brien. Drunkenness and Night Walking. Born in Boston. Father died 1862. Mother 1872. Harlot for five years in houses of ill fame on North and Richmond Streets. Used up with Syphilis—died here January 31, 1878 aged 22 years.

Margaret Fallon. Common Drunkard. 6 months. Born in Ireland. About 47 years old. Married John Fallon 18 years ago. Has had nine children. Now pregnant. 5 children dead: Rosa, John, Mary, Ann, Maggie. Has been intemperate 11 years. Child born here.

Bridget Coggins. Born in England. Deaf and dumb. Enc [impregnated] by one of several young men with whom she had been criminally intimate, resorting to the woods for that purpose. Child born and died here. Left Jan. 30, 1879. Said she was going to Uncle in Hudson.

Stuck beneath this entry was an undated newspaper clipping, perhaps half an inch square:

FATAL ACCIDENT

Hudson, Mass. Sept 16: The 7:35 train from Marlboro ran into and killed a deaf and dumb domestic

named Bridget Coggins at a sharp curve near the
East Meadow reservoir. Her skull was fractured,
and she lived but about half an hour.

That first year just 3 violent criminals were incarcerated at Framingham, along with 243 behavioral ones. Most of the charges were for
what seemed more like personality traits than crimes: being lewd, stubborn, intemperate, or idle. Even the more specific charges of "illegal
cohabitation" and being "illegally intimate" translate, of course, as living with a man, and sleeping with a man, and they were punishable, in
the late nineteenth century, by prison terms of up to five years.

Of course, not all women engaged in extramarital sex were locked
up in prison. Almost exclusively first-generation immigrants, few of
Framingham's first inmates had access to the protections of the more
comfortable middle classes. Hardly any had even the most rudimentary
education. None had money. Locking up society's most marginal citi-
zens in the name of law and order is nothing new. Even back in the sev-
enteenth century, when Massachusetts was still known as the Bay
Colony, it was almost exclusively poor, isolated women who ended up
on the wrong side of the law. Back then, more women were punished
for witchcraft and adultery than for all other crimes combined. Only
one couple—the unfortunate Mary Latham and James Britton—were
ever actually executed for adultery in Massachusetts, but literally hundreds of isolated, poor women were executed for "consorting with
malevolent spirits." The trials at Salem were only the most dramatic of
these persecutions. They continued throughout the eighteenth century,
and while women were convicted of less than 20 percent of serious
crimes in Massachusetts, more than three times as many women were
convicted for witchcraft than were men.

Witchcraft was stricken from the list of capital crimes in the 1770s.

But I couldn't help thinking, as I sat in the library, checking off common nightwalker after common nightwalker from the logbooks, that perhaps the fears that lurked behind those accusations remained. There has to be some explanation for the fact that men are still punished mostly for crimes against property and people—theft, assault, and murder—while the majority of women continue to be punished for transgressions against conventional morality, namely, for having sex and getting high.

Adulterers and "consorters with malevolent spirits" in the eighteenth century, drunks and prostitutes in the nineteenth, drug-addicted single mothers in the twentieth. Perhaps these were all witches, still.

MIRRORS

YOU CAN ALWAYS tell when people are visiting a prison for the first time because they don't know to empty their pockets. Or to take off their watches. Or to put the key upside down in the lockers provided to store these things in. Or the fact that the machine that dispenses cards for snacks in the visiting room takes only five-dollar bills—old five-dollar bills, no new, crisp ones—in fact, only old five-dollar bills that you've run along the edge of the fake-wood table upon which the card-dispensing machine sits. Never before have they stood, sometimes for as long as ten minutes, facing a bulletproof window on the other side of which sits a uniformed employee who resolutely ignores them. He might be talking to a co-worker or catching up on paperwork. Perhaps he is just cleaning his fingernails. And when this uniformed employee finally does look up and address these newcomers, they always flinch because even in the welfare office they've never been spoken to with such disregard.

Not surprising, then, that after twenty or thirty minutes of this sensory confusion these now beaten-down newcomers are heard to say something like "Psssshhhh! They sure make things tough around here." If it weren't for the kindness bred of solidarity with the other visitors waiting to go inside, most people, I think, would simply turn around and walk away.

Similarly, you can tell the new guards from the rest because when they summon people into the tiny room with the metal detector where you take off your shoes and pull your pockets inside out, they call them by name instead of by number. I've seen this happen only once, and I saw the same surprised look on everyone's face, a look that shamefully turned to scorn almost immediately, as though the families of the incarcerated, like the incarcerated themselves, knew that here, finally, was someone in an even more precarious position than themselves—a "new Jack," a guard learning the ropes.

After a while, though—a surprisingly short while—you, like they, become an old-timer. It happens imperceptibly. One day you're anxious and wary and not a little on edge. The next you're sitting in one of the orange plastic chairs in the entranceway, reading the paper, calmly prepared to wait perhaps five minutes, perhaps a couple of hours, until being let in. This is how you begin to recognize the other old-timers too—by their passivity.

There were a few of them, three or four, who were there every time I went to Framingham. There's the short man with the drooping, oval eyes and the figure that is disarmingly like a woman's, and the man wasted by AIDS, folded up in his wheelchair, skinny legs crossed beneath him like some kind of guru. There is a middle-aged woman with a clever little girl, her granddaughter—the daughter of her incarcerated daughter—who, at five, sometimes sits with me and reads the paper; and there is the old man who speaks through a metal amplifier, which he holds to his throat where his Adam's apple must once have been. But there are never more than a handful of visitors at the prison. One unintended result of our incredibly high incarceration rates is that for men, going to prison has become a rite of passage in many communities. For women, because they are comparatively so few, it is still very much a disgrace. Of everyone I met at Framingham, only Denise gets regular visits from her family. Most get none at all.

I was the first visitor that a woman named Susan Grissin had received in more than three years. It had been so long since she'd been in the visiting room that I had to show her around, taking her first to the hot-food vending machine and then to the soda and the snack machine on the other side of the room. All the choices—the Sun Chips and the pretzels, the hot dogs, cheeseburgers, and boneless barbecue-rib sandwiches—dazzled her into stunned indecision, the way one hears people from former Eastern-bloc countries respond to American supermarkets.

Also, Susan is one of the women at Framingham with terrible teeth. She has only two, and because they are both upper-jaw incisors, she finds eating much of anything difficult. But she has lived most of her life as a homeless crack addict, and she would never let a purchase of otherwise unavailable—and therefore highly valued—junk food pass her by. We spent almost twenty minutes hovering in front of the hot-food machine that first day, pressing the oversized button that clunked the food carousel around one shrink-wrapped dish at a time. Then we sat together for another half hour as she made her way through a tray of cheese nachos, munching for whole, silent minutes at a time until I couldn't help remembering that William Carlos Williams poem about the old street lady eating plums:

> *They taste good to her*
> *They taste good*
> *to her. They taste*
> *good to her*

This was back in September, that first heady week when I finally gained access to the prison and went there almost every day there were visiting hours so I could meet women I'd been writing to for months.

There were five of them back then: Denise, Susan, Riza, Charlene, and Carmen. As a sample of the women at Framingham, it was more or less representative. Three were convicted of nonviolent, drug-related offenses, one for theft, and one, atypically, for murder. They ranged in age from their early twenties to their mid-fifties, and among them they represented the African American, Latin American, and Anglo American populations that more or less define prison society. Because of the racial makeup of the state as a whole, Massachusetts prisons tend to look more integrated than most. Nonetheless, the rate at which women of color are incarcerated is almost triple that of women of European descent.

Of all of the women I met in Framingham, though, it was the white Anglo Saxon, Susan Grissin, who'd lived the harshest life. Homeless for decades, she was preternaturally thin and had the gray skin and toothless grin of a longtime addict. She'd been in and out of prison more or less continuously for fifteen years and was by far the most comfortable at Framingham. She calls it "Good old MCI!" And though there is, of course, a vein of irony winding its way beneath the endearment, Framingham did seem to have become a comfort to her. After years of chaos on the street, it was as if it had come to represent some kind of steady and reliable reality.

Susan was twelve when her mother left her on a randomly chosen street corner in Boston.

"What are you going to do when DSS arrives and scoops your kids?" she'd asked her mother during a beating one day.

"You don't like it, pack your bags," she remembers her mother replying.

"They're already packed," Susan said, and with that her mother threw her in the car, dropped her on a street in Boston, told her to wait, and never came back. Susan didn't try to get back home to the frequent beatings with leather belts and Wiffle-ball bats. She didn't see her mother even once for the next ten years. At the age of thirty-three, she has been in and out of Framingham twelve times—mostly for theft, criminal trespassing, and drug possession.

Her sense of comfort in prison becomes still less surprising when you realize that she is one of the more than 60 percent of female inmates who have open mental-health cases. She was diagnosed as bipolar when she was still a teenager, but she'd been drunk and high at the time and never placed much stock in the diagnosis.

"I-mean-yeah-I-have-little-depression-problems. I-get-depressed-a-lot," she told me, the same way she said everything, in one long breathless string, so that sometimes, listening to her, I felt like a spontaneous translator. "To-me-I-always-wanted-to-have-a-mother-you-know?"

At one point she said, "I'm-like-Freddy-from-*Nightmare-on-Elm-Street.*" Another time she said, "I'm-not-all-here-I-do-like-people-I-just-don't," and she often referred to herself in the third person, as in "Susan-Grissin-and-her-stinking-thinking." When I asked about medication, she said, "I-do-want-to-get-put-back-on-my-meds-but-I-don't-want-to." And though she was ultimately placed on regular doses of the antidepressant doxepin, it's hard to tell whether this helped or hindered her day-to-day progress. Like all tricyclic antidepressants, doxepin can unleash mania in bipolar patients. But prison itself tends to work on your personality like one of those funhouse mirrors at the fair. It doesn't distort so much as simply exaggerate what's already there—giving prominence to personality traits that might never have developed in the outside world. After almost sixteen years of circling through prison doors, Susan may well have become a caricature of herself, with or without the help of the drugs.

The last time she was released, she told me mischievously at the end of our visit, she'd lasted just seven months. She'd elected to go to a sober house in an attempt to keep clean, but she'd soon snuck out to the Cape, where she got "totally shitfaced."

"Less-than-a-year-later-I-wound-up-back-in-here," she said. "Yup. Back-in-good-ol'-MCI!" Then she slumped against the back of her orange bucket chair and began to swing her feet against its spindly metal legs like a happy, overfed kid at a birthday party.

ALMOST ALL THE women I've met at Framingham have become exaggerated versions of themselves in one way or another. It is as if, lacking different experiences to reshape themselves, they repeat the same responses to the same stimuli over and over, until only those components of their character evolve.

Riza Stots is thirty-eight years old, exactly my age. Tall and pale, with long auburn hair, she grew up on a farm in northern Maine and still carries herself as if hard physical labor were part of her fixed daily routine. The first time I met her I remember being so impressed by her fresh-faced, all-American robustness that I couldn't help imagining her in a commercial for butter, lilting out the enticing refrain "Churned on our farm just for you!"

She was by far the most outwardly composed woman that I met at Framingham. But the intensity of her composure unnerved me, because it was prison-born, I think, like some weird mutation in an otherwise delicate hothouse plant. She was always so exceedingly concentrated. The way she spoke seemed overly careful as well, consciously clipped around the edges of each word as if she had learned English as a second language. Perhaps it was just this exaggerated speech pattern, then, and not the knowledge that she was in prison for murder, that made me feel nervous around her. Or perhaps it was the muffled silence of the sealed interview room the guards sometimes let me use when I was there, or the suspicion I couldn't help harboring that in her own quiet way, Riza was trying to hoodwink me.

As I'd done with all the women I met at Framingham, I tried to be very clear about the purpose of this book when I first wrote to Riza. I emphasized that it was not about getting cases reheard, or freeing women who believed they had been wrongly convicted. I don't know any lawyers, I always told them, and know nothing about the legality or illegality of criminal-court procedures. But Riza is serving life at Framingham, *life,* and I suppose any chance, even a chance that isn't really a chance, is worth reaching for. So maybe all I felt was her desperation. Desperation sharpened and refined by the five years she'd already served. Or maybe not. Maybe she did kill an innocent old man during a bungled attempt at robbing his home. I'll never know.

I certainly found her boyfriend's claim that she shot Mr. Eccles from behind, and that, facing him, he had seen the old man's eyes fill slowly with blood, hard to forget. The image of the scene haunts me to this day, though Riza certainly has her own version of the story to tell. On my second visit she launched into it, and became visibly anxious—really quite agitated—when she did so.

At one point, I remember, she took my notepad and drew a map. She didn't seem to care if the correctional officers who routinely milled around the visiting room saw her using a pen. It's a punishable infraction, and like most lifers, Riza had long since settled into a more or less trouble-free relationship with the authorities at Framingham. But at that point Riza wasn't in the visiting room anymore. She was reliving the crime.

She drew a box first, and labeled it "garage." Then she drew another, adjoining box, which was the kitchen. She drew stairs in the middle of this, which she said went down into the cellar. Outside the house she made a squiggle and wrote "woodpile." Then she drew a window frame next to it. She had been hiding behind this woodpile when her boyfriend, Gary, shot the old man, she told me. She heard the noise and looked through the window and Gary had seen her and had forced her back into the house at gunpoint. That was when she'd first seen the body, lying in a pool of blood at the bottom of the basement stairs.

As if she knew the power that other image held over me, the old man's eyes filling up with blood after she shot him, Riza seemed determined to paint another picture just as vivid. Staring at me in such a way that it would have been impossible for me to look away, she said: "He forced me to go down to the cellar to clean up the blood. But there was just so much of it. So much of it. There's no way he could be alive. I asked Gary what happened. He said, 'Never mind, just clean it up or you'll be next,' and I didn't need much convincing. I was seven and a half months pregnant, sloshing through Mr. Eccles's blood, and Gary just kept bringing me more towels. More and more towels."

I'D NEVER MET anyone with such stories to tell—stories that included the loading of Mr. Eccles's dead body into the trunk of his own car and then throwing it into a ravine several hundred miles away in Vermont. Until then I'd never heard stories of the kind of abuse—the beatings, the rapes, the forced prostitution—that Riza's boyfriend so regularly subjected her to before the murder either.

Forced into prostitution to support herself and Gary, Riza had been beaten and threatened with her own death so many times that she'd come to think of it as inevitable. ("What would you do with a favorite pet in a situation like this?" Gary asked her one rainy day when they had nothing to eat and no place to go. "You'd put it out of its misery, right?")

Her childhood had been complicated too—there were questions about whether she was her mother's or her sister's child, and she'd been sent to live with her grandparents almost as soon as she was born. She'd enjoyed life on the farm, though; the feeding of pigs, the gathering of eggs. For a time she was a successful high school student and a part-time waitress on the side. But then Gary showed up, all greased hair and charm, and before she knew it she'd fallen in love with him— and then in hate and fear of him too—but by then she was working as a hooker on a curb in L.A. someplace, climbing in and out of cars, and trucks, and once even an off-duty bus, in a desperate attempt to keep him calm.

She tried to leave him on numerous occasions. She slipped onto buses and flagged down strangers, but he used to tell her that he knew what she was thinking, and because he really did seem able to read her mind, she began to believe him. There was the time she got on the bus to the airport and turned around and saw him there, right behind her, "because he knew." Or the time, when she was six months pregnant, when he found a note she'd written that read: "I'm with someone I can't get away from, please help me."

"He took his hands and banged them into my ears like this when he saw that," she told me in the visiting room, slamming her ears startlingly hard with her own flattened palms. "It felt like something burst when he did that," she whispered, looking down at the table for the first time all day. "Clear fluid ran from my ears for days. It was like my ears were crying."

None of this makes the death of Mr. Eccles any less shocking, of course. Riza is the first to admit that. Almost every woman in Framingham has a horror story to tell, and only a tiny handful end up committing crimes as senseless as that which left Mr. Eccles dead in his own home in the middle of the day. There are a few, of course, who respond to the abuse they receive by lashing out violently themselves. Women who, in the end, become so distanced from their own humanity that they seem able to do things the rest of us find incomprehensible. On the other hand, not one of the women I met at Framingham—not even Riza, not even during those moments I felt convinced of her guilt—left me feeling secure in the knowledge that I wouldn't have done the exact same thing if the tables were turned.

Charlene Williams certainly did nothing I wouldn't have at least considered doing myself when I was in my teens. Born in Saint Croix but raised in Boston, Charlene combines Caribbean laissez-faire with a tougher, more sardonic and urban approach to life that people in Framingham—inmates and guards alike—find hard to resist. She is funny, loud, and, sometimes, disrespectful. And, like many of us, she can be foolish too.

One summer, hot and bored and fed up with hanging out with her friends at the baseball field in Boston's Franklin Park, Charlene agreed to an offer of ten thousand dollars to smuggle drugs into the country in her underwear. Nineteen at the time, she wasn't even certain if the offer was serious. Less than a month later, however, Charlene found herself on a flight to Jamaica. She couldn't believe her luck. Apart from occasional trips back home to Saint Croix, she'd never left the country before. Now she was being put up in a fancy hotel, spending the weekend drifting along the beach buying presents for her mother, whom she adores, and sipping at brightly colored cocktails at the bar. It wasn't until the night before her flight back to Boston, when her contacts showed up in her room with a package of specially bought clothes and an additional, drug-filled panty pad, that reality hit.

Twice during the flight she'd gone to the bathroom to get rid of the drugs, but twice she'd thought better of it. There were consequences to flushing thousands of dollars' worth of merchandise down a toilet, she knew. The men had been clear enough about that when she'd tried to get out of the deal back in the hotel. Sitting on her bed in the strange beige shorts suit and the bulging underwear, she'd begun to cry and had begged them to let her board the plane clean. But the men were unmoved. In a halfhearted attempt to reassure her, they asked if she believed in God. When she said that she did, they handed her a Bible and told her not to worry. Just read Psalm 27, they said; it would make her feel better: "For He will hide me in His shelter in the day of trouble;/He will conceal me under the cover of His tent . . . ."

CHARLENE HAD KNOWN nothing, back then, about the mandatory drug laws that covered offenses like hers. She had no idea that for attempting to import more than two hundred grams of cocaine, she would be subject to a mandatory sentence of fifteen years in prison. By the time she found out, it was too late. As in many states, judges in Massachusetts have no discretion in the sentencing of drug offenders. Prison terms are fixed by state lawmakers, many of whom feel pressured to produce "tough on crime" legislation to placate their constituents. Despite the fact that this was Charlene's first criminal offense, therefore, and that it would cost state taxpayers almost half a million dollars to hold her in prison for the prescribed minimum sentence, the judge who heard Charlene's case had no choice but to send her to Framingham for fifteen years and a day. There would be no probation. No parole. No time off for prison-earned "good time." Charlene was twenty-one by the time she was finally sentenced. And she had a sixteen-month-old baby as well.

The little girl, Trinada, was born almost exactly a year after that terrible day at Logan when the security guard had casually asked Charlene to please step back inside. She'd been out on bail awaiting trial, working as a data-entry clerk in a big office building downtown and had had no intention of getting pregnant at all. For a time she didn't dare let anyone know. But then she started to get sick, nauseous to the point of vomiting every morning, and her mother soon figured things out. Trinnie was born, easily, eight and a half months later in Brigham and Women's Hospital. Her mother and the baby's father, Derek, were there. And though it was a mixed blessing, bearing a child from whom she knew she was soon to be separated, there was something about the little girl's face—the too-heavy eyebrows, perhaps, or the tautly flared nose—that made distance from the child impossible.

Still, Charlene realized it had been a mistake to bring Trinnie to court the day she was sentenced. She'd known she'd do time. Her lawyer was telling her she might do five years. When the judge announced that she'd serve fifteen years and a day, Charlene crumpled. She felt, she said, as if someone had hit her. A guard came up from behind, shackled her hands, and then led her away. "The most hurtful thing was to see my daughter waving for me to come over to her as they was shackling me," Charlene told me. "They took me away without even being able to kiss her good-bye."

LIKE DENISE, CHARLENE has also forced herself to settle in at Framingham as best she can, struggling to keep sane without succumbing altogether to the mindless monotony of prison life. For Charlene, this balance is most readily achieved by giving way to the occasional furious outburst—not at the horror of having been apart from her daughter for almost five years but at something much smaller, something over which she has at least a semblance of control.

The first time I met her, Charlene stormed into the visiting room in a self-conscious and, I can't help but think, partly parodic rage because of the problems she'd been having with her new roommate. Norma weighed three hundred pounds, Charlene told me as we settled around a small square table at the back. And she smelled bad, and though she had plenty of money from a sugar daddy she saw every now and then in the visiting room, she never spent a penny on toiletries. The smell in their room grew more pungent by the hour. For the first few days Charlene had shared her own meager supply of soap and deodorant on the assumption that she would be more than repaid when Norma's first store order came through. But just yesterday when Norma struggled back from Canteen with her first order—a huge, transparent plastic sack stuffed with fifty dollars' worth of Little Debbie cakes and English muffins and cocoa and sodas and banana Moon-Pies—there was no cleaning stuff and there were no toiletries. None.

Setting her steaming barbecue-rib sandwich aside for a moment on the table between us, Charlene now became almost operatic in her outrage. Because—well, imagine it! Here was this newcomer, this large woman prostitute named Norma (in prison for the hundredth time probably), sitting outside their room on a chair she'd placed there for the purpose, eating her breakfast of three banana MoonPies and a cup of hot cocoa, as relaxed as she pleased, while Charlene, the old-timer, swept out the room!

"I'm not a neat freak," Charlene told me then, straightening the pieces of brown paper towel that serve as napkins in the visiting room. "But I am clean and tidy. And I don't want no trouble. But everyone should know about basic hygiene issues—even in here. See, for me coming to jail is a downfall. But not a total downfall. I still have my life and I still have my family. I never lived on the street. And I didn't have no kids when I *committed* my crime. Nuhh-huhh," she cheered herself on. "When that woman smiled at me all condescending and told me why didn't I have no john to provide for me, I told her, Fuck you! You have no authority to judge me! I'm not the one who comes to prison and still keeps being a whore."

SEX

BY THE SUMMER, time had slowed to a not quite crawl again. Back to the endless round of counts and lockups, lines for group and for twelve-step meetings, longer lines for meals and strip searches, and endless gossip, and urine samples, and phone calls home, and the dull satisfaction of successful twenty-four-hour-a-day rule following. Denise tried to keep distracted by her power walking and by the college-level correspondence courses that her father had finally paid for. But too much philosophy and sociology made her head ache. All that sitting around thinking allowed the horror of Pat's aloneness to become real again. Sitting there on her bunk, trying to study while her current roommate, Alma, watched the television too loudly beneath her, Denise slipped into daydreams about the fishing outing she and Pat had gone on the week before she came to Framingham, and the Italian and Chinese restaurants they'd eaten at, and the games of Nintendo they'd played, and the hockey match they'd gone to, and the camping trip too, because it was important to do everything they enjoyed together in that one week. Then she'd start crying and wish that her boyfriend, Joel, had just done as he was asked and developed two copies of the roll of film that documented all this, one set for Pat, one set for her, so that she could relive some of the magic now, and imag-

ine Pat doing it too, out there in Hawaii, where, she couldn't help remembering, he was the object of bitter teasing for being the only white
kid in his class. But Joel had never developed the photos. Or if he had,
he'd never sent them to her, or to Patrick, and anyway, he hadn't come
to visit or even written a letter for five or six months, so there was no
point wishing for them now. He'd probably thrown the roll away.

This kind of thinking got her nowhere, she knew. It made for what
her friend Louise called a "jail day," where you allowed yourself to surrender entirely to the powerlessness that was prison. This was still as
occasionally appealing to Denise as it was to everyone at Framingham,
but she'd been in long enough by then to know too that if the momen-
tary surrender held a certain listless pleasure, it led nowhere in the end.
Prison was too rigid, she'd learned, its hierarchies too defined, for lan-
guor.

It was a relief, then, to have crazy Julie Kelly transferred to her room.
A pretty twenty-two-year-old, Julie, the daughter of a cop, was serving
three to four and a half years for a series of dry-cleaner robberies she
helped her boyfriend commit. Her dad had been horrified, of course. But
it had been hard for him to keep track of his daughter since his wife
passed away, and he'd long settled into a grudging acceptance of the situation. Better in prison than dead, he concluded. She'd been in trouble
with drugs for years. Supposedly the getaway driver, she'd been so high
on heroin at the time of the heists that it was all she could do to twiddle
the dial of the radio, searching for something to nod off to while she
waited for her boyfriend to come out. Once he'd even had to push her
out of the driver's seat and take the wheel himself as they drove away.

Julie had been fairly wild since arriving at Framingham. She spent
plenty of time in the Hole. That's why their unit's block sergeant had
engineered the move, thinking Denise might be a good influence on the
much younger woman.

Denise had had her share of whacked-out roommates, and the latest one, Alma, had particularly grated. It sounded petty, but she snored so loudly that Denise had had to buy earplugs from Canteen the month before, and she'd worn them so much that her ears actually hurt now when she put them in before going to sleep. Alma watched too much TV during the day. Spent her time brain-dead and depressed on her bunk, watching soap opera after soap opera.

Julie, though, was different. She needed help and responded to the slightest of attentions with adoration. She was no more than a kid, really. Just turned twenty-two, and though she'd been in the prison for a little less than a year, she had a completely different story to tell. Turns out, Denise told me, about a month after Julie's arrival in her room, that prison didn't run the way she'd thought it did at all. That underneath the stark divisions between guard and inmate that Denise had always assumed were sacrosanct lay a complex web of intrigue and desire the force of which actually propelled the day-to-day reality there. Sex, she said, eyes wide with disbelief, between guards and inmates. Especially on the three-to-eleven shift when the administrators and the teachers and the other white-shirt types had all left.

There was Sergeant O. and Lisa. Sergeant C. and Ann. Officer K. and Robin, Officer G. and Shevaun, Officer F. and Mayi—even Lieutenant E. was in on the act. Denise was incredulous. Like a child who first discovers that her parents had to have sex to give birth to her, she simply refused to believe what she was hearing. But Julie insisted. Everyone did it, she said. And everyone but Denise seemed to know. Sergeant H. had the women talk dirty to him, Officer L. liked blow jobs, and Officer G. had had countless affairs—and was widely thought to be responsible for Shevaun's pregnancy—before being walked off the property.

The list was endless. There were the officers who liked to be touched and the officers who liked to touch; officers who dared only to kiss and officers who liked to go the whole way. There were a couple of officers who liked to watch girls together, and one whose preference it was to get blow jobs by thrusting his penis through the food slots that the rooms in the Smith Building still had, lugging a towel with him to clean up the mess as he progressed down the corridor of the unit. The feasibility of this Denise understood. If the women were all locked into their rooms, the risk of being seen was substantially reduced. But how could the rest of it work—and how could she never have known?

Julie was happy to explain. On the units, she said, it happened during count. The guard simply unlocked an inmate's cell door, leaving her free to come to his office and to fool around with him there with relative equanimity for the half hour or so it took for count to be completed. When the guard wasn't a unit officer, as many of them weren't, she said, hastily grabbed moments in broom cupboards, supply closets, and small side offices with solid doors that closed was more or less all you could expect. Rough, but sexy, Julie said, grinning. Grabbing her thin prison-issue pillow and holding it close, Julie pretended to kiss it, the way guards had kissed her. Laughing, she darted out, checked the corridor for officers, and then stood in a shower stall holding the pillow from behind, thrusting, thrusting. Denise couldn't help laughing. It was too surreal not to be funny. Still playing the role of amorous guard, Julie mimicked the sound of someone coming. She pushed the pillow away and hastily did up invisible flies.

PERHAPS THERE IS something inevitable about guard-on-inmate sex when you have a building full of constitutionally disempowered women being ruled over by uniformed male guards. Even the most cursory of glances at X-rated videos shows just how widespread the fantasy of such mandated female powerlessness extends. Perhaps for this reason, the United Nations Charter of Human Rights insists that female inmates should be guarded exclusively by women.

As far as I know, every country in Europe stands by this ruling. The United States used to as well. Male inmates in this country had always been guarded by men, and women by women. Rules have changed on a piecemeal basis, state by state, since the early seventies. In Massachusetts they changed after a woman became incensed at her inability to work as a guard in one of the state's numerous male prisons. During the 1970s she brought suit and won, ultimately forcing the Department of Correction to enforce nondiscriminatory gender-hiring practices in prisons for both men and women. The same thing happened in most states, and while numbers of women guarding male inmates never grew dramatically in the nation at large, a recent survey found that an average of 40.3 percent of the correctional officers working with female inmates are now men, with that figure rising as high as 55.5 percent in Massachusetts, 68.9 percent in Kansas, and 67.8 percent in California.

In general, prison policies prohibit male staff from viewing undressed females and from conducting strip searches and body pat-downs unless in an emergency. But not always. A Nevada court ruled that men could conduct searches of women even when they involved the touching of breasts and genital areas. In New York too it remains legal for men to pat down female inmates, though the methods and circumstances under which such searches are allowed have changed since a 1998 lawsuit that described the authorized method of pat searching as follows: "An officer begins by ordering the inmate to stand against a wall with her back to him. The officer then approaches the inmate from behind, placing his hands on the inmate's neck inside the collar of her shirt. He works his hands down every inch of the surface of her body. Probing for small items, the officer runs his hands under and over the woman's breasts, brushing her nipples. Searching the woman's legs, the officer grips one inner thigh. His hands press against the woman's vagina before moving down her thigh toward the ankle. He then grips the other thigh and repeats this procedure on the woman's other side."

Even in states where such procedures are not allowed, however, physical encounters like these still occur. Washington and Hawaii have both had to settle lawsuits about male-on-female body searches, and in 1997 Massachusetts settled a suit brought by 112 Framingham inmates after masked officers of both sexes burst into their rooms in the middle of the night demanding urine samples and strip searches. Women in Framingham also insist that despite existing rules to the contrary, male guards pat them down routinely and that men are frequently in a position to see them naked as they pass by the showers, for example, or the glass-walled room where, until recently, women were taken to provide on-the-spot urine samples.

The issue of actual sex between inmates and guards, however, was different. While almost everyone I met at Framingham acknowledged it, many did so only obliquely: a new officer would come into the visiting room, and they might shake their heads and say something like "Now, *there's* a dirty officer." Some kept quiet about it for months. Giving a CO a blow job could get you a couple of cigarettes, or a box of matches, or an order of take-out Chinese food, delivered direct from the restaurant and still hot, and the last thing they wanted was to get themselves or their friends in trouble.

What they probably didn't know was that there have been reports of liaisons between inmates and staff, as well as records of pregnancies, illegitimate births, and secret abortions in prison ever since records have been kept. Even in Framingham in the 1930s, well after it was established as a facility with an all-female staff, women were frequently caught dallying with visiting male engineers and electricians in exchange for snuff, cigarettes, and small packages of angel cake that the men brought them from home.

Not surprising, then, that the problem has worsened since men have become guards. For obvious reasons, departments of correction have always downplayed the issue in public. During the incarceration boom of the 1990s, however, most jurisdictions were forced to privately recognize that staff-on-inmate sex was becoming a problem. In 1996 the Association of State Correctional Administrators identified sexual misconduct in female institutions as one of its major management concerns. By then, at least twenty-three departments of correction had faced class-action or individual damage suits related to such sexual misconduct.

In 1994 a court found that female prisoners in three facilities in Washington, D.C., were frequently subjected to violent sexual assault and harassment. The same year the Justice Department found evidence of widespread sexual abuse and rape in female facilities in Michigan. And in 1997 a similar investigation concluded that authorities in Arizona failed to protect women from systematic rape, sexual touching, and fondling at the hands of correctional officers.

The list goes on. In 1997 the sheriff of Grant County, West Virginia, was sentenced to seven years in prison for forcing female inmates to engage in sex acts with law-enforcement officials. In 1998 the Federal Bureau of Prisons was forced to settle a lawsuit that reported, among other things, that guards had taken money from male inmates in exchange for allowing them to enter women's cells so that they could sexually abuse them. In that same year alone, one or more correctional officers were found guilty of rape or sexual assault of incarcerated women in Florida, Idaho, Illinois, Maryland, Michigan, New Hampshire, Texas, Virginia, Washington, and Wyoming.

An Amnesty International report released in March 1999 asserted that MCI-Framingham was also plagued by increasing levels of inappropriate sexual behavior by guards. Shortly thereafter the state charged a twenty-five-year-old guard named Anthony Maddix with two counts of rape and two counts of indecent assault against women at Framingham. It was the same old story. He'd unlocked the women's door during count. According to the prosecutor in the case, Maddix told them they were needed in the Health Services Unit. Instead he took them to a dark corner somewhere and forced them to perform oral sex. At first both he and the DOC were vocal in their denials of the accusation. Then a DNA sample provided by Maddix matched a sample removed from the women's clothing. Maddix pled guilty, and the department spokesman at the time, Anthony Carnaevale, was reduced to the assertion that "this was an isolated incident."

This, however, is clearly untrue. Though correctional jurisdictions across the country have failed to compile systematic data or analysis of reported sexual allegations, making it impossible to know precisely how often such encounters occur, every woman I met at Framingham—save, initially, wide-eyed Denise—told me that sexual relations between guards and inmates are commonplace.

For many women at Framingham, in fact, it seems as if sex is the only thing that keeps time clicking by. Young, lithe, and plausibly available, Julie had attracted hasty fondlings almost as soon as she arrived. The fact that she allowed it made her an immediate favorite of the guards and had ensured her other creature comforts. She always had a cotton blanket, for example, instead of the scratchy wool ones that "didn't even let you sleep they were so nasty." She'd been given it by a property officer, that and her supposedly illegal second pillow, in exchange for, well, some attention. And Officer G. had been good for a cigarette here and there, or some gum, until he was walked off the property. Even Officer C. would come through with some pizza if she let him watch her fool around with her roommate.

It wasn't until she met Officer F., however, that Julie really began to see what a relationship with a guard could do for a woman in prison. She'd met him back when she was placed "on eyeball," or round-the-clock suicide watch, after overdosing on pills. She'd been given them—Xanax, she thought—by a girl in the holding cell of the courthouse she'd been sent to for sentencing. They'd been ground to powder so Julie had no way of knowing how much there was in the small plastic baggie. She didn't much care, to tell the truth, and without really thinking about it, she took the whole package and nearly died. After that she was placed on eyeball in the prison Health Services Unit. Isolated in an empty cell, naked except for a thin, paper robe, and under constant surveillance through a peephole in the door, Julie became agitated. After the first couple of hours, the robe started to tear, making her body increasingly visible to the guard stationed at the door. Framingham has a stated policy of using only female guards for this eyeball duty, but almost everyone I have spoken to there—including former superintendent Barbara Guarino—has contradicted this. Sure enough, Julie's first memory of F. is of him sitting on a stool on the other side of her door, telling her repeatedly to "lie down."

"Fuck you," Julie remembers saying. "Don't you want to see me naked?"

"Not really," he said.

That had been in July. By the time she got out in early August, after twenty-five days in solitary, they had taken a liking to each other and she asked him for a job. F. led a work crew of seven or eight women. "Can you cut grass?" he'd asked. She said that she could and got a position on his crew the very next day, though the rules state that an inmate needs clearance from Inner Perimeter Security before being given that kind of work.

F. was forty-five at the time, more than twice Julie's age. ("He's got, like, wrinkles on his forehead, you know how old men get those?" she told me. "And he's real tall, walks with wicked bad posture.") At first glance he seemed virtuous enough. He was married, had a pair of young twins, and got on well with his workmates. There was an air of danger about him, though, and he'd swaggered under a glow of infamy at Framingham ever since he was hauled down to Inner Perimeter Security for allegedly striking an African American inmate while she was in handcuffs. Nothing had come of the charges, and like most stories in prison, this one was impossible to verify. But I'd heard the same tale from Denise a few weeks before—she'd heard it from the victim herself in group therapy, where the woman repeatedly broke down in tears about it—and when I asked Julie if she thought F. might be capable of such a thing, she said: "Oh yeah. Definitely he coulda. He's real, real prejudiced. He's wicked bad. But he makes me laugh," she added after a pause. "And I've always gone for bad boys. I love him, Tina, I really, really do. It's not just sex. That's the thing. It's a relationship."

THE FIRST TIME they touched, they were in the utility closet, shortly after she started to work on his crew, Julie told me. She'd been trying to get down a box of mops and dropped them on his head by mistake. He made use of the confusion to grab the back of her jeans and turn her around to face him. Thinking, "Fuck it, why not?" she let him kiss her. From then on they did it everywhere—in the basement where they keep the lawn mowers, in the broom closet right by the entrance to the institution, even in the small chapel. "That's wrong, I know. The little chapel downstairs? It's ugly, I'm sorry, it's just nasty. But we can't fuck in the units because he's not a unit officer, and there's too many people, sixty women in each one, you know what I mean?"

For a time things seemed great. She wrote him love notes and he slipped her gifts: a G-string, some pizza, an order of take-out Chinese food. But it's hard for Julie to reject overtures from any man, and when F. threatened a rookie in the locker room after Julie smiled at him, she knew the stakes had changed. Shortly after that he started to hit her. The worst had been when he heard she'd been fooling around with the packages officer. F. became so enraged that he forgot himself and smacked her in the face, leaving a bright red mark on her cheek. This seemed particularly cruel, as any inmate found with a mark on her can be sent right down to the Hole, no questions asked. Usually Officer F. was more considerate. The last time he heard she'd been talking with another male officer he escorted Julie into the mop room and told her to fetch something from a top shelf. Then he yanked her down by her hair and told her never, ever to make him look like a fool that way again.

NOT ALL GUARDS at Framingham were like F., of course. The majority performed their duties professionally, and even among the less upright, F. stood out. This disturbed Denise. She didn't care that Julie was fooling around, but couldn't she at least have picked a nicer guy? Someone like Officer V., for example, who worked on their unit. He was a middle-aged, slightly balding, earringed man who always managed to be polite without seeming weak. Denise had never really noticed him before Julie moved in. But now she did. Especially when she took sick with the flu. Her bones ached and her head screamed and she hadn't left her bed for two days when V. opened her door one afternoon and asked, "You sick?"

"Yeah," Denise replied lethargically. "Got any chicken soup?"

V. laughed. The next day he again opened the door to Denise's room and threw a roll of throat lozenges on her bed. "They got vitamins in them," he said, and gently closed the door.

He was sweet that way, she had to admit. Good-looking too, if the bald spot didn't bother you. Despite his sometimes leering references to strip clubs and sex-for-hire encounters, he wasn't able to completely hide his gentleness either—a sensibility that struck Denise as odd in an officer. He had even taken her side about the bird who'd made a nest outside their window. It wasn't anything fancy, the bird—something small and unimpressive and noisy in its work, but its arrival thrilled Denise. Julie hated it. Swore the bird's chirping disturbed her sleep and talked increasingly of poisoning the damn thing. She'd even asked V. to send up some rat poison, but he refused to put in the request. Denise noticed how shocked V. had been by Julie's attitude and was surprised by his insistence that having a bird like that was a wonderful thing, a blessing.

"Two nerds together," Julie said when Officer V. left that day. "You were made for each other." At first Denise thought that this was just how Julie's mind worked. But now things seemed different. She even felt flattered when Julie told her he liked her. It wasn't just a physical thing, he'd told Julie. He'd been watching her running, and was impressed by the way she "stays apart from it all and isn't crazy like the rest of them."

Perhaps it was just this unaccustomed boost to her ego that led Denise to do herself up the next morning, and to then linger in the corridor of her unit and smile as V. passed, asking, as casually as she could, if he might spare a piece of gum. He motioned for her to follow him into the glass-walled office that lay across the corridor from the showers next to Denise and Julie's room. The phone was ringing as he went in, and he pointed to the extra chair. Denise sat. It was the first time she'd ever been in the guards' "bubble," and she felt self-conscious.

"So," he said, finally, when he got off the phone. "You want a piece of gum?"

Denise managed to stop herself from saying, "I'm not going to sit here and beg for a piece of gum, asshole." Instead she smiled and said, "Yes, it's been a long time since I've had a piece of gum."

"You haven't had a lot of things for a long time," V. said with the kind of smile that lets you know what's coming next. "You haven't driven a car, you haven't had a good meal, haven't had a drink, haven't had, well, we both know what else you haven't had for a very long time, and all you want is a piece of gum?" Denise managed to laugh and say, "Yeah," and tried not to watch as he peeled back the wrapper from a package of raspberry-flavored Bubble Yum.

Denise felt like a fool in V.'s office, by turns enraged, belittled, and singled out in a nice way somehow too, but all that was eclipsed now by the solid actuality of the gum. She went straight to her bed, carefully unwrapped it, then lay back and started to chew. The raspberry flavor was unfamiliar. But she had always liked the smooth sweetness of Bubble Yum. It was as if they used tiny granules of icing sugar instead of the regular-sized ones, and it made her mouth water. Once the flavor faded, which happened just about as quickly as she now remembered it always did, she began to blow bubbles, and for a time, she was mindlessly, almost idiotically happy. Then, just a little before three, V. came in and said, only half jokingly, "You owe me one."

"Yeah? Like what do I owe you?" Denise parried, trying desperately to banish the notion that she might just have sold herself for a piece of gum.

BACK IN 1990, burgeoning relationships like these would have been legal in forty states. Though physically coerced sex was as illegal inside prison as it was on the outside, sex of the kind between Julie and F. was seen as consensual and so was treated, at most, as a mere breach in procedure. When sexual-misconduct issues began to snowball in 1996, however, experts began to conclude that sexual relations between staff and inmates were inherently abusive and could never be truly consensual, even if initiated by inmates. Reasoning that there could be no true consent in an area of such power imbalances, and that a prison guard has "all kinds of authority and power and potential means to exert influence and pressure," many states outlawed even nominally consensual sex between guards and inmates. By July 1999, forty-one states and the federal government had passed such laws, leaving just nine, including Massachusetts, without one.

Massachusetts finally passed such a law, tacked on as an amendment to the budget, at the end of that year. It made any sexual contact between guards and inmates a felony offense for a correctional officer, punishable by up to five years in prison, a ten-thousand-dollar fine, or both. It was a tough bill, tougher than most, and for a time it filled advocates with optimism. Four years later, however, only one man has ever been convicted under the statute. Only two have been criminally charged.

Instead, the department continues to address the situation the way it always has when it discovers sexual misconduct: by placing the offending woman in the Hole and quietly transferring or retiring the officer from MCI-Framingham itself.

In 2004, the department did finally provide me with figures for sexual-misconduct investigations in Framingham. According to them, sixty-two official investigations have occurred in the past five years. Of these, they assert that thirty-one accusations were "unfounded," twenty-one "unsubstantiated," and seven substantiated. For some reason only two of these seven were referred the D.A.'s office.

To be fair, it isn't entirely the fault of the DOC that so few criminal cases have been pursued. Women in prison themselves have little incentive to report sexual relationships with guards. The reasons for this are numerous. A horror of publicity is one driving factor. Female inmates across the nation have complained that they face harsh retaliation if they speak up. A woman in the Federal Bureau of Prisons reported that she was beaten, raped, and sodomized by three men who told her, during the course of the attack, that they were retaliating against her for the statement she gave to investigators about sexual misconduct in the prison. In 1997 a Michigan woman also reported acts of retaliation including sexual and physical assault at the hands of guards for speaking out, and a former officer there claims to have been attacked by "an unknown person in an area of the prison where no prisoners were permitted access," after publicly denouncing guard-on-inmate abuse.

Even when punishment isn't the stated goal, most correctional systems remove a prisoner to "protective segregation" when they make an allegation of this kind. Protective segregation usually means being locked in a cell by yourself for twenty-three hours a day, and as this generally lasts for months—or as long as the investigation takes to complete—the effect, if not the intent, remains punitive.

Perhaps most damaging to an effective reporting process, however, is the difficulty of proving the claim, particularly when, as is almost always the case, the only evidence is the prisoner's own account. Even when witnesses can be found, conviction is rarely a foregone conclusion. In 2002, for example, three separate women accused the same officer at the minimum-security facility in Lancaster, Massachusetts, of sexual assault. One of them, a thirty-eight-year-old former heroin addict, testified that the officer, Daniel Tessier, fondled her breasts while she slept and then made small talk about a movie on TV while he touched her hair. According to her testimony, the woman "froze with fear" as Officer Tessier unbuttoned his pants, knelt on the floor with one foot against the door, and began touching himself while he "penetrated her digitally." When he was done, she said, Tessier looked at her inmate ID card, asked if she was going to "give him up," and then put three cigarettes on her shelf before leaving the room.

The woman had two witnesses to back up her testimony. They hadn't been in the room at the time, but they'd both seen her directly after the assault, holding the three cigarettes and sobbing. "She felt dirty and was scared and didn't know what she was going to do," one testified. "She wanted everyone to keep quiet about it."

The two other alleged victims told similar stories about Tessier entering their room and touching them. In this case, there was no physical evidence like the semen-stained garment that convicted Anthony Maddix. In the end, all Tessier's attorney had to do was tell the jury: "He pleads not guilty. He tells you, I didn't do it. They have the wrong man," and they voted to acquit.

As in so many cases, the alleged victims soon found themselves back in medium-security Framingham instead of in the far more comfortable minimum-security facility in Lancaster. They present a living, breathing warning to other inmates about the danger of reporting guard-on-inmate abuse. But there is another, more subterranean and complex reason for incarcerated women's silence on this issue. It has to do with rebellion and desire.

All human contact is illegal in prison. Even a touch or a sympathetic hug between inmates is punishable by a stint in the Hole. I'll never forget the time I saw a husband and wife clasp hands in the visiting room only to have an officer storm over to the husband shouting: "Get your hands off her!" Voluntary physical contact of any kind, then, represents both a liberating defeat of these rules and a rare moment of connection with another human being. It needs to be said that many officers at MCI-Framingham perform their work appropriately. A few, like Maddix, abuse their power appallingly and literally rape at will. A sizable group, however, I have come to believe, simply succumb to the temptations that surround them.

Even on the outside, that power attracts is a truism. In prison, where powerlessness is the ultimate, daily reality, it becomes magnetic. When I asked Julie who initiated the romance between her and F., she didn't hesitate. "Oh, me definitely," she told me. "I sweated him, I followed him everywhere. Sucker didn't have a chance." But she was quick to admit too that she wouldn't have looked twice at most of the guards if she were out on the street.

"No, ickkk!" she said when I asked, trying hard not to sound as exasperated as she was clearly starting to feel. "You gotta understand, it's a different world in here. Ninety percent of these officers could fuck whoever they want in jail, no matter how smoking she is, no matter how good-looking. It's a power thing, Tina!" she said then, referring not to the power the officers wield but to her belief that it rubs off on inmates in close enough contact with them. "I fucking walked around the three-to-eleven shift like my shit didn't stink," she went on. "Nobody gave me D reports. Nobody did anything because they all knew I was going with F. If we walked by Officer T., who's one of F.'s friends, if we walked by T. going somewhere unusual, do you think he's going to say anything?

"Like one night we was coming out of the Smith Building and Officer T. was at gate C, in between HSU and the Smith Building. He goes, 'And where are you two going?' and F.'s like, 'Mind your business,' joking around. He knew where we were going. We were always doing it. Always balling!"

Julie's eyes were sparking now, and it was clear she was feeling not only empowered but triumphant. Sitting there watching her, I had to recognize the thrill she was feeling then; the glee of self-assertion and the inner swagger that breaking all the rules entitles you to. So however twisted the logic, I understood too when Julie told me sternly one day that if I wrote about any of this, I would only "ruin it for everybody."

For a time I remained uncertain about how much to reveal here. I couldn't help feeling that even such a clearly self-destructive choice as Julie's remained a *choice,* and therefore a precious commodity in a world where your every minute is controlled by the state. It's not that I ever doubted that the consensual-sex law is a good law, or that it needs to be enforced. It's just that until it is, I couldn't help thinking that claiming a relationship as your own—as a conquest, a victory even— was, at least in some ways, healthier than succumbing to the legal as- sertion that you are incapable of consenting to something as basic and elemental as sex.

BUT THEN I met Marsha Pigett and all that changed. Marsha was a case of involuntary sexual relations being tagged as voluntary. A case that occurred before the law was passed and an example of what must have happened all the time.

A long-term victim of both physical and sexual abuse, Marsha had served three years of her five-year mandatory drug sentence at Fra- mingham before being transferred to the lower-security facility at Lan- caster. As a prerelease inmate at Lancaster, she was given work on the town's graveyard-maintenance crew and was placed under the direct supervision of two male city employees, Bob Jones, and a younger man named Max, who was in charge of the graveyard.

Bob was in his early sixties back then, and he was friendly enough to the inmates at first. He bought the girls cigarettes and let them smoke when the correctional officer who accompanied them to the graveyard every day was out of sight. He was even careful to get the brand that each woman liked: Newports for the most part, though

Marsha preferred Marlboro Lights. After about a month, though, his friendliness became a little overwhelming. Sexual innuendo crept into his conversation with increasing regularity, and soon he was telling Marsha—and a couple of other girls too, it turned out—that he wanted to "lick her pussy" and do all kinds of other things with her that were pictured in the porn magazines he used to store in a locker and bring out for further elucidation.

Marsha says she tried to keep away from Bob after that. But since she'd grown up in the countryside—the Spanish girls used to call her *jíbara*, "hick," because she knew more about farm machinery than all the other women put together—she was often left alone in the building where they stored the machines.

The first time Bob actually touched her, Marsha told me in a small-town diner near where she now works as a kitchen aide, was underneath the loft in the equipment shed, where she was sharpening blades for a lawn mower. "I had sweatpants and a sweatshirt on," she said. "And he came up from behind me and stuck his hand underneath my clothing and right up inside of me.

"Soon he was sticking his hands down my pants, sticking his hands up my shirt, whenever he could."

For months, from July to October 1998, Marsha told no one about this. She hated the way such behavior made her feel—"like I deserved it, like I didn't deserve to be treated any better than that"—and she wanted it to stop. But in part because Bob had a number of friends in the state police force who dropped by the graveyard all the time, she thought it safest to keep quiet. In fact, if one of the women who worked on the crew hadn't filed a complaint about Bob on the day she was released from prison, no one would have been any the wiser.

As it was, the DOC was forced to pursue an investigation into the freed woman's allegations. As almost always happened before the passage of the consensual-sex law, they seemed to find it easier to argue that the sex between Bob and the women he supervised was consensual rather than try to disprove the allegations altogether. They argued that the women agreed to Bob's fondlings in return for the cigarettes that he bought them, and the story quickly became known as the sex-for-cigarettes scandal. Because cigarettes are strictly forbidden in Massachusetts prisons, all the women involved were shipped back to Framingham for breaking the strict no-smoking rules. Bob, who in this scenario had done nothing illegal, was left to continue his work.

Marsha continued to keep silent about the nonconsensual nature of Bob's sexual approaches even after she was shipped back to Framingham. Bob had always said that no one would believe her if she dared tell the truth. But when investigation teams from both Lancaster and Framingham, as well as representatives from the state police, all got together to interview her, she finally broke her silence and related, in detail, the forced touchings and probings she had suffered for months. She also told them that she was afraid.

"I *was* afraid," she told me. "Bob, I knew, had friends who were cops. He made that very clear to me when he told me that nobody would ever believe me, because if I told people, who were they going to believe, an inmate or a cop's friend? He had said that to me more than one time."

"What did the police tell you?" I asked.

"Nothing. I think they understood why I was afraid. And the state cop told me if I was afraid, then I should write a statement that I didn't want to press charges at that time. That way that would protect me. So that's what I did."

"You signed a paper declining to press charges?"

"*At that time,* yes. See, at the time I'm still thinking that I'm going to end up in big trouble over all this. That was my mind-set because the whole time this was going on Bob would tell me that if anything ever got said, then I would be the one who gets in trouble, not him. And I believed that."

In the end, of course, Bob was right. Bob Jones remains an employee of the town of Lancaster even today. After declining to press charges, however, Marsha suffered a very different fate. While bringing an end to the sexual-relations investigation, she remained charged with the possession of cigarettes. For this infraction, she suffered a transfer back from a minimum-security facility to Framingham, a six-month loss of the right to buy food or toiletries from Canteen, and a six-month loss of visiting privileges. The repeated sexual assaults she had suffered at the hands of a city employee were, apparently, forgotten.

PERHAPS IN PART because of examples like Marsha's, Officer F. felt no need to be particularly careful about his involvement with Julie at Framingham. He seemed to rely more on the discretion of others than on any kind of wiliness of his own. People knew. People had always known. But after four months, word had started to seep out beyond the reliable community of officers and their similarly implicated women. On Labor Day the Inner Perimeter Security team hauled Julie in for questioning about her "inappropriate relationship" with F.

The IPS officers knew Julie well. She'd been sent to them twice before, once for the alleged suicide attempt with the ground-up Xanax, once for losing her temper with a female officer and calling her "a cunt." As they always did, they put on kind expressions when she came into the room, told her to take a seat and to tell them everything. They understood her position, they said; no harm would come to her if she just told the truth. But that wasn't Julie's style; she wasn't even tempted to "come clean." Besides, she knew F. would kill her if she did. He was married, after all, had his twins to support; it might cost him his job if she talked. So she said nothing. Later, when she told F. how worried she'd been for him, she told me that he said, "Listen, there are three kinds of officers. There's temporary officers, there's transfer officers, and there's permanent officers. I'm a permanent officer. It would take an act of Congress to get me out of here."

They did have to cool it for a while, he said. People were watching. Julie was despondent about this, and when I asked, the next time I saw her, if she was seeing him at all, she dropped her head onto the visiting room table and said, "I wish." The collapse was only temporary, though. A couple of weeks later they were back together. He even finagled a way to visit her in the Hole, where she'd been placed for fighting with a girl named Trina ("She thinks she's so great just because she's with a guy with stripes on his arm"), and after a month or so you'd never be able to tell that IPS had ever been involved.

DENISE, FOR HER own part, had backed off V. almost entirely after the bubble-gum incident. She had spent a couple of days in front of the mirror, applying foundation, lipstick, and eyeliner in the mornings, but she was mostly furious at herself, wary and scared and not a little regretful at the turn their relationship seemed to be taking. She wasn't Julie, she kept telling herself. Julie lived for this stuff—she moved in a cloud of sexual energy and got through her time fairly easily that way. But Julie was young, and Denise was thirty-four and a mother—someone who knew better. And who was she anyway to be laughing or fooling around with makeup or enjoying a piece of Bubble Yum when she was in prison so many thousands of miles away from her son? A few weeks before, she had slumped back in the bolted-down visiting-room chair and said, "It makes me feel so guilty. I mean, here I am in prison, and I'm laughing my head off until two o'clock in the morning, and my son is so, so far away."

It was a complete surprise, therefore, when V., now known to Denise and Julie almost exclusively as Bubble Gum Man, popped the lock of their cell during count one afternoon. This was how it always happened, Denise knew by now, and the sound of that lock being undone prompted something close to panic. She'd allowed herself to chat with him for a few minutes earlier that day, but she hadn't meant anything by it. She certainly didn't want to go out to him now. Didn't want to fool around at all. Not with Bubble Gum Man. Julie, of course, was thrilled. It was safe, she kept saying. No one would ever know. All the girls were locked in their rooms, and he was an officer, for chrissake. Didn't she want some? All she had to do was walk out of her cell and across the corridor maybe five feet to the bubble, and there he'd be, waiting for her. He was wicked good-looking, she said, even by outside standards (maybe), and his cute little earring? Just go! Go!

But Denise couldn't move. The seconds ticked by and the door hung there, heavy and open and alarmingly expectant. She could picture V. sitting there in his bubble, straightening his uniform, maybe turning his earring as he watched the door. He wouldn't get up and close it now, any more than she would walk through it. Time slowed. She wanted that door closed again more than anything in the world.

Almost a full hour later the intercom screeched, "End of count!" and the doors of all the other rooms finally popped open. Denise left the unit for the rest of the evening and spent the next few days in her cell when he was on shift, watching a lot of bad daytime TV and flicking through the magazines her mother sent her every month.

Part of it was guilt. He was a good officer and a good guy, and she'd given him the come-on and then bailed. He wasn't the kind to mess around, she berated herself, and he'd seemed genuinely to like to her.

She needn't have worried, though. Bubble Gum Man wasn't as crushed as she thought he would be. Or as good. Just a couple of weeks later he was abruptly transferred to the front desk. A short time after that he left the premises altogether. He'd been caught in a closet with another inmate from Denise's unit. The woman involved had been sent straight to the Hole, a place Denise had never, until now, even risked being sent to. Denise was enraged at first. Then embarrassed. But the experience hurt her pride more than her heart, and after a couple of weeks she was relieved to get back to the less scintillating life of quietly serving her time, of toothbrushing and muscle building and occasionally, just occasionally, thinking about Pat.

ELIZA FARNHAM

RAPE HAD ALWAYS been a problem—really *the* problem—for women in prison in America. The eighteenth century's use of pillories, stocks, and hangman's nooses had given way, by the nineteenth, to less violent punishment behind the walls of a prison. This was progress, undoubtedly. Especially for men whose punishment was now designed to reform, instead of only to reprove. For women, however, the move to incarceration held a number of problems unassociated with the public, physical humiliations of the town square.

Prisons—or penitentiaries, as they were then known—were designed to bring about spiritual and moral reformation of criminals. For decades arguments raged about how best to achieve this—to keep prisoners in solitary confinement with only the Bible for company, or to have them work communally at profitable labor for the duration of their terms. The problem for women at this time, however, was that unlike men, they were seen as entirely unreformable.

Worshipped almost as a goddess while she conformed to the confines of home and hearth, the nineteenth-century woman was subject to a vicious double standard if she ever strayed. In the words of one Belle Époque historian, even one episode of extramarital sex brought her "a rotting, a decomposition of human virtue and dignity. Even a single sexual experience made her capable of any crime." One misstep and a woman was beyond redemption, beyond reform. And, like the proverbial apple in the barrel, just one was enough to corrupt every man she came into contact with.

This was especially true in prison. "The reformation of girls who have contracted bad morals, is a chimera which it is useless to pursue," correction officials of the time advised. So while the men in some prisons were allowed to work, and those in others only to contemplate the errors of their ways in seclusion, female convicts were simply herded into the airless basements or attics of these shiny new prisons and, thereafter, ignored.

Conditions in one New York prison, Auburn, were more or less typical. Here, where men were carefully classified and segregated into rooms of their own, women were held, unsupervised, in a sprawling attic room from which they were let out only once a week in order to walk down a corridor to a closed wooden grate behind which they huddled for church. In Auburn, as around the country, the windows in this room were blackened and sealed closed all year round in order to prevent the spread of the women's "moral pestilence" to the men of the prison. Ironically, however, a detail of male prisoners entered the women's quarters each day in order to deliver necessities and carry out refuse. Sometimes these men lingered, and prison-spawned pregnancies were not uncommon despite the fact that as many as thirty women were often crowded together in the dark, airless room. Lack of fresh air and exercise also led to the rapid spread of disease among the female convicts. But because the prison guards and prison doctors were male, the women's infirmities frequently went unnoticed.

"To be a male convict in this prison would be quite tolerable; but to be a female convict for any protracted period, would be worse than death," the Reverend B. C. Smith reported after visiting the women's quarters, yet some women spent as long as fourteen years locked inside. So many went mad that workers in the prison began to complain about their shrieking. When a group of inspectors were sent to investigate, they found that the women's room presented "a specimen of the most disgusting and appalling features of the old system of prison management at the worst period of its history. We know of no subject of legislation which, in our opinion, calls more loudly for immediate action than this."

It wasn't until a woman named Rachel Welch died in this attic room in 1825, however, that any real support for a separate women's prison got under way. Welch had been admitted to Auburn about a year before. Like many women inmates of the time, she'd become pregnant during her incarceration, probably at the hands of one of the inmates who brought the women their meals. Five months into her pregnancy, a guard named Ebenezer Cobb flogged Welch brutally, and shortly thereafter she died. Such was the extent of the beating that a grand jury later convicted Cobb of assault and battery. Tellingly, they fined him twenty-five dollars but let him keep his job.

Such conditions were by no means extraordinary across the States, or indeed in the world at large. Though the first ever women's prison, the Spinhuis, was in Amsterdam, most European countries left criminally convicted women to languish in dark corners of men's prisons where they were at best ignored, at worst, beaten and raped. The eighteenth-century governors of the London Bridewell prison, for example, ran their institution as a highly profitable brothel by persuading women inmates to provide sexual services. Those who would not prostitute themselves "voluntarily" were coerced by threats and beatings to do so.

Even then it seemed clear that female supervision of female inmates would have prevented the worst of these abuses. But it wasn't until the early nineteenth century, when a few privileged women began to emerge from the confines of the home, that a series of tentative experiments in such female supervision began to take hold. Under the influence of the British reformer Elizabeth Fry, women opened and ran a handful of separate female wards in men's prisons on both sides of the Atlantic. The apparent success of these programs in the United States lent impetus to reformers' requests for entirely separate, female-controlled prisons for women, and in 1838 such a prison was finally constructed.

Described as "an imposing marble structure, after the model of a Greek temple, with massive columns," the first women's prison in the United States stood on the grounds of the now famous men's prison at Sing Sing in New York. This was, wrote a deputy matron of the time, a "charming situation. . . . The broad and beautiful Hudson is widened at this point to a bay and its banks were rich in color till the late autumn. Groups of locust trees and tall shimmering poplars helped to give picturesqueness to the neighborhood. Small craft like happy spirits used to flit up and down the river continually."

Despite its stately appearance, however, and the good intentions of its supporters, the new institution quickly proved defective. Though under the nominal supervision of a female warden, Mount Pleasant, as it was called, remained under the real control of Sing Sing's male administrators. Thus, windows in the women's building continued to be sealed for fear of male prisoners' morals. Punishments were corporal, frequent, and harsh; food was poor; and the lack of adequate hospital and nursery facilities meant mortality rates remained extraordinarily high.

Conditions became so bad so quickly, in fact, that less than five years after it opened—and after a riot during which women threw food at the warden and, seemingly worse, "made the air ring with ribald songs and lusty yells"—inspectors recommended that the place be shut down. The problem was that no one wanted the women. If nothing else, Mount Pleasant had at last freed the state's male prisons from the ordeal of housing what one official of the time called these "purveyors of moral pestilence." With little alternative, then, administrators were forced to keep Mount Pleasant in operation. Desperate, they hired an independent-minded woman named Eliza Farnham to run it.

Like only a handful of progressives of the time, Farnham believed that the reform of female criminals was not only possible but plausible. To this end, and to the chagrin of many contemporary penologists, she took the then radical step of instituting communal schooling at Mount Pleasant. With funds gathered by the sale of the women's own handicrafts, the prison library (which up until then had housed only seventy-five copies of a book entitled *Call to the Unconverted Sinner*) became the new focal point of the prison. Classes and lectures were provided. Women who could read were given books to take back to their cells. Illiterates were allowed instructional picture books.

Such educational initiatives, however, were only the beginning. Farnham believed the whole atmosphere of Mount Pleasant—its isolation, darkness, and gloom—could have only a negative influence on the women in her care. Flowers were placed on windowsills; donated maps and paintings were hung on walls. Large lamps were hung from ceilings. Visiting speakers were welcomed. Holidays were celebrated, and music became a part of institutional life.

In an environment where good behavior led to increased privileges, disciplinary problems were dramatically reduced. Illiterate inmates now spent the bulk of their time learning to read, while others attended workshops and training programs. For a time the possibilities seemed limitless. Activists and reformers traveled across the United States to see firsthand the changes Farnham had wrought at Mount Pleasant. But there were dissenters as well. The prison chaplain in particular was upset by Farnham's emphasis on secular education and her encouragement of novel reading, especially Dickens's *Nicholas Nickleby* and *A Christmas Carol.*

When Farnham later fired him, the chaplain went public with his complaints and asserted in the New York tabloids that she had inculcated in the women "a love of novel reading averse to labor," and that she was willfully neglecting even the most basic religious instruction at the prison.

Such indulgence of female criminals made for good copy in the nineteenth century, and more headlines materialized: Farnham was capricious in her administration of discipline; she used prisoners as hired help for her family; she was loose with prison funds. No proof was ever offered for these claims, but Farnham's increasing notoriety weakened whatever political support she may have held until then. In 1847 two conservative prison inspectors finally ended her experiment when they sent the legislature a statement condemning Mount Pleasant outright, not on the grounds that its warden was inefficient or corrupt but on the far more rudimentary supposition that reform should never be the aim of a prison in the first place.

When they visited the institution, they saw, apparently, what Farnham had been so avidly trying to create: a prison as a place of reform and education and hope. But instead of being impressed, they were frightened.

"Let prisons cease to be a terror to the depraved," they argued, ". . . and the period will arrive when insurrection, incendiarism, robbery and all the evils most fatal to society and detrimental to law and order, will reign supreme."

It apparently mattered little that crime was actually being reduced through the successful reformation of the women at Mount Pleasant. The charge of pampering criminals had already become an easy one to

level, and politicians no more dared to disagree with it in the nineteenth century than they do today. Under pressure, therefore, and in
disgrace, Farnham was finally forced to resign in 1848. Funding to the
prison was dramatically reduced. Programs were cut. And two years
later, after a series of inmate riots, the prison was shut down for good.
Across the state, women were sent back to the unsupervised and darkened garrets of men's prisons. It would be decades before the memory
of Mount Pleasant became blurred enough for another women's facility to be opened in America.

STEPS

THE ADMINISTRATOR IN charge of MCI-Framingham while I was researching this book was a small, plump woman named Barbara Guarino. She didn't seem like a prison warden at all. In fact, her vague, hovering smile and her distracted air made her seem more like a good-natured volunteer—perhaps a flower arranger—than the woman in charge of almost 250 correctional officers and 600 inmates.

The first time I met her she was wearing a soft green floral suit and carrying a handbag just like the queen of England's: black and shiny with one of those U-shaped handles that hang from the wrist when your arm is just so.

We had met, by chance, at a DOC-sponsored press event and then again, briefly, at a farm stand afterward. Guarino was puttering around, choosing perennials for her garden. At nine dollars the tiger lilies were so much cheaper than those near her home. She couldn't resist buying several, though she did worry about leaving them parked in her car at Framingham for the rest of the day. "I could take them into the facility with me," she said to herself wistfully. "But no, I don't want to do that," she corrected herself, and then smiled again at the waiting cashier.

When I told her that I was headed to MCI-Framingham myself just then, she smiled sweetly and said: "Really? How nice! Good luck!"

This sense of good-natured vagueness became particularly incongruous when I learned that Guarino had worked for the department for thirty-two years. Of these, all but five had been at MCI-Framingham. Back in 1971 she was hired as a junior clerk at the prison—"A junior clerk and typist," she told me when I met her more officially, obviously proud of her humble beginnings. And now, here she was, in charge! The idea seemed surprising even to her. Certainly the inmates were not much impressed with her leadership capabilities. She rarely showed up in the dining hall for "Happy Hour," when women were supposed to be able to ask questions directly of the administration, and she never walked around the prison on her own. She did, however, occasionally tour the facility with a phalanx of staff. Once she stumbled upon an inmate named Flora stirring a can of spaghetti with a spoon she had constructed herself. Utensils are not allowed on the housing units, but Guarino seemed unaware of this. "Oh, how creative!" she'd said. "Let me see how you made that." After chatting amiably with Flora for a few minutes more, Guarino wandered off. The next day officers came to confiscate Flora's "creative" work. This seemed typical. Guarino was, everyone seemed to agree, a "hands-off" superintendent.

"She doesn't run this prison, DOS Oxford does," Flora's girlfriend, Janine, told me a few weeks after the event, referring to the prison's director of security. "He wants to make this into a men's prison, and she's out of it. She don't know what the hell's going on."

Guarino did allow that changes, both big and small, had taken place during her tenure at Framingham, but she denied even the possibility of it becoming like a men's prison. She wished it weren't so, but the institution she ran didn't have the luxury of being a straightforward state prison the way men's facilities were. Framingham held state prisoners for sure, but also federal prisoners and county inmates. It held both women who'd been sentenced and those awaiting trial; women at every level of security classification, those seriously in need of drug treatment, and those who, in an ideal world, would best be housed in a mental facility. Each of these groups would have had their own facility if the population were male—there are eight prisons for men in this state alone. But Framingham was pretty much all there was for women. Other than a few dozen beds at one minimum-security facility, this was where you went if you were a woman who broke the law in Massachusetts. Framingham was a "different world," Guarino kept saying. "But then, of course, the biggest difference is that the female offender is very receptive to educational programming."

I asked her why she thought this might be.

"I'm not sure. It could just be one of those men/women things—what's that book? *Men Are from Mars, Women Are from Venus*?" It could just be that, you know, a group of women together, they like to feel like they're doing something constructive, and it could simply be that."

We were sitting in an upstairs room at MCI-Framingham when Guarino told me this. Every year the prison opens its doors to the media for a partial and guided tour of the facility. The tour includes a rather flashy, full-color folder describing the facility but omits the Health Services Unit, the punishment block, the dining hall, and the unit reserved for the mentally ill, and while I'd been reluctant at first to grant the DOC the legitimacy such pseudo-openness seems to claim, I soon realized it was the only way I'd ever see even a portion of the prison and signed up.

There wasn't much that was newsworthy about such a well-chaperoned, circumscribed tour, and only one other reporter showed up. We weren't officially supposed to be interviewing anyone. Nonetheless, Justin Lantini, the media-relations man, paid close attention to my chat with the superintendent and jumped in as soon as she started to talk about programming.

"Women are very receptive to treatment," he repeated. "But while over the years we've had various fluff programs, feel-good programs, today we've finally figured out what inmates need."

When I asked, Lantini wasn't able to be specific about either the fluff programs or the ones women needed. And then Guarino jumped in again, grinning blissfully: "Yes, yes," she said incongruously. "If we build it, they come!"

THE DEPARTMENT OF Correction frequently acknowledges the special needs of incarcerated women during meetings like this. They have little choice. Over the past twenty years a rising stack of governmental reports has outlined just how numerous these needs are, as well as how little served they are in most prisons. In 1998, for example, the National Institute of Justice produced a report with the following findings: "Women offenders have needs different from those of men, stemming in part from their disproportionate victimization from sexual or physical abuse and their responsibility for children. They are also more likely to be addicted to drugs and to have mental illnesses. Many states and jail jurisdictions . . . have little special provision either in management or programming for meeting the needs of women."

Perhaps in response to this, DOC officials such as Lantini repeatedly state that MCI-Framingham has more programs and opportunities than any other prison in the system. Its website indicates a long list of programs available to the women of Framingham, including adult basic education, the Boston University program, building trades, computer technology, GED and pre-GED classes, but when you take into account the diversity and breadth of its population, it remains a fact that each woman at MCI-Framingham has access to fewer programs, and therefore to fewer privileges and less prison-earned "good time," than most male prisoners in the state.

On the guided media tour, for example, we were able to walk around parts of the building where classes are held and meet the institution school principal, Ann Marchitelli. She'd been working at the DOC for twenty-seven years, and when the other reporter asked if the most recent round of cutbacks had affected her programming, she almost started to speak and then checked herself and, looking around at the group of administrators surrounding us, asked: "Is it okay? Can I . . ." Someone must have nodded then because she focused on the other journalist and me again and said with an audible tinge of anger: "I lost half my staff this January. Five people. And I ended up losing more than fifty percent of my population of students. I lost almost *sixty percent* of my population. It was, and this is an estimate, it was close to two hundred women that we lost with those cuts."

Most dramatically cut were English as a second language, which was closed down altogether, and the GED program, which was reduced by half. The manicure program had been closed entirely, and construction arts was cut by 50 percent. There is a waiting list—twenty women long—for the computer class, which is everyone's favorite, and long waits for everything else that is offered. The computer course lasts ten months, so it can take years to get a slot in the class.

In this way, programs at Framingham both exist and do not exist. Therapy, exercise, educational opportunities, behavior modification, and drug treatment can all be said to exist in the prison. Most, however, are unavailable to the majority of women incarcerated there. Many programs have been so shredded by cuts that their actual function is hard to decipher. Catch the Hope, a program designed to provide prenatal and birthing care to pregnant women, for example, is currently run by a staff of one—a woman who has no experience or training in prenatal care. With between 3,600 and 4,000 entrances and releases each year, this makes providing any actual, practical help more or less impossible. And for various reasons, this drives the women at Framingham crazy.

Especially as, despite strict rules forbidding it, they are in frequent and continuous touch with their male counterparts across the state. In Massachusetts, communication between prisoners in different institutions is punishable by time in the Hole. Officials stress the potential danger of such interprison communication. It happened, for example, that a gang leader in one New York prison was able to order a hit on an inmate in another institution—even from solitary confinement. By far the bulk of the interprison letter writing from Framingham, however, is more humdrum in nature. Many of the women's boyfriends and husbands are also behind bars; most were their co-defendants in court, and because of the interconnectedness of these personal relationships, letters from Framingham tend to make their way to their destinations despite correctional officers' attempts to prevent them.

Valentine cards and photos of kids, promises of lives reformed, news of classes and programs graduated, word of relatives, of births and deaths and familial or neighborhood scandals, make their way from woman to man and man to woman via a system known as the "three-way mail." Here's how it works: an inmate in one institution mails a letter to an inmate in another by enclosing it in an envelope addressed to a friend on the outside. This friend then forwards the enclosed to its intended receiver free of the mandated warning that is stamped on the back of all mail sent directly from a correctional institution.

Because the DOC retains the right to open—though not to read— all incoming mail, communications in these letters are, of necessity, vaguely phrased ("Life in this apartment complex continues to get worse and worse"). But codes have long been established to get around that. I think I'm safe in saying that there isn't a woman in Framingham who hasn't at one time or another been in communication with her co-defendant, or, lacking one, with a friend of her roommate's co-defendant at least. With visits so few and programs so reduced, any contact with the outside world is better than no contact at all, and they go on risking their hard-won privileges in order to support ex-boyfriends, or husbands, or sometimes even strangers in the way that, as one man wrote, "only a woman knows how."

One or two women at Framingham, however, keep in contact with male inmates for altogether different and ulterior motives. A lifer named Janine Arloise, for example, keeps tabs on shifts in DOC regulations in the men's prisons through the three-way mail. In this way she is generally in a position to know when a rule change allows men in prison to buy fresh fruit and vegetables almost on the day that it happens.

Janine is fifty-one years old. After thirteen years at Framingham, though, she looks seventy-five. Her skin is powdery and soft. Not pale, exactly, but translucent, made solid only by the myriad creases of age that mark her skin like a cartoonist's crosshatching. She couldn't stand up to greet me when I first met her. Her hip had given way, and she had a pair of wooden crutches leaning against a chair. She ordered me around the room, first to get a meat sandwich, then a soda, then a bag of chips, with the proud entitlement of a woman who'd beaten the odds simply by surviving so long.

But then, she'd always looked older than her age. When she was just thirteen, she told me, her mother had been able to sell her as a wife to a neighbor for three hundred dollars. Her mother and her father were abusive, she explained, drinkers who were seldom around and who were violent when they were. But her husband was worse. In a calm voice, as though it had happened to another person long ago, she began to detail the physical and psychological abuse he'd subjected her to. But I was stuck on the detail of the "selling." I asked her what she meant exactly by that. She looked at me, blank and angry all of a sudden, and said:

"What part of it is it that you don't understand? My. Mother. Sold. Me. For. Three. Hundred. Dollars. I. Was. His. Merchandise."

IT WAS 1988 when Janine first arrived at Framingham—and it really was a different world then. All the women had more freedom, as well as a greater array of educational options to choose from. But lifers especially led a different kind of existence. They had their own unit, a "family-like setting," with carpets in the dayroom, and plants, and they were allowed their own sheets and blankets and shades on the windows. They had a family day twice a year during which they could eat outside, walk around the "compound," and go to their rooms with their families "so that the kids could see where Mama lives." They even had pizza once a month, paid for with money raised from selling their arts and crafts at a stand in the main prison entrance. They put on talent shows, plays, and fashion shows for the rest of the prison and were allowed regular peer-support groups too.

Through her active three-way correspondence, Janine knew that many of these advantages were still offered to male lifers. With little left to lose, male lifers are seen to pose a threat to security, and it's generally acknowledged good policy to keep them as happy as possible. All such privileges were removed from the women in Framingham in 1992, and since then they've had to live just like everyone else at the prison. Housed in rooms with nonlifers, they are now forced to compete for recreation activities and programs with people who are there for less than a year.

It's just one more example of women being stepped over for men, Janine is convinced. She keeps a list. Most egregiously, men in prison are able to earn twelve days a month good time because they have the programs and educational classes to do it, while women who aren't in the drug-rehab program (which grants seven and a half days) can earn a maximum of five. The whole concept of earning good time was that it was supposed to act as an incentive to learn. Paradoxically, it now does the opposite, encouraging inmates to fail classes so that they can keep earning their two and a half days of good time month after month after month. Susan Grissin had been in the pre-GED program for a year and a half and seemed in no hurry to get out. When I asked how long most women stay in the class, she smiled and said: "Well, there's the good time, right? We ain't stupid."

After years of trying to rebalance the system in the women's favor, Janine has concluded that the main fault for these continuing inequities lies with the women themselves. "My main goal," Janine told me, "is fighting where women are afraid to fight." Male prisoners are prepared to stand up and fight for their needs, while women are not, she said. "We are afraid of creating any turmoil, so it just doesn't work out for us."

This is at least partly true. Journalists, politicians, and legal-aid groups all report receiving virtually no mail from the women at Framingham, while they are swamped by complaints from male inmates in the state. There has been no protest against reduced programming or long sentences in the Hole. No voiced outrage over coerced guard-on-inmate sex, or high prison suicide rates. The women of Framingham came together only when DOS Oxford tried to ban tampons from the premises. After a woman tried to kill herself by swallowing one, leaving it in her throat and then drinking water to cause it to swell, he'd insisted the women make do with panty pads. Threatening to sue on the grounds of "cruel and unusual punishment," the women grew so incensed, however, that Oxford finally backed down—partway. The women continue to get toilet paper and panty pads for free, but tampons, regarded as a luxury, have to be purchased from Canteen.

It was the ban on T-shirt wearing, however, that most undid Janine. The regulation change had come about because COs were taking off their jackets on the job and authorities were worried that confusion might arise if inmates were allowed to wear clothes the same color as the COs' regulation black or blue undershirts. Prisoners would therefore be allowed to wear white T-shirts only. This seemed simple enough. Except that women in prison have never been allowed to wear white T-shirts. They are too see-through, supposedly, and are only allowed to be worn under DOC-approved "dress" shirts. The new regulation thus effectively (and unintentionally) barred women from wearing T-shirts at all.

Janine had seen the list of approved clothing shrink with almost every year she'd been at Framingham. But this was the final straw. If it was visible flesh they were worried about, why did the DOC force county inmates and women awaiting trial to wear men's stiff gray uniforms with Vs cut out at the neck that on women became deeply revealing? According to Janine, and as soon as she mentioned it I could see she was right: "All you have to do is bend over in one of those, and everyone sees *everything.*"

For once, she was determined to organize a protest. Not a big thing, just a group of women marching out to the yard wearing plain white T-shirts with no dress shirts on top. Bras were fine. She wasn't out to incite anyone. She just wanted to draw attention to the absurdity of it all. Janine had a lot of pull at Framingham. As the self-proclaimed mother to the family of lifers, she was particularly influential with women serving ten years or more, and after a few days of canvassing, it looked like a sizable crowd might follow her. In the end, though, and when the time came, no one dared join in. Undaunted, Janine, in her white T-shirt, marched out to the yard on her own. She lasted just a couple of minutes. Then a CO sent her back to her room to change.

DENISE HEARD ABOUT Janine's plan but wanted nothing to do with it. Like almost everyone else at Framingham, she knew Janine at least by name—she was as close as you can get to being famous there. But the two women were not friends. Janine had her hands full with her thirteen lifer "kids" ("They don't ask anything from me but love. Not money, but 'Can you rub my head, Mom?' and 'Do you love me?' " to which Janine replies: "I love you immensely.") But her relationship with her lover, Flora, a manic-depressive who played abusive husband and father to Janine's doting wife and mother, upset Denise. As far as she could make out, Janine spent half her time ironing Flora's shirts, polishing her shoes, keeping her room neat and tidy—and for what? More abuse? Wasn't it bad enough they all shared the same miserable histories on the outside? Did you have to go looking for it even in here?

Since she'd come to prison, Denise had been revisiting her relationship with Alan. She'd even made a list of the times he had physically abused her. He'd pushed her down the stairs when she was pregnant, hit her in the head, choked her—once until she passed out— and repeatedly made her watch him cut his wrists with a knife. He raped her twice, threw a phone at her head, held her against a wall by her neck while slamming his fist inches from her face; dumped a full ashtray over her head, and locked her and Patrick in a closet when she threatened to leave. On separate occasions he drove her car into a ditch and broke its every window. Once, in the middle of the night, he forced Denise and Patrick into his van and then stopped in the middle of the highway and turned off the lights.

The worst, though, had been that long-ago Memorial Day weekend when Denise first gathered up the courage to leave him. She'd filed a restraining order against him and then packed up Patrick and moved over to her mother's house. But it was late on Friday by the time the restraining order was ready, and no one found Alan that night. As Denise expected, he became enraged when he discovered she had left. With no legal order to restrain him, he charged around to her mother's house and spent ten minutes trying to "bust down her four-inch-thick front door." When he failed to break anything more than the frame, he crashed through the back-room window instead, hopped on the dresser, and then jumped to the floor with a carpet knife in his hand. He grabbed Denise and told her he would kill himself if she left, that there was no way she *would* ever leave. Upstairs thirteen-month-old Patrick screamed in his crib. Denise's mother, Nancy, dialed 911. Undeterred, Alan frog-marched Denise down the hallway and out the front door. Then he threw her in his van and screeched off down Middlesex Turnpike, banging the steering wheel and screaming, "You're not leaving me! You're not leaving me! You're not leaving me!"

Denise tried to sound calm. She told him that of course she wasn't leaving him, that all he had to do was pull over and she would never leave him; that she loved him, she loved him, all he had to do was stop the van. Cop cars were behind them by then, sirens wailing, lights flashing, but it wasn't until others materialized in front of them as well that Alan pulled into an industrial park and stopped the car. Denise took off running.

Physically, at least, she was more or less unharmed. But the story made the local papers, and Denise lost her temp job as a result. Nothing personal, her boss told her; they just didn't want publicity like that involving their firm.

FLORA WASN'T AS bad as that, of course. No one could get away with behavior like that in prison. Besides, when abuse occurred among the women, Janine herself confessed, it was most often emotional, not physical. "Flora is pigheaded, and she has that hardness about her like a man," she said. "But other than that she's supportive. She's really a good person—if she'd only let herself be . . . a person."

Denise couldn't for the life of her see the attraction. There was almost no casual sex between women at Framingham. What the women there needed were *relationships,* and she'd long grown used to seeing these ties ensnare rather than liberate. Just like in the real world, really. But Janine should have been different. If only because of how she stood up for herself in other ways. It might sound petty to people on the outside, but makeup and clothes and food really did become all-important to women who'd lost everything else. Granted, half the women wanted the cookies and the cakes and the starchy dinners the DOC laid out for them night after night. But Denise put this down to ignorance. Maybe, just maybe, some of them would increase their self-esteem, and even lose some weight, if they were ever given the option of healthful eating. As it was, they all gained thirty pounds at Framingham. Many couldn't wait to get out so they could get high and lose the extra weight.

It was the opposite of how it was for men. Men arrived in prison flabby and lax and left fitter and stronger than they'd ever been in their lives. There was an exercise program at Framingham—the full-sized gym had caused a scandal when a progressive superintendent had it built in the 1910s. And though it was more run-down now, volleyball, basketball, and softball teams still used the facility. Unlike at men's prisons, however, physical fitness remained peripheral at Framingham. The prison housed more than six hundred women, but the teams catered only to a small group of diehards. This drove Denise crazy. Here was a chance to force-feed healthfulness to women who'd spent years undermining their health through drinking, drug use, prostitution, depression, and abuse. For all the philosophy and sociology she'd been reading for her correspondence classes, it was this question of nutrition and physical health that had begun to grab her. Soon Denise was taking her stand against apathy by hauling women off to the gym to take part in an aerobics class a fellow inmate named Kayla had started to run for the recreation department.

It was pretty much all she talked about for a while: how exercise produced a natural drug in your body that made you feel great. How it gave energy, didn't use it up. How it improved your looks, your figure, your self-esteem. Julie was first bored, then irritated by it all. But Kayla and Denise were so relentlessly enthusiastic that even she started to show up in the gym at three-fifteen for an hour's jumping around before count. The truth was that it was a relief to Julie, and to many women—a release, all that crunching and jumping and sweating under the self-banishing *thump-thump* of the tape player and the exhortations of the two crazy women up front.

The class grew so popular so fast that, later, Denise would add a second step class, which she called "Buns and Abs," and which sometimes brought in as many as fifty women at a time. Not being an official employee of the recreation department, she wasn't paid, though she ran the class on her own. But she appreciated the dance tapes the rec officer brought in specially for her class, and she didn't much care about the $2.50 she could have been earning each week. It wasn't about that. It was about giving the women something they needed. And giving herself something too.

When she was called up for her biannual classification meeting, then, Denise was less eager than usual to perform at her best. The classification process is supposed to provide a realistic security level for every inmate individually. The higher the level, the higher the security level of the facility in which you are housed. Just as with men, these hearings were provided once every six months at Framingham. But while for men they were all-important—being successfully "classed down" could mean a change from a maximum- to a medium-security facility, or from a medium- to a minimum- —for women they were pretty much symbolic, since aside from a few dozen beds at MCI-Lancaster, Framingham was the only place they could be.

Perhaps that was why the meetings were always so weird. Three officers—a unit manager, a CO, and a social worker (who usually knew nothing about you)—summoned you into an office, read a description of your crime out loud, and then belittled you for having committed it. It happened every time. Denise assumed it was some kind of psychological test to see how you responded, and she always replied with the requisite remorse, though she knew it made little difference. Everyone knew the possibility of being transferred to Lancaster was based on numbers more than merit.

It was right there in their own regulations—any inmate with five years or less to serve was eligible to be considered for minimum-security clearance. But it was only when numbers fell low at Lancaster, or grew too unmanageably high at Framingham, that women had a chance of actually being "classed out." Until now, Denise had been determined to get to the minimum-security facility one way or another. Lancaster housed both men and women, the prospect of which didn't much thrill her, and they had nothing in the way of programming, she knew. But it did have a trailer fully outfitted like an apartment for kids to come stay in. Denise had spent whole nights imagining herself and Patrick together in that trailer. It had a kitchen, she'd heard. And a bath. She'd even told him about it when she'd finally reached him by phone after her block sergeant took pity on her and sent Alan's number in Hawaii all the way to the system's headquarters in Denver, where it was added to the list of available numbers for Framingham.

Patrick seemed to like the idea, though she hadn't been able to tell him if it had a TV. He sounded well, she had to admit. Fine. There was the occasional bout of alarming information—like the time Alan confessed he was so broke that the two of them had eaten nothing but rice and water for weeks. But through it all, Patrick seemed to be doing all right. He was very tall, even for an almost eleven-year-old, he told her—"five feet eight!"—and he'd gotten over the racial harassment at school and wanted to go to Boston University when he grew up, he said. BU was the college that offered classes to the women at Framingham who had sixteen credits or more, and when Denise said she was hoping to go there too one day, they both laughed.

Alan was a different matter. "He's right on schedule," Denise wrote me one day. "He works on an annual cycle. I can predict it, almost exactly to the day. He goes to bed every year for a couple of months in December and January. Just takes to bed and doesn't get up. During this time he acts out sexually, using the phones mostly. By the end of February he is either hospitalized or has been prescribed medication. By March or April he starts to feel better and goes out and has fun and has lots of affairs. After a while he starts to think he's fine again and stops taking his medication. That's when he starts to get violent and crazy until he finally takes to bed and gives up altogether again in the winter." It was May. He was, as she said, right on schedule. She could hear it in his voice. In his excitement that first time she got through, his rambling, manic chatter about things that couldn't possibly interest her while she stood in the frieze-block corridor of her unit, waiting to hear her son's voice. "You want to speak to Patrick?" Alan finally asked, and though it felt like more than she could cope with right then (she almost hung up the phone in panic), being able to speak with Patrick regularly over time had become the mainstay of her equilibrium.

So perhaps it wasn't worthwhile to transfer to Lancaster. It would be a relief to be out from behind the layers of fencing and barbed wire that surrounded Framingham, to escape the endless lockdowns and rigid hours for movement. Lancaster was beautiful, she'd heard, and you were more or less free to roam around when you liked. But who knew how long it would take to get the phones there set up to call Hawaii? It might be months before she spoke to Patrick again. On the other hand, Alan wouldn't stay out in Hawaii forever. The last time she heard anything of him he was making noises about coming back to Maine. Her mother had gotten the time difference confused when she last called him and woke him up in the middle of the night. In his fury he cursed and screamed about how he needed the money to get back out here and then hung up the phone. Three minutes later he called back and left a similarly raging message on her machine saying, "I'm going to kill you, you bitch!" Who knew how things really were out there?

The classification hearing was the same as it always was: the three officials, the crime, the belittling. The numbers were different, though. Framingham was packed and everyone knew it. So despite her lack of enthusiasm for the process, Denise wasn't altogether surprised to find she'd been classed out. She'd be at Lancaster in six weeks if all went according to plan. Things at Framingham frequently didn't go according to plan, of course. It was often the case that women who'd been told they were leaving were then told, on the day, that plans had changed. "I'll be excited when I'm there," Denise told me. "Although it's kind of scary too—you know, it's a new place and I'll miss Julie, and the girls, and the Buns and Abs, the step class. I'm not sure about the men there, either. Maybe, at least, we'll get better food?"

PART

LOSSES

TWO

MANDATORIES

"YOU GET TIRED of the same old routine, you know? It sometimes feels like there's only the count. Just the standing up for count four times a day. Ughhh! Sometimes I just can't cope with it. *This week* I haven't been able to cope." Charlene, the young woman who smuggled cocaine into the country from Jamaica, arrived in the visiting room late that day, and sleepy-headed. She'd been expecting me, but I was kept waiting by the officers outside, and when it got to be past two, she figured I wasn't coming and decided to take a nap. She'd been sleeping a lot, she said, since hearing that her appeal had been turned down.

As an inmate sentenced to a mandatory fifteen years at MCI-Framingham, Charlene was not able to earn a reduction in her sentence with earned good time, even if there were the programs to provide it. Nor was there any chance of parole. Mandatory sentences are just what they profess to be—mandated lengths of prison time that no established system can reduce. Unlike most violent criminals, then, Charlene would serve every day of her bizarrely specific fifteen-years-and-one-day sentence unless a judge overturned her conviction. This was unlikely. Charlene had been caught red-handed. She'd been so nervous stepping off the plane in Boston that customs people had picked her up right there in the airport. The drugs sewn into her clothes and stuffed into the panty pad were found just a few minutes later. There remained one last appeal, and after that, a one-off chance of a pardon from the governor, but neither of these seemed promising. Besides, Charlene didn't like to think like this. Fifteen years at Framingham was, frankly, unthinkable. Fifteen years would be her daughter's entire childhood. Kindergarten and grade school and all the way up to high school. Instead Charlene preferred to think about lawyers—about her first one, the privately hired Mr. Asuni, and how he'd always seemed so on top of everything, and then about her second one, state-hired, whom she'd barely even seen until the trial. She spent hours going over their various strengths and weaknesses, whole days planning how to rehire Mr. Asuni for a reduced fee, or how her sister, or perhaps one of her brothers, could help her find some other competent and capable lawyer, a better one, cheaper than Asuni but at least privately hired. Usually thinking strategically like this transformed despair into pragmatism, which at least kept time ticking by. Today, though, it couldn't sustain her.

"I cried last night," she told me suddenly, emerging from a silence that had hovered for minutes. "I laid down on my bunk and I cried from a daydream." She'd told me once that her favorite fantasy was of standing up in church and giving testimony after her release. She'd been a little embarrassed about this and used to wonder why this of all images was the one she so recurrently conjured up. After speaking to a couple of friends about it, though, she found that it was very common, that in fact everyone she asked fantasized the exact same thing. This time, though, the defeat in court had weakened her, and she allowed herself to imagine the unimaginable: returning home, ringing the doorbell, and then falling into her mother's astonished and disbelieving arms right there on the porch.

"I don't usually cry in front of my roommate because that affects her too," Charlene told me. "I don't want to depress no one. But I did cry last night. I did. I looked at my mother's picture and I kissed her. I love my mother. You see how I want my mother? That's how my daughter want me."

CHARLENE IS THE youngest of eight kids. Four boys, four girls. For years after her older sisters immigrated to the States from Saint Croix, she'd been the only girl living in the house. Because her mother worked two jobs, cleaning houses during the day and office buildings at night, Charlene took over the homemaking duties. Every afternoon she cooked, cleaned, and laundered. She reserved each Saturday morning for ironing, "five shirts each for each of my brothers and five shirts for me," in preparation for the coming school week. It was hard, shouldering all that responsibility at the age of eight, but she enjoyed the centrality of her role and the special treatment she received as the only girl-child in the house. Every year, no matter how hard times were, her mother gave her a birthday party. No one else had such a thing, and even as the guests arrived, she used to worry that her brothers might get jealous. She got sent to a real typing school on Saturdays too, in town. She was the youngest in the class by ten or fifteen years and had to sit on a book to reach the keys. But her mother wanted her to know how to look after herself, she'd said, and Charlene loved the grown-up feeling of sitting with the other women in class.

She remembered this every time she saw her daughter. The way Trinnie's legs dangled off the prison visiting-room chairs brought back images of that sun-filled room and the *clack clack clack*ing of the old typewriter keys: "cat cat cat, car car car, care care care." There were other memories too: when she was very little, her parents having fights; later, her big brother being hit by a car; her grandmother's funeral; and, when she was ten, getting her period for the very first time the day after she'd first kissed a boy and panicking that the baby she and that boy must have made was falling out of her into the toilet. Little Trinnie was still a scrawny five-year-old with heavy eyebrows and legs so thin they looked like a fawn's. But there was something about her, a "little womanness" Charlene said, that reminded her of herself as a child. "She's just so grown," she told me. "She's too grown. I want her to interact with people, but since I came in here she don't want to talk to no one. She's in and out of her own little world. I feel like I'm losing her sometimes, Tina, I do. And it don't ever get easier.

"Fifteen years," she said after a time. "This place breaks you down to where you don't even know who you are no more, or what you're capable of doing. You don't know nothing. Some days you wake up and you're so depressed you don't want to be bothered. You just want to be left alone. It's terrible. I can't get over it. I can't get over it. I feel like I'm losing my kid."

MORE THAN 30 percent of the women in Framingham were serving mandatory drug sentences like Charlene's. Most of them were first-time, nonviolent offenders who'd been caught up in a system originally designed to trap big-time dealers. As with so many things that turn out badly, mandatory minimum sentencing began with good intentions. During the 1970s widely divergent sentences were being handed down for more or less identical crimes depending on which state, or even which judge, the offender was tried by. It was in an attempt to eliminate such disparities that Congress stripped federal judges of nearly all sentencing discretion, instituting instead a set of prespecified, mandatory sentences for a variety of crimes. This idea was nothing new. As early as 900, King Alfred of England prescribed mandatory fines for every conceivable injury, including one shilling for an inch-long wound (if it fell under the hair); a thirty-shilling fine for a severed ear; and sixty-six shillings, six and one-third pence for a knocked-out eye.

In the United States too, mandatory sentences were imposed for crimes such as murder, piracy, and causing a ship to be run aground by use of false light as early as 1770. Then, as now, most of these standards were established following specific, heinous, and well-publicized crimes. This most recent bout of federal mandatory sentencing began taking hold after a young man named Len Bias, an all-American basketball player from the University of Maryland, collapsed and died in his dorm after using cocaine on June 19, 1986.

Crack cocaine had been a mainstay of inner-city life for years by then. But perhaps because its horrors had infected mostly urban, poor, and minority communities, it had been largely overlooked by mainstream politicians. Bias, on the other hand, had been chosen as a first-round draft pick by the Celtics two days before his death. His overdose made headlines across the country and, more than any other single event, galvanized public sentiment against drugs. The Reverend Jesse Jackson, among others, used the occasion of Bias's death to promote his vision of a national war on drugs. Just a few days later, President and Nancy Reagan made a joint television appearance in which they urged the nation to pull together for a new crusade. This was the beginning of the famed "Just Say No" campaign.

The public's response was overwhelmingly positive. In an attempt to placate their now riled-up constituents, lawmakers scrambled to make their own views clear. Harsh new drug-sentencing laws were passed with huge majorities in both the House and the Senate, and within a month, the massive Anti-Drug Abuse Act had been signed into law. Combined with its successor, the 1988 Anti-Drug Abuse Amendment Act, this law would change the direction of the criminal-justice system for the next twenty years.

Mandatory ten-, fifteen-, and twenty-year sentences were now imposed for drug dealing, and a minimum of five years in prison was now mandated for simple possession of five grams of crack. As well, "drug conspiracy" charges had been altered to allow the equal application of mandatory sentences to both major dealers and low-level hangers-on. From now on, prison sentences were to be based exclusively on the amount of drugs involved in an arrest rather than on the role of the offender in the crime. So it was that fifteen-year mandatory sentences began to be handed out to bottom-rung drug mules like Charlene, and to women like Mariselle Gonzalez, another young mother, whose involvement with drugs was so peripheral that her conviction was ultimately overturned.

Gonzalez had moved into her boyfriend's apartment when she lost her own place out in Fitchburg, Massachusetts. Unbeknownst to her, the apartment had long been under police surveillance, and soon after she moved in, a DEA raid uncovered bundles of cocaine hidden in the basement and tucked up in the rafters of the backyard shed. Gonzalez was out on the landing at the time of the raid, getting her children dressed for school. She had no criminal record and insisted she knew nothing about the drugs. No evidence proved otherwise, but under the mandatory minimum laws, her presence in the apartment alone was enough to convict her. Reluctantly, her judge was forced to sentence her to fifteen years in Framingham for drug trafficking. It took more than three and a half years to have her sentence overturned. By then her children were living in Puerto Rico with her mother and her life had been shattered.

In part because the majority of mandatory drug convictions were against small-time dealers and hangers-on like Gonzalez, the wave of crack-related crime remained unabated despite an ever-growing number of mandatory sentences at both the state and federal level. Fueled by the public's fear, members of Congress continued to compete to be the toughest of soldiers in the by now well-established War Against Drugs. By 1995, Republican congressman Newt Gingrich had begun to call for mandatory *life* sentences for first-time drug offenders, as well as a "two strikes you're *dead*" statute for second-time offenders. "If you sell it, we're going to kill you," he said.

That such dramatic sentiments held a visceral appeal to the nation at large is undeniable. At the same time, however, the nation's prison population had begun to swell so massively as a result of increased drug arrests that tens of millions of dollars were now required to build new prisons. The problem was that even seven years after the passage of the Anti-Drug Abuse Amendment Act, the great majority of these new prisoners remained low-level drug dealers instead of the much dis-cussed "drug kingpins" the laws had been designed to ensnare.

In 1995 *The Boston Globe* found that drug kingpins regularly avoided long sentences by trading a reduction in time for information on other dealers, or by making forfeiture deals in which police departments received thousands of dollars' worth of drug-related assets in exchange for shorter sentences. It was a kind of legalized bribery, a quid pro quo that quickly became a national phenomenon as one police depart-ment after another began to rely on seized drug assets to pay for further drug probes as well as, frequently, basic operating costs such as over-time and rent. In a review of major trafficking cases featuring ten thousand dollars or more of forfeited assets, the *Globe* found that "seventy-five percent of the drug dealers ended up charged with lesser crimes and were allowed to plead to substantially lower sentences. In a few cases, they walked away with no time in prison at all." Low-level drug dealers, on the other hand, rarely have access to this kind of money and are mostly in no position to barter information for a reduc-tion in sentencing.

"The real traffickers should be in prison forever," the *Globe* quoted Judge Thomas E. Connolly as saying. But he rarely got the chance to preside over such eminences. Instead, "ninety to ninety-five percent [of the cases that he heard] are drug or alcohol addicts, or both," he insisted. "Small-timers, kids making terrible mistakes. So we're putting away drug addicts for long-term sentences, and this does not help the drug problem."

DENISE WOULD AGREE. After placing a call to a drug-dealer friend on behalf of an undercover cop, she'd been arrested for dealing cocaine. An addict at the time, Denise had been haplessly vague even during the arrest. When the undercover cop came out with the drugs and asked "Hey, Denise. You got a scale?" she went to get the bathroom scale for the officer—"It was always five pounds off either way, that scale, I couldn't think what he wanted it for," she told me. "But I wanted to be helpful."

Like many other low-level dealers and hangers-on, Denise had been offered a reduction in time if she provided information deemed useful by the police. The problem was that she had none. Nor did she have any money. She'd been trying to figure out how to pay her three-hundred-dollar phone bill when she was arrested. One of the men she spent time with at the club, a one-eyed Chinese gangster who owned a bunch of restaurants and who always treated her like a lady, agreed to pay for a good lawyer. Following this lawyer's advice, Denise pled guilty to the charge and earned a five-year-and-a-day mandatory sentence.

Back in those early days at Framingham, Denise had tried to fight her way out of the institutionalization fog by joining a lobbying group called Families Against Mandatory Minimums. Created in 1991, FAMM, as it is known, comprises judges and lawyers as well as families of the incarcerated. With chapters in most states, FAMM lobbies for reform of the sentencing statutes. Denise spent a lot of time and energy getting petitions filled out by other women serving mandatory time. But it was hard to convince most of the women even to sign their names to any kind of official-looking protest sheet, and though many paid lip service to the idea of organized protest, Denise found herself writing their letters to the statehouse herself most of the time (albeit in ingeniously and variously disguised handwriting styles) and then paying for the stamp and the envelope out of her own pocket. This quickly became demoralizing. And what good would it do, anyway? The thorough and penetrating four-part series the *Globe* had run on the injustice inherent in mandatory sentences had had no effect on Massachusetts law. In fact, in the intervening years the laws had only stiffened. Now so many nonviolent offenders were being incarcerated across the state that it seemed there wasn't enough room left to house violent felons. But this was old news. Even back in 1995, the *Globe* found that violent armed robbers and men convicted of aggravated rape were having their time reduced by as much as 25 percent while sentences for nonviolent drug sales almost doubled. The difference was that now statistics like this merited just a couple of small wire articles in the local press. Denise mailed me a copy of one of them:

> Tina—I am *so* mad! I found the below information in the Boston Herald. I had to do something with it! So you came to mind ☺

STATE RECORDS REVEAL
LIGHT SENTENCING

The tough rhetoric stops at the courthouse door. While prosecutors and politicians say crimes against children demand the strongest possible punishment, the result in Massachusetts is often quite the opposite. Consider these sentences handed down in Suffolk County in 1999, the latest sentencing data available.

Eugene Casey was convicted of rape of a child, indecent assault and battery on a child under 14 and disseminating matter harmful to minors for crimes committed against an 11-year-old girl and her 10-year-old sister over a three year period. He received ten years probation from Judge David Roseman.

Raul Vasquez was convicted of two counts of rape of a child and four counts of indecent assault and battery on a child. He received four years for the rapes and three years probation for the indecent assaults from Judge Barbara Rouse.

Joseph Moody was convicted of rape of a child and indecent assault and battery upon a child. He received three years in jail from Judge Carol Ball.

Darryl Rankins, previously convicted in New York for forcible rape and in Suffolk County for indecent assault and battery against a child under 14, received three and a half years for four counts of rape of a child and probation for five counts of indecent assault and battery on a child under 14 from Judge Isaac Borenstein. Rankins had three victims. Although he was sentenced in 1999 he got credit for time served and was released in September of that year. Less than a year later he was arrested for two counts of indecent assault and battery on a child under 14 in Middlesex County.

These guys also received good time, parole eligibility and work release! I do every day of my 5 years. I have over 120 days that I've earned—I cannot use them towards reducing my sentence. These #!@##@** can! Imagine! Then studies prove that kids who are molested or raped have a much greater chance at substance abuse. So take a group of 10 kids who were molested or raped, follow their lives for 15–20 years . . . Guess who's in prison? Non-violent, drug offenders!

I was molested at age 11 by my neighbor. Julie was raped at 14, Susan Grissin was repeatedly raped . . . And the people who kick start the beginning of our destinies go free, or do so little time?! I'm doing two years more than a child rapist!?! I feel sick to my stomach. My molester never even saw a local police station, never mind years in jail away from his family.

Also, taking all of these mothers from their children leaves these kids more vulnerable to these types of predators. Then they grow up to use drugs? More in prison, where does it end?

Ok I feel better now. I vented.

See you

—love ya, Denise

The director of the New England chapter of FAMM, Nancy Brown, had been trying for years to convince someone to do a major story about women serving mandatory sentences. A tireless advocate, her efforts had been mostly fruitless so far. She was hopeful this year, however, because there was a mandatory-sentencing hearing scheduled on Capitol Hill the Friday before Mother's Day, and she thought that afterward the press might just be enticed to a small room to listen to some more personal testimonies next door. To this end she'd gathered a group of inmates' relatives—and Charlene's mother, Anna-May Williams, was one of them.

Anna-May is the mother of eight and the grandmother of seventeen, the oldest of whom is eighteen years old and in college. A qualified nurse's aide, she has worked in an old-age home since moving to the States from Saint Croix fifteen years ago. It's a job she enjoys, she says, because "who wouldn't like helping people who cannot help themselves?"

Close to seventy, however, Anna was increasingly feeling the strain of her life. She was tired most of the time and had heavy dark circles under permanently bloodshot eyes. Her back wasn't as good as it once was, and aside from her long bus ride to work, she rarely strayed from the confines of her crumbling Boston neighborhood. Recently she had become afraid of things like snow and driving, zoos and tunnels. "I don't take no chances," she said often.

The first time I met her, Anna showed me into her living room, a tiny space with crimson shag wall-to-wall carpet, a four-piece seating set, and a large wooden console holding a big TV. A vase of brightly colored paper flowers sat in the middle of the coffee table. The windows were draped with shimmering crimson valences, and the off-white walls were covered with framed color photographs of her children and grandchildren. A wooden plaque that hung on the door read THE LOVE BETWEEN A MOTHER AND DAUGHTER IS FOREVER, which made me think of Charlene in far-away Framingham. But the plaque could have been a gift from one of Charlene's three sisters, or could have been intended as reassurance for Trinada, who, like most children of incarcerated women, has lived with her grandmother since her mother "went away."

The whole building was inhabited by family. Anna's second daughter, Tonya, and her husband and kids lived on the top floor. A niece lived between them on the second. Roaming through the house was also a cat named Nanook. Trinada liked to think that the cat ate rats for breakfast and cat food for lunch and dinner, but when Anna heard this, she chuckled and said, "Oh Lord, she don't even know what she saying now—the cat eat cat food *all* the time, Trinnie!" On this, however, Trinada was firm. "No, Grandma," she said. "He eats rats for breakfast. I seen him!"

Trinada was small, skinny, and pretty. Charlene had told me that she looked just like her, except for her eyes, which she inherited from her father, and it was true, she did have the big eyes and long flat brows of a man on a little girl's face. This made her look serious a lot of the time, but she was a bright, enthusiastic child, pliable enough that after ten minutes of playing with her I felt she would have gone anywhere with me. That first time I met her I made her a paper airplane with a bent nose and sharp wings. I told her it was supersonic, and she liked that. "Like Grandma," she said. "Grandma's supersonic!" which made Anna chuckle proudly. Then Trinada got excited and started running around the room skidding the plane along the edge of the television console, and Anna whispered tautly, "Hush, girl! Be quiet now, don't make me spank you in here!" which sent Trinada straight to the edge of the sofa and to a careful, quiet stroking of the plane with her finger.

Anna was proudly self-sufficient and extremely private, and I'd been confused at first by her vehement decision to take part in Nancy Brown's press conference. "I will do that, yes I will," she'd said. "What is the date? I'll try to get it off from work." It quickly became clear, however, that it was concern for Trinada that was propelling Anna-May beyond her natural reticence. Trinnie had been having difficulties in the kindergarten her grandmother had enrolled her in across the street from their apartment. She didn't like to play with the other children and tended to cling to available adult females. She cried every morning too, Anna told me, and almost every evening as well, and though some of her loneliness might have been alleviated by transferring her to another preschool, one attended by her cousins downtown, Anna was reluctant to move her so far away from home. "The little girl is grieving," she told me. "She is grieving for her mother. So while I may be tired, and I may be sad, and I may just want to lie down and sleep, I have to do something to help her. I have to get some help for that little girl.

"Still to this day, every morning, every night, every time that child turns, it's, 'Grandma, when's Mummy coming home? When we went to see Mummy, Mummy told me she coming home soon. Why Mummy can't come home?' That is what she ask me, over and over and over. Call her right now and she'll say if I'm telling any lies. All the time it's, 'Where's Mummy? Nobody can go to get Mummy? Auntie Fran has a car. Auntie Gina has a car; Uncle Melvin has a car, why can't any of them go to get my mummy?'

"See how she's so small?" Anna went on after a pause, wiping her own tears with the flat edges of her thumb. "She will not eat the food! Even at school she is not a hearty eater. You know what I do now in the afternoons—like around five or six? I sit down with Trinnie and put her food on the table and put mine next to it, and I say, 'The two of us is going to eat.' But she always say the same thing: 'Oh Grandma, I don't want no food. I'm full. I'm full.' 'No sweetheart. You are not full,' I tell her, but gently, and then I start to feed her like a baby. Yes. I put her on my lap and I feed her with a spoon. Then she will eat. With a spoon, yes. A little ice cream anyway, a little Ensure."

I HAD SEEN Trinada with her mother only once, when I drove her and Anna out to MCI-Framingham for a visit. It had been the first trip the family had made in more than four months, and after an hour-long drive and a two-hour wait, we had only been allowed to stay for forty-five minutes. I knew how desperate Charlene was to see her daughter; how she often felt betrayed by her family because she saw her so rarely, and how conflicted she felt about her belief that even women whose children were with the Department of Social Services seemed to see their kids more regularly than she did. This wasn't in fact the case. Over 60 percent of women in prison nationwide are incarcerated more than a hundred miles from their kids, making visits difficult and often financially prohibitive. In part because of this, less than half report even one visit with their children since going to prison. Still, it seemed that at least some mothers with kids in DSS saw their kids more often than Charlene did. Once, when a woman taunted her about this, she flew into a rage and slapped her. Ten days in the Hole for that slap, but it was worth it. Kids are sacrosanct in prison. Especially when you're looking at fifteen years.

Now, though, Charlene walked into the room as poised and open as if the family met like this every week. She greeted her mother first, buried herself for a moment in her chest. Then, smiling, she crouched down to rub noses with her daughter, presenting me with two identical profiles, one large, one small, the same high cheekbones, aquiline noses, full lips. Only then did Charlene speak. As undramatically as if she'd seen her just the day before, she asked Trinada about school and about the nice new yellow sweater she was wearing. Her auntie had given it to her, Trinnie said with a smile. "Mmmmm," Charlene replied appreciatively and then took her daughter onto her lap and began to play, gently, with her hair.

Charlene lived for moments of contact like this, I knew. She slept with letters from Trinnie under her pillow and carried a photo of her in her pocket wherever she went. Recently, when the DOC reduced the permissible number of bathrobes from two to one, she elected to keep her highly impractical black satin robe instead of the warmer multicolored terry cloth because she had worn it when she was pregnant and believed that some ineffable connection to her daughter still lingered there.

I had been expecting tears and long, clinging hugs. But there was no visible desperation at all. Instead things felt weirdly flat, as though Trinada didn't wake up every morning crying, asking why her mother was having such a long "time out."

I still don't know whether each of them was performing in turn for the comfort of the others, or if this was how the meetings had become formalized over the years. Whatever it was, the quiet but determined cheeriness they all shared lent to the visit a distanced air—friendly but polite, careful, above all, to avoid the reality of where we were and just how long Charlene was going to have to stay there.

Trinada, at least, seemed happy enough just to sit with her mother. She was all dressed up in her finest new clothes, and though her grandmother didn't let her eat candy at home, here she was allowed to buy a whole packet of mini Reese's peanut butter cups from one of the vending machines. Sitting on her mother's lap as the adults chatted about nothing at all, she hummed as she riffled through the identical, gold-wrapped candies, deciding which one to unwrap. Even as we made our way out of the prison she seemed fairly content. Still humming to herself, she practiced ballet steps as we stood in line to pass through security, waving sweetly to her mother as she pointed her toe and bent her knee just so. But in the car she sank into silence. "I wanna go home," she said softly at one point. "I wanna go home now, Grandma."

FOUR MONTHS LATER, in May, outside the golden-domed State House in Boston, Anna still looked worried. "I look good?" she asked me, trying to assess the effectiveness of her pink linen shirt and beige jacket set above a floral, ankle-length skirt. I told her she looked lovely. Unconvinced, she frowned and asked again, "Really-really? I want them to know that I look after my granddaughter good. That I . . . well, you know," she said, trailing off. "I'm a little nervous. I slept not much at all. I'm just a little nervous."

The hearing turned out to be a typically dry, politic kind of affair. Seven or eight legislators sipped coffee as a slew of judges spoke out in favor of their sentencing guidelines. Anna and I sat all the way in the back, and it was impossible to hear just what it was they were saying. A photocopied document let us know that the men sitting in front and above us in their imposing brown leather chairs were members of the Massachusetts Joint Committee on Criminal Justice. They were considering, among other things, the sentencing commission's recommendations on mandatory drug sentencing. In its original version the bill contained a provision allowing judges to depart from mandatory minimum sentences. Their own version of the bill, however, included changes suggested by the District Attorneys Association that significantly limited this provision. The lackadaisical atmosphere in the room gave the distinct impression that their minds were already made up.

A majority of the voting public still supports severe punishment for drug dealers. Even when they become aware that tough sentences target mostly low-level dealers, a wide margin of voters continue to believe that harsh mandatory sentences do more good than harm. Fearing the political fallout of even appearing to be soft on crime, most lawmakers remain reluctant to challenge the status quo. This hearing certainly seemed perfunctory. It ended at twelve o'clock, exactly as scheduled. It had been fairly well attended by both the public and the press, but perhaps because of the confusion caused by a false fire alarm earlier that morning, only one reporter from the *Globe*, pregnant and weary-looking, even bothered to show up at the press conference afterward.

Nancy guided Anna ahead of a couple of interested congresswomen and introduced her to the reporter. For a time Anna stood there, stiff and nervous, answering questions with monosyllables. She became a little more eloquent when she was asked about Trinnie. But the journalist, clearly tired by then, soon moved on.

Nancy was trying hard to come to terms with yet another disappointment when a cameraman from Fox Television News turned up. I always forget the impact that television cameras have when they suddenly materialize this way. People stop slouching, chewing, or picking at their fingers and, filled suddenly with purpose, fix their expressions to whatever seems most appropriate and stare. Nancy, especially, was excited. She had been organizing this event for more than a month. She'd traveled down from New Hampshire to be there, had made countless phone calls, sent out hundreds of information booklets, met with dozens of people, all in an attempt to get some kind of Mother's Day story out to the media, and now here, at last, was a television camera. She grabbed Anna and ushered her over.

"This is Anna-May Williams, the mother of a woman serving fifteen years for a first, nonviolent drug offense," she said to the cameraman.

"Okay," he replied, game enough, turning on his light so that it shone right on Anna-May.

"Could you tell me your name first, and spell it for me, please—look right at me, now, not at the camera."

"Anna-May Williams," said Anna, erect now, drawn up.

"Anna spelled the usual way? A-N-N-A?"

"Anna-*May*, yes," said Anna. "Anna-May Williams."

"And your daughter is serving time for drugs?"

"Yes, she is. Fifteen years in prison for first attempt. Nonviolent."

"Could you tell me how she got involved in drugs in the first place?" It was exactly the same question, phrased in exactly the same way, that the *Globe* reporter had asked. Unfazed, Anna answered it just as she did before. "I do not know. I really do not know anything about that."

"But you think something was wrong about the sentence your daughter received?"

"Yes. I do."

"Mmmm-hmmm."

"Well, I don't think that fifteen years is really fair."

The cameraman said nothing.

"I don't think it's fair at all," Anna repeated. And when the cameraman again failed to respond, she added: "I think that what my daughter did was wrong, but it was first attempt, nonviolent, and if they sent her to prison, they should have given her a lesser time. Not mandatory fifteen years. She got a daughter, and I think it's time for her to come home now, to her child. Because the little girl, Trinada, she is really going nuts for her mother. She wants to know why her mummy can't come home."

"So what do you want to see happen?"

"Well, I am not saying that my daughter wasn't wrong. But what I'm saying is that they could have done something else. Done something other than to send her in there for fifteen years—for first attempt! Because children need their parents! Kids need their mothers to grow up strong. I know that many people believe it is punishing the mother to send her off to prison for fifteen years. But I am here to tell you, no. You are not punishing the mother, you are punishing the child. You are punishing the children. So please, soften your hearts. My daughter was wrong, but mercy. For one little child, mercy. Because if I wasn't alive, what would happen to this kid? They would just take her and send her to anyplace, and she might not ever even know her family when she is all grown up! I'm not saying that what my daughter did was right, but do something else please! Don't keep punishing the children like this.

They need their mothers. They need their *mothers*. Trinada gets all the love from her grandmother. All the love from her aunt, her cousins, everybody. But she still needs a mother's love. She needs a mother's love! That is what the kid needs. She needs a mother's love."

Anna sounded, suddenly, like an old-time evangelist. The crowd started to grow. Women, other mothers, nodded in agreement. Congresswomen turned to look, and Nancy, surveying the scene, began to relax and even to smile. But having lugged around cameras like the one the Fox TV guy had on his shoulder, I knew what was happening when he flicked the switch just above the index finger of his right hand halfway through Anna's speech. He had turned the camera off.

For the next couple of minutes he stood there politely, I have to admit, holding the camera with the light turned on as if it were still recording. At the first possible moment, however, when Anna paused to collect her thoughts, he flicked off that switch too, said, "Thanks, thank you, thanks," and without any warning slid the heavy camera from his shoulder and walked away. Or rather, he disappeared, taking with him only half of Anna-May's story and half of her name and an obvious intention of doing nothing with either.

JAIL BABES

Do you know that there are hundreds of beautiful ladies sitting in prison, just waiting for someone to love and care about them? Well it's true! Every day we have beautiful women signing up and joining as members of Jail Babes, our Pen-Pal and Singles Introduction Service!

These ladies have nothing but time on their hands and can't wait to hear from you! Whether you just want a friend, pen pal, someone to talk to or are looking for that special lady in your life, you could find her here.

Yes, these ladies have made some mistakes in their past, but now they are looking forward to a much better future! So, go ahead, browse our profiles, make your selection, submit your order to us and we will do our best to help you find the dream-girl or special friend you have been waiting for. Believe me, she's out there . . . and she's been waiting for you for a long time!

So began the Internet dating service www.JailBabes.com, a website that specialized in selling the names and addresses of female prisoners. Ken Kleine, the retired paralegal who came up with the idea, worked at it out of his suburban California home for five years until August 2003, when the site abruptly disappeared. Today the domain name is for sale. But during its heyday, he had about ten thousand active customers and received between sixty and seventy thousand hits a day. For a few months, after he appeared on *The Howard Stern Show,* Kleine received upward of two million hits. When I asked just who would be seriously interested in starting a romance with an incarcerated woman, he told me, "My customers cover the entire spectrum of society. I've had airline pilots and attorneys, doctors and bus drivers. It's natural for a male to want to help a damsel in distress—to want to rescue them, to be a hero. I think it's a macho kind of hero situation—guys want to feel needed. They want to be respected, to be the provider, and they can be all this to women in prison. I've even had a judge and a couple of police chiefs as clients," he added, though when I asked if I might be able to talk to them, he told me that he doubted it. The last time he asked them to talk to a reporter, they were furious, he said.

Certainly there was no lack of interest among the women at Framingham. Massachusetts inmates are not allowed access to the Internet, so most women never actually saw the Jail Babes website. The way Kleine had it set up they didn't need to. There was no charge for a woman to sign up. All she had to do was provide some basic information (education, measurements, sexual preferences), along with a photograph and a brief, personal statement, which Kleine broke down into three sections: "Describe your personality," "Describe some of your interests," and "Something special."

Denise's young roommate, Julie Kelly, never hesitated. She'd been in prison for just over a year when she first heard about Jail Babes. By then the initial stream of letters and visits from friends and family had begun to dry up. Denise had recently left for MCI-Lancaster, and without her around, Julie was bored, lonely, and broke. Meanwhile, friends of hers were receiving steady streams of letters and, more important, money from Jail Babes pen pals. She'd already sent off information to another service, WomenBehindBars.com, but she'd never heard anything back. Anyway, just by glancing at the tasteful logo of a heart trapped behind bars on the much photocopied application form, she felt sure that Jail Babes would serve her better.

For a time Julie was the first Jail Babe you would see if you clicked on "Massachusetts." Underneath her "vital statistics" (Height: 5′6″. Weight: 120. Measurements: 36-23-37. Marital status: single. Education: some high school. Occupation: exotic dancer. Smoker: frequently. Drinker: frequently. Release date 6/30/2003.), Julie had written the following thumbnail description of herself: "I am real easy going and I like to have fun. I am very comical and your basic 21 year old. I enjoy riding on a Harley. I am really into nature and S&M. I just want someone who I can have a good time with and stay real." For some reason she sent along a goofy picture of herself smiling gawkily into the camera like a high school freshman at her first dance. But it didn't seem to matter. It took just two weeks to get the first letter from a suitor, and she got forty more in the almost two months that she kept her photograph up on the site.

This was just the response Kleine hoped for. He insisted he was performing a much needed service for women in prison, and it is true that he was generally respectful of the women he showcased. He never allowed nudity on his site, and though the women did have to describe the reason for their incarceration, Kleine never posted this information. There might, of course, have been a commercial reason for this. The damsel-in-distress fantasy must have been easier for his clients to maintain without the words "drug trafficking" or "prostitution" staring out at them right next to all those pretty pictures. But Kleine told me: "I don't include that kind of information at the request of the women.

They don't want to be prejudged by their past mistakes. They'd rather have the opportunity to make first impressions by correspondence and telephone conversations. Usually, after the first or second letter, if you ask them, they're more than willing to give you all the details."

Kleine's claim that Jail Babes was the premier women-in-prison dating service on the Internet seems to have some merit. If his site was florid with the promise of soft porn and kinky sex, then at least it was up front about its purpose and was remarkably easy to navigate. Another site, www.PenGals.com, attempted to sort women by race, a feature that might be helpful to some people, but it seemed to have difficulties with its search engine and routinely crashed. WomenBehindBars.com had racier photographs but endless disclaimers made its home page a little off-putting. And while VerySpecialWomen.com offered a monthly pinup calendar that was easily downloadable, it didn't have a comprehensive state-by-state listing and was not updated as often as Jail Babes.

Kleine was adamant about the importance of this. Keeping his files current took up the bulk of his time, and he routinely added photographs of fifty new women a week. Besides, Jail Babes was the only women-in-prison site I found that attracted mainstream advertising of any kind. There was a banner for Visa on every page.

Kleine, however, received no revenue from Visa. All advertising income went to Skyworm, his website host, which provided free service in return. He did, however, make a substantial amount of money by charging seven dollars for each name and address his customers requested. And while he could be seen as a kind of Internet pimp, Kleine would rather be perceived as a man providing a much needed service to women in prison.

He came up with the idea, he said, when seated next to a pretty parolee from Florida at a party. As a former paralegal for the Ford

Motor Company, Kleine wasn't used to mingling with ex-cons—especially female ones. Intrigued, he'd asked her what the most common feature of life in prison was. "She said loneliness, and I thought, that's a pretty common denominator among single men, too. I mean—I'm a lonely divorcé myself!" The idea for an Internet dating service came to him that night, he told me, and with the parolee's help he contacted Floridian women in prison to propose the idea for a website. Their responses, he said, were uniformly positive, and by spring of that year, 1998, Jail Babes was launched.

In the beginning the website showcased ads for just one hundred women. By 2001 there were upward of forty-five hundred. Kleine doesn't deny that the idea for Jail Babes (which he initially called Jail Bait before he wised up to the possible legal consequences) was "very profitable—an excellent retirement supplement." He did emphasize, however, that he was one of the customers as well as the owner. He was corresponding with three women in prison when I spoke with him—and was seriously involved with one. Though he'd heard of at least nine couples whose Jail Babe introductions had culminated in marriage, he was hesitant to make such predictions for himself. "We just decided to take it slow and easy," he said. "Let's leave it at that for now."

Julie, however, finds it hard to take anything slow and easy. It's just not how she operates. She's an enthusiast, albeit a wayward one. But even she had to admit that most of the guys who wrote to her didn't share Kleine's honorable intentions. One of the things she liked about Jail Babes was that it encouraged men to send gifts of money. But most didn't send anything to begin with, and anyway, they sounded like jerks—abusive perverts and losers who had no interest in maintaining any kind of supportive relationship, financial or otherwise. She never bothered to write back to most of them. Why waste the stamp? In desperation she did start a correspondence with a charming dwarf named

Fletch. Predictably, he quickly became just a friend. "He's real, real short, but he's a really nice guy," she said. "Other than the fact that he likes to be kicked in the face. I think being a midget has affected him."

A man named Leggy sounded more promising. He lived nearby and had a steady job and sent a twenty-dollar money order with his first letter to prove it. After a few letters back and forth they even made a plan to meet. Julie still thinks it would have been better if he'd warned her about his tattoos. The way he did it, just showing up in the visiting room one day, as casual as could be about the fact that he was covered—literally covered—in multicolored skulls was just a little too much. "Oh my God! I took one look at him and wanted to go right back inside," Julie told me. "But, you know, he had some money, so I hung around until he said it was too bad I had buck teeth, and I'm like, whatever, asshole, fuck you if you don't like my teeth."

Julie had never been that choosy about men—put her in a room with fifty of them, she said, and she'll end up "catching feelings for them all." She'd been a stripper and a dominatrix before coming to prison, and told me once, "You know, sex is like drinking a can of Coke—it doesn't bother me at all." But she was clear about the division between work and real life and had managed to maintain a fairy-tale approach to romance more typical of a high school cheerleader than a convicted felon. So it wasn't that surprising to discover that she had found her "soul mate" through Jail Babes a few days after her visit with Leggy.

Since he lived in L.A., she called him California, and she fell for him hard. "Oh my God I'm in love with him!" she told me one afternoon. "He tells me he loves me. He's real smart, he analyzes handwriting. He sent me two books already, *The Cynic's Dictionary* and *The Millionaire Next Door*. He wants to be a millionaire, that's one of his dreams. He wants to own an airline and to open a bookstore for, you know, books that everyone should have, like how to hide your assets. I'll say one thing for him, California's real smart. Real, real smart."

In many ways, in fact, California seemed to be the perfect Jail Babes customer, just the kind of upright, if slightly lost, young man Kleine had been at such pains to convince me was typical of his clientele. He held down a steady job and sent Julie twenty dollars a week alongside letters that were only tantalizingly kinky and filled with enthusiastic plans for his future. He even sent her a year's subscription to *Rolling Stone* for her birthday and promised to buy her a TV for Christmas.

Once he took the time to analyze her handwriting: "So, what does your handwriting say about you?" he wrote. "You like to be noticed, and you're unpredictable. Whatever you choose to get involved in you tend to be passionate about. You have a true ability (and need) to relate to other people and be in contact with them. As a child I would guess that being made to stand in a corner or stay in your room was a far worse punishment than being spanked or having your mouth washed out with soap. You're also feeling physically deprived right now." For some reason this made Julie lose her head entirely. Even when he sent a photo of himself in an Einstein T-shirt, looking geeky and out of place in front of a big church in California somewhere, Julie refused to get downhearted about their long-term prospects. "He's wicked ugly," she confessed. "But at least he's honest. He couldda sent a fake photo, you know. Most people do."

In fact this was one of the biggest concerns of Kleine's customers— that the images of women they saw and the stories they read on the Jail Babes website were just so many put-ons. Kleine felt compelled to place a disclaimer on his site—if in a quiet paragraph near the end of a little-viewed section called "Our Services"—absolving himself of all re-sponsibility for the truthfulness of the women's claims. He did make his women sign a statement affirming the truth of everything they submitted to him, but, when pressed, he acknowledged that in most cases he had no way of knowing just what was true and what was not. Customers interested in women incarcerated in Kentucky, Texas, Florida, and Pennsylvania, however, didn't have to worry about this at all, he told me. The departments of correction officials there oversaw women's submissions to check for their veracity. In Kentucky, he assured me, they'd actually started to "discipline girls if they submit the wrong information."

Elsewhere, though, Kleine did recommend that his customers verify basic facts about the women—their crime, age, and background—through public records. He also repeatedly insisted that everyone should meet his Jail Babe face-to-face before making too many plans for the future. Kleine himself changed his mind about a woman he had been writing to for months when he went down to meet her. "The chemistry just wasn't there," he told me, though he added that it had been in that very visiting room that he spotted another Jail Babe, Lori, whose prospects seemed so much more promising now. Lori and Kleine wrote to each other for months. Kleine visited numerous times. They even planned to go into business together when she got out, he told me. When the website disappeared I couldn't help hoping that the two of them were making a new start for themselves someplace else.

For his part, California asked Julie to take her name off the Jail Babes website after two months of writing back and forth. This was the Jail Babes equivalent of an engagement, and Julie happily agreed. Soon they were discussing their future together ("Kids, marriage, he doesn't want me to work"). Then California took the red-eye from Santa Monica to Logan, rented a car, and drove right out to Framingham to see her.

Julie spent all morning preparing for the visit. She pulled her hair into a soft ponytail, careful to leave a strand dangling tantalizingly across her forehead, put on makeup, and pressed her jeans and matching jacket. She was ready and waiting for him when she got word he'd arrived, and her heart was pounding the way it always did when men were around. It was just too romantic. He'd come all this way just to see her—"No other reason, honestly, Tina, he's coming just to see me!" She was used to getting favors from men. Officer F. had long been giving her gum, and sometimes even underwear, in exchange for a quick bit of foreplay in a dark corner somewhere—but no one had ever crossed a continent to see her before. By the time she walked into the visiting room, her mind was spinning with plans for the future.

But one look at California sitting there, sweating, in a long trench coat and it was all over. It wasn't the way it had been the first time she'd seen Leggy. She'd often worked with guys like Leggy back when she'd been a dominatrix. But California was different. He was ambitious and open and viable—she'd loved him—and now here he was, sitting right across from her in the almost empty visiting room, holding tiny hands out to her, whispering her name over and over. "The way he kept saying Julie-Julie-Julie like some kind of devil worshipper freaked me out," she told me. "He was a creep—fat and sweaty and ugly—way uglier than he looked in the picture. And he was wicked pasty! Gotta be the only guy from L.A. who doesn't even have a tan. I don't know. He gave me the creeps. His teeth were wicked pointy. And when he laughed he sounded like the Joker in *Batman*."

It was the embarrassment of being seen with him that most worried Julie. She'd been talking about him for weeks, and now, as if being heartbroken and demoralized weren't enough, she had to deal with the humiliation of being courted by a freak. Julie tried to make her displeasure with California clear by sulking and pouting and slouching across the table like a disenchanted teenager. But the visiting room at Framingham is a public space, a space where reality often bumps up against the stories that are told in prison and news travels fast. Here loving, successful boyfriends are routinely exposed as ugly, cruel, and dumb. Some are so abusive that COs are posted nearby to prevent them from attacking the women they've come to visit.

By the time Julie met California I'd grown used to scanning my fellow visitors for genuine family members instead of the johns and tricks and Jail Babe subscribers that I now realized were everywhere. But it had been Julie who'd first pointed them out to me. She who'd first persuaded me that many of the people there paid, in one way or another, for the privilege of meeting with their incarcerated "women friends." Even the fragile and elderly man with the softly curling white hair and the voice amplifier that he held to the outside of his throat was not the doting grandfather he so utterly epitomized I knew now, but a john, paying twenty dollars a month to sit with the surly, heavyset woman he visited.

But California was worse even than him, Julie insisted. At least that old man was cute, and devoted. California was just creepy. Even her friend's mother, who happened to be visiting at the very same time, commented on the fact that he looked like some kind of psychopath.

At first Julie thought she might give him the boot and leave. But life in Framingham was hard enough without having to worry about where your next Canteen check was coming from, and for all of Jail Babes' promise, California seemed to be the best it could come up with. Whatever he was like in person, he had sent her money for a TV, just like he'd promised, and he did send checks regularly. Besides, he lived in California—how often was he going to be able to visit?

It was a tough decision to make, though, to keep seeing him. Almost everyone in prison strung someone along for money, but for Julie, having to sink so low was humiliating. Perhaps to prove her independence, she made a big show of calling him up one evening and, while laughing with her girlfriend and sticking her finger down her throat, giving him a story that wheedled fifty dollars out of him right then and there.

For a time things were fine. He'd write every week and always send money, and she only had to call him occasionally. But he couldn't keep away. Two months later he again flew into Logan and hired a car and then drove out to see her. This time Julie was so repulsed, even frightened, by his simmering obsession that she told him not to come back the following day. Her grandmother had died unexpectedly, she said. She had to go to the funeral. Meekly, he complied, and two days later he wrote her another letter with another check and with plans for his next visit. He just wouldn't give up.

Then the week before Valentine's Day he showed up in a tuxedo and a bow tie. He'd decided to surprise her, he said, as a Valentine's gift. "Will you marry me?" he asked once she'd settled down at the table, before she'd even had time to unwrap her sandwich. "Will you please, please, marry me, Julie?"

"I couldn't believe it!" Julie told me. "I swear my skin was crawling just sitting with him, and he was asking me to marry him! I was wicked scared and wicked embarrassed. Even the officers said stuff to me later—one of them said she had to twist her chair around because she was laughing so much. . . . As serious as I could I told him I was kind of committed to getting my act together in this place and that I really couldn't promise him I would marry him. I thought I was going to die! I left the visit early because I had to pee. He asked me to 'think about it'—and gave me twenty dollars too, so I pretty much got what I could from him."

One week later Julie got a letter from California saying he was planning on returning to the prison for her birthday. He included yet another check for twenty dollars, but by then it was all too much for Julie.

His letters were becoming kinkier and kinkier. They were getting increasingly violent in their fantasies too. Embarrassed by her failure to prevail, Julie whispered that she'd written him a "Dear John" letter. "I just can't suffer through another visit with him, Tina. I'll die if I have to. I swear, I'll die." She'd written:

> As you've noticed, I've been very distant. I realized I need time to get my shit together. I'm not ready to commit to anyone. I haven't even started to do the work on myself that is needed. I really hope you understand. I do appreciate all the support you've shown me. I just think we should stop writing for a while. I hope this gives you enough time to cancel your plans and trip out here. I will refuse a visit so please don't waste the trip.
>
> Thank you,
Me.

Now, instead of letters and checks, Julie receives weekly postcards from California. He has tried writing to other Jail Babes, he tells her, but no one can replace her. The cards sometimes show pictures of dungeons and chains, sometimes of kittens playing with twine, and every time she gets one now, Julie shares them with Officer F., who has asked her to remove herself from Jail Babes permanently.

ELLEN CHENEY JOHNSON

ISOLATED, BORED, AND frustrated, the women of Framingham rioted in 1888. Historians do not know what sparked the event. The prison was well under capacity at the time, and the superintendent reported only that "the participants in the trouble replied to all questions put to them by the commissioners . . . that they had nothing to complain of, and only did it 'for fun.' "

Contemporary annual reports from Framingham, however, give an impression of widespread discontent at the prison. A report five years after the riot states that for the first time ever, discipline was being well maintained and that the "number of cases calling for severe punishment" was declining. Even then, though, logbooks show long lists of women being locked in solitary punishment cells, and continuing requests for the construction of additional isolation cells. As the end of the nineteenth century approached, life seemed to be getting harder for the women of Framingham. It hadn't always been this way.

In the early 1870s, questions relating to female penal reform had been, once again, at a premium. As a result of the Civil War, women, particularly women of privilege, were beginning to be recognized as capable actors in the public sphere. Nurses, charity workers, and administrators, reluctant to return to the confines of the home, settled on the new "penology for women" as an avenue to further this more public identity. The demise of New York's Mount Pleasant almost two decades before had diminished the zeal with which many regarded the prospects of improving conditions for women in prison. But in Massachusetts, at least, interest was once again fermenting, and in 1871 a group of women began to demand the construction of a prison to be run for and by women.

Many men in the state were reluctant to comply with this request. With 227 female prisoners in Massachusetts, there was a clear need for such a facility, but the idea that it could be effectively controlled by women still seemed far-fetched. It took three annual requests from the state's prison commission and two directly from the governor himself for the nation's second all-women prison to be commissioned. But in the end the women got their way. In the fall of 1874 a unanimous vote of the prison advisory board allowed for the purchase of thirty acres near the South Framingham railroad station. Architect George Ropes was hired to draw up the plans for what was then called the Reformatory for Women, Sherborn.

Here again, the women had to compromise. They had sought a cottage-style reformatory consisting of a group of intimate housing units, each more reminiscent of home than a punitive institution. Instead, Ropes created a single, monolithic building more in line with traditional prison design of the time.

The reformatory was designed, nonetheless, to be "less Spartan, less militaristic, and less secure" than contemporary prisons for men. Instead of cells, for instance, women were to have private "rooms" ranging in size from fifty to ninety square feet, and according to Ropes, the "whole construction and fittings have been planned on the theory that it is not necessary to construct an impregnable fortress to confine women; and as a *reformatory* institution, to relieve it as far as possible, from *prison like* features."

Despite the fact that Ropes also quietly made provision for more "refractory prisoners" by constructing sixteen solitary work cells (each just twelve feet square), as well as several basement punishment cells, the completed building stood in stark contrast to the dank and filthy quarters inhabited by incarcerated women of the state until then. A female inmate in Massachusetts would no longer be confined in haphazard spaces in some dark corner of a men's prison but would now be provided with her own room complete with an iron bedstead and crisp white linens. If she was among the best-behaved inmates, she would be allowed to decorate her room as she liked and to have windows without bars. At the very least she would have free access to the grounds, as well as to the chapel, library, workroom, infirmary, and school.

The actual crimes committed by these women were, of course, still startling for their pettiness: most of the inmates were drunks and prostitutes; many were "disobedient" wives or daughters; and some were simply homeless. The question as to why they were being incarcerated at all, when men convicted of similar activities would not be, remained pressing. In the meantime, however, they were at least now to be "treated" rather than "punished" for their crimes. It was a premise strongly held by reformers of the time that such treatment could be achieved only by an all-female prison administration, and the posts of matrons and undermatrons, as well as of superintendent, prison doctor, and chaplain, were all held by well-qualified and professional women at Sherborn.

Outside the prison walls, however, men were still in control. All financial decisions had to be approved by a male financial officer. Also, in order to "calm the fears that inmates would overrun their too gentle female keepers," a handful of men were kept on prison grounds in the capacity of carpenters, engineers, and firemen.

Nonetheless, reformation of the female inmate was once again on the ascendancy. By 1879 women were being sent to Sherborn from men's prisons and jails all over the state. That year 409 women were resident at the prison, along with 35 children under the age of two. Prison doctor Eliza Mosher recorded that there was also one marriage and fifteen births. The prison library contained 816 books ("they are read with much interest and pleasure"), and in addition to learning how to read, women were being trained in sewing, knitting, farming, gardening, and dairying.

"I wish thee could see me!" Dr. Mosher wrote to her sister. "I cannot describe my surrounds. I might as well be in the desert of Sahara for human companionship at this moment.—no hark! In the distance I hear the rumble of a railway train which means *life*. But I am separated from it by a high red fence—and from the other inmates of this building by wings—and corridors and doors."

Mosher believed the prison's first superintendent, Eudora Atkinson, was too stern and complained that she interfered with necessary medical treatment by inflicting "unduly severe punishment" on the women, confining them in solitary at an average rate of ten a day. When Mosher herself was appointed superintendent the following year, she did all that she could to replace such punitive measures with more progressive reforms.

First she stopped the inmates from being called "girls" and insisted they be addressed as "ladies" or "prisoners" instead. Then, like Eliza Farnham at Mount Pleasant before her, she set about reducing the dehumanizing effects of incarceration by attracting volunteers who helped provide individual teaching and training for the women. Mosher herself spent a large part of her time reading to them. When some of the women requested Bible readings in addition to the novels she read aloud for them, Mosher wrote that "they really were stirred."

Mosher's enthusiasm for her work grew with each implemented reform. Though she sometimes had doubts about its effectiveness ("It is so hard to know how much is superficial and how much is heartfelt in

the words and actions of those under our care"), she believed passion-
ately in the importance of bridging the divide between the incarcerated
and the free. To this end she instituted a series of lectures, musical per-
formances, and recitations that were attended by people on both sides
of the prison wall and organized numerous "entertainments" that
brought celebrities such as feminist Lucy Stone into contact with the
women in her care.

Then, in 1882, a new governor was elected who had "little sympathy" for women in prison and who consequently "took a great deal of
pleasure out of state work" for Mosher. Governor Benjamin Butler had
been a major general in the Civil War, serving as commander of the occupation forces of New Orleans. He gained a certain notoriety there for
his "Woman Order," which stipulated that women who insulted Union
soldiers were to be treated as prostitutes. Now a staunch conservative,
Butler maintained this aggressive stance toward women by threatening
to cut off funds for Framingham altogether after Mosher finally re-
signed—or appoint a male superintendent.

Instead, the prison commission induced perhaps the only woman
Butler believed capable of running such an institution to take over:
Clara Barton, creator of the American Red Cross. Barton's proven ability to provide aid to Civil War soldiers placated even Butler's concerns
about female abilities. But nothing prepared Barton herself for the
kinds of women she would find at Framingham. The year she arrived,
just three women were convicted for violent crimes—one for assault
and two for manslaughter. The other 221 were there for nonviolent offenses, including 97 for being drunk, 29 for prostitution, 14 for idle-
ness, 13 for being lewd, 11 for being stubborn, 6 for vagrancy, and 5 for
adultery.

Barton did what she could to alleviate conditions at the prison.
Taking a personal approach, she made it clear to inmates that they
should feel free to voice worries and complaints directly to her. Con-

tinuing Mosher's work, she also worked hard to expand educational opportunities both in the classroom and on the farm and pushed for a greater flexibility in the enforcement of discipline. Appalled by the injustices she saw as inherent in a system that penalized women so differently from men, however, Barton spent more time questioning the underpinnings of the system than tinkering with its details. She believed in the work that Framingham was doing and was aware of the challenging social and political pressures that swirled just outside its gates. But she was moved, most of all, by the seemingly unjustifiable fact of so many women's incarceration in the first place. She wrote:

> In the interest of that portion of the community which still questions the management of a prison by women, doubting if it be possible for them to maintain government and enforce discipline, and amuses itself by styling the institution "gilt edged" and its inmates "boarders" I beg you, if it not be out of place, to accept my testimony.
>
> It is to be remembered that, in your state prison for men, every inmate stands convicted of high crimes or felony. That on the other hand three fourths of the women in this prison are neither convicted of, not sentenced for, crimes deemed worthy of trial by jury, but rather offenses against the good order and customs of society. Drunkenness, vagrancy, disorderly conduct, lewdness, ill-temper, idleness, are not so much crimes against others as against the offender herself. Often ignorant of the dangers to which such misdemeanors expose them; often more weak than wicked; often more sinned against than sinning, girls of fifteen, worn women of sixty-five, trials to the community or disturbers of its peace, tempted, stupid and dazed, they stray and blunder into Sherborn. Yet I find the re-

quirements made of, and the restrictions laid upon these women differing in no essential particular from those meted out to the hardened criminals of [the men's prison at] Concord. The power, the wit, the *brain* of the crime of the Commonwealth are in Concord—or *ought to be;* the wrecks they have made are in Sherborn.

The women of Sherborn loved Clara Barton. In her time there she brought to bear all the kindness and warmth she'd become famous for during the Civil War. But she didn't stay long at Sherborn, and later superintendents had difficulty maintaining the standards she set. More typical was Ellen Cheney Johnson, who succeeded Barton and stayed at Sherborn until her death in 1899.

To Johnson, both personally and professionally, the institution on the Sherborn-Framingham line was of central importance. An early and steadfast proponent of an all-female correctional facility, she had been a frequent visitor even before she became superintendent, as well as an avid correspondent with both inmates and administrators. When her husband died in 1881, she wrote to Clara Barton: "There is no place so dear to me as that prison now." Adding that even on vacation "my mind often wanders back to the Prison," and to thoughts of uplifting an inmate so that "at night I should not feel so absolutely *good for nothing.*"

Convinced of the importance of rehabilitation, she once donated a painting made specially for the purpose named *Christ and the Erring Woman,* which she had hung in the chapel hoping that "the lesson of forgiveness and mercy taught by it sink deep into the hearts of those for whom it was intended,—a downcast, but not forsaken, sisterhood." For the most part, however, Johnson differed from her predecessors in that she saw no contradiction between reformation and discipline. For her, rehabilitation came primarily through control. "No lesson is more important than that which teaches respect for the law and dread of its wrath," she wrote. "At the same time, it is a fundamental point in our theory that every criminal can be won by gentleness and patience."

Of these two strains, however, Johnson seemed mostly to emphasize the former. In 1884, her first year in office, she requested increased punishments for escapees (there were, tellingly, three that year alone, though all were "speedily captured"), proclaimed her intention to "do away with recreation which can only be productive of harm," and requested the construction of additional solitary cells for "refractory" prisoners.

Despite the fact that she was occasionally willing to break the rules for inspiration's sake—once even waking the women and sending them outside to look at a gorgeous, night-blooming flower—she stressed formality over intimacy and rigor over the more organic daily structure that existed before her tenure. Misbehavior at meals, for example, now led inexorably to solitary dining; "further insolence" to confinement in a solitary workroom for up to three weeks. "Extreme insubordination" meant a stint in isolation without books or company on a diet of bread and water, for as long as it took for the offender to declare her penitence.

There were, by then, just five women serving time for violent crimes (two for manslaughter, one for assault, one for brawling, and one for "poisoning—attempted"), but Johnson became increasingly adamant in her requests for lengthier sentences for the women in her care. "We strive . . . to teach obedience to authority, and control of self; to rouse ambition and establish a disposition to resist evil," she wrote. "The short sentence is unfavorable to this because self-control and steadfastness against temptation do not follow a life of license and vice without a struggle, which must not only be determined but *protracted.*

One year will not overthrow the habits established by the sins of fifty years, or thirty years, or fifteen years."

Many employees at the prison—and, judging from the 1888 riot—many inmates as well, resented this shift away from the progressive reforms of Barton and Mosher. Once so optimistic, sometimes even joyful, life at the reformatory now seemed gray. The same methods that disgruntled those inside the prison, however, gave it legitimacy to men in power on the outside. Suggesting it was Johnson's more traditional approach that allowed the experiment of women's work there to be considered legitimate, the Massachusetts Legislature declared during her tenure that the prison had "attained a degree of success far exceeding the most sanguine expectations of its projectors."

And so it went on. Over the years Johnson removed infants over the age of one from the institution, restricted personal items, reduced direct inmate access to herself, and separated older women from the general population in order that they not "contaminate" the more innocent in her care. Though she continued, always, to emphasize the importance of education, she also maintained a strict hierarchy in which only those in the highest "divisions" were allowed access to books and other so-called privileges. Despite the continuing disciplinary troubles that arose inside the prison as a result of these measures, however, her fame on the outside continued to spread. Described in the suffragist *Women's Journal* as "a living demonstration of women's ability to govern," Johnson was heralded as the first person, male or female, to have "achieved such success in reforming criminals as well as controlling them." And at the World's Columbian Exposition she was awarded a bronze medal "for evidence of a model management in every detail."

However, it wasn't until 1990, a year after her death, that the prison finally became a facility where "every officer, from the head down to the lowest matron, is female." Johnson's successor, Frances

Morton, moved even further in the direction of austerity. Finding recreation to be a great source of "evil and detrimental to discipline," she removed it from the schedule altogether and told the women they would do better using the time learning to sew. "Obedience is the first lesson taught each woman," she told visiting colleagues repeatedly. The long dance of confusion over just exactly what we should do with female prisoners in this country continued in its antsy way: one step forward, one step backward; two steps forward, two steps back.

TRAILER TIME

"WOW WOW WOW WOW! I'm kind of numb! Pat is back! He's in Maine! I'm so excited, but I feel like something awful will make this end. I don't know why . . ." Denise couldn't calm down, hadn't been able to properly function since her father had dropped by for a surprise visit with Pat in tow. Her father often surprised her with visits, so when a CO called her name at ten past six one Saturday evening, she headed over to the dining hall, along with the five other women who'd been called for a visit, without thinking much about it. On their way up the hill, though, they passed the shift commander sitting on a bench, watching the guys play baseball, and he called Denise over and told her that next time her son came to see her he needed a birth certificate. "I let them in this time, but next time I won't," he said, and Denise's heart skipped a beat.

"What?! What-what-what are you talking about?" she said, grabbing his forearm without realizing it. "I haven't seen my son in two years. He's here?" The shift commander nodded and said, "Yeah."

Denise panicked. She wanted to walk back to the women's house. She wanted to run up the hill. She wanted to throw up. Then she decided that there'd been a mistake. Pat couldn't really be there. It was impossible. Perhaps he was just on the phone. With help from the other women, she walked, shakily, to the chow hall and saw her father through a window. He was alone. Yes, Pat must have called from someplace else. She pulled open the heavy, wooden door. And that was when she saw him, her son, Pat, grown but otherwise the same, hunched over a bag of unopened chips in the corner.

Denise doesn't remember this, but her father told her later that she ran over and grabbed Patrick, sobbing, almost unable to breathe. Pat burst into tears too, and clung to her. Across the room, her father started to cry, the officer in charge of the visiting room that night started to cry, and one by one the inmates and even their visitors started to cry along with them. Through it all, all Denise could think to say was, "I can't believe you're here, I can't believe it."

"I ran out of words quick," she told me later. "But they will come. And just holding each other, the naturalness of that was so great. It was as if the past two years had never been missing. He was so beautiful! Taller. But what a gorgeous, sweet kid! So gentle and grown up yet still my pumpkin, still my baby. 'Whew! Pat!' I kept saying—'I can't believe I'm seeing you tonight. I never even could have imagined it!' Wow, I'm still in shock. Still kind of numb. He has such old, gentle eyes. And he played with my hair—his hands were bigger but still little like a child's, and the same with his face—and we hugged and held hands and clung to each other. I am so happy. I was beginning to think that I'd never see him again.

"When I came back, the whole house, most of it anyway, was ecstatic. Five girls were waiting to talk to me, and one really hugged me, just hugged and hugged me and cried. Some of these women really are good people. I love Patrick so much, I pray for the day we can have a trailer visit. God thank you."

IT TAKES A while to find MCI-Lancaster. It's not like Framingham. The facility has no walls or barbed-wire fences. No signs of being a prison at all, in fact. I'd been told it stood just up the hill from a winding, country road, but I spent fifteen minutes driving back and forth along it, passing the prison over and over, mistaking it for a college campus. Even when I finally drove right up into it, I was convinced I was in the wrong place. Only the absence of people made me linger. I wandered around the clusters of distinguished-looking, turn-of-the-century buildings for at least five minutes before I saw a man barbecueing. Turned out he worked not for the prison at all but for a social service agency that operated out of the same compound, and was undivided from MCI-Lancaster by even the semblance of a fence or a gate.

Denise later explained that a whole world existed up on that hill. In one two-story building were the incarcerated women; in another, the male inmates. Across a lawn and down a path was the prison dining hall, which doubled as the visiting room, and which looked like a cafeteria in any national park: exposed wooden beams, colored diamond-pane windows, brown ceiling fans. Across the way, another Victorian red-brick building housed children in trouble with the law, and in a similar structure, on the other side of the campus, children who'd been removed from their families for their own safety were housed. It was bizarre. Men, women, and children all living more or less together but all kept apart too, not allowed even to speak to one another. Invisible barriers replace walls in a minimum-security facility.

On the other hand, the wide open spaces and sloping, green lawns were as real as they were pleasant. So too the squirrels and the birds that nested in tall evergreen trees, the antique, wrought iron lampposts and the signs directing visitors from one place to the other that were hammered out in a quaint, forestry-commission style. It was disconcerting at first. Even the COs wore regular clothes instead of uniforms, so that when I stopped to ask the second person I saw where the visiting room was, it was impossible to know whether I was talking to a guard or an inmate.

Denise looked well here too, even before Pat appeared. She'd cut her hair into feathery layers and was sporting a big yellow scrunchie wrapped around one wrist and a shiny new watch around the other, loudly and gladly asserting her new right to own them because both were prohibited in Framingham. She was also wearing a stylish new pair of Velcro-strap sandals that her mother and brother had just smuggled in for her, she told me. All she'd had until then were state-issue shoes, and because security was so relaxed at Lancaster, she'd written to her mother and asked that she come for her next visit in a new pair of sneakers. These could be exchanged for her own under the table without anyone noticing, she wrote. Denise's mother was usually a stickler for the rules, but when they'd next spoken on the phone she'd dropped her voice suddenly into a conspiratorial whisper and told her that she'd got them—"Not what you asked for," she said obliquely, "but something else—something better!" Hence the sandals. Denise had needed the sneakers for working out. But she wasn't complaining. The sandals were comfortable for padding around in, and though her mother had chickened out in the end, forcing her poor brother to wear them into the dining hall though they were way too small for him, she'd been so emboldened by the success of this plan that she now had another under way. Her mother was to fill up an empty pot of cheap, prison-approved face cream with fancy antiwrinkle eye cream instead.

Exchanges like this could never have happened at Framingham. As a minimum-security facility, Lancaster had an easiness to it that made life in prison seem almost bearable at first. But the place could be crushingly boring too. Most of its residents were on prerelease status, which means they went out to work every day—the women in a nearby Burger King mostly, the men in a high-tech factory that paid almost twice as much. Inmates serving mandatory drug time, however, are not allowed to participate in work-release programs and are never allowed to leave the premises. In this way, murderers, child molesters, arsonists, abusers, and thieves in MCI-Lancaster on prerelease end up working for businesses located in or around the town, while nonviolent drug felons are kept trapped in a facility that offers virtually no programming at all.

Denise felt, at first, as if the weight of time might smother her at MCI-Lancaster. She'd taken a job in the horticulture department, and she enjoyed digging and planting and weeding the plots around campus. But she was only allowed to do this during the afternoons, and she spent most of the rest of her time alone in her room—a single!—trying not to think too hard about much. Now that Pat was back, though, everything began to orbit with new and vigorous purpose around the family-visitation trailer. Reserved for overnight visits with children under the age of thirteen, the trailer sat in the middle of a field, back maybe twenty yards from the road, on its own. It held "a wicked nice apartment inside"—two bedrooms, a kitchen, and a living room. Outside, a rectangular patch of grass was enclosed by a pretty wooden fence, so it even felt as if it had its own yard. And though COs occasionally dropped by unannounced, there was enough sense of normalcy there, and enough privacy, for a mother to live out whatever kind of kid-centered fantasy she was able to construct.

Denise had been imagining spending weekends in the trailer with Patrick since she'd first heard about it in Framingham. But she hadn't dared hope it would happen so soon. It had been a fantasy, something to plunge into when she felt really down, and now here he was, her eleven-year-old son, taller even than she'd imagined from the photos, and a little heavier too, riding a perfect-attendance record at his new school in Maine, his dream of becoming a navy pilot once again intact. It took a while to sink in. Patrick was back. Patrick was real. Patrick was surviving, flourishing even, though of course it couldn't all be easy with Alan.

They were broke, for a start. Almost every day Denise heard from her mother that Alan called asking for money. First it was money for a car, then for a muffler. Then there were clothes for Pat to wear to school and for sheets and a comforter, even a CD player so Pat wouldn't feel completely left out by his friends. After a time, Nancy began to feel as if Alan was blackmailing her—either she wrote the checks or she wouldn't see her grandchild. Denise doubted this. Alan wasn't that calculating. Still, since he'd turned up in Maine, her dad had given him more than three thousand dollars, and not counting some as yet unpaid dental bills, her mom had sent one thousand one hundred and change.

At least now that he had a car Alan might be able to get a job. He was a carpet installer by trade, and the temptation was always there to tell him to use the knife he still carried on his belt for the job it was intended. But Denise had to be careful in her dealings with Alan. She needed to see Patrick for a string of twelve-hour visits before getting him for the night, and she relied on Alan to get Pat down to her from Maine. One misstep and he'd call the whole thing off. As it was he was already yakking down the phone about how Patrick had it too easy. How when *he'd* been young, his dad used to bloody his nose and blacken his eyes and his mom never did anything to stop it. He'd moved all the way from Hawaii to be closer to his mom now that she was getting on in years, he said, tumbling again into his usual pit of alcohol-induced self-pity. And how did she repay him? By slamming the car in reverse and driving backward down the street in an attempt to run him over! Denise tried to make sympathetic noises, but what she really wanted to know was where Patrick was when all this was going on. She felt so damn helpless in there.

There were weeks of phone calls back and forth. Should Pat come down on the bus by himself, or would Alan bring him over? Perhaps

Nancy would drive up to get him, or would meet him halfway, on the highway someplace. In the end he came down on the bus by himself, which he enjoyed, he said, because it made him feel grown-up. He stayed with Nancy for a few days (they spent a lot of time at the mall) and had a twelve-hour visit with Denise in the trailer.

They still didn't really have words. But they played Scrabble and cards and even cooked together in the small, well-stocked trailer kitchen. They started with pizza, but it had been a long time since Denise had been in a kitchen and they burned it and had to throw it away. Next they tried a chicken-and-broccoli dish, complete with a cheese sauce, and it turned out better than either of them would have dared expect. "Real food. Good food," Patrick said as he ate.

After that, they spent a couple of hours drawing. Denise had always had a talent for it, and when Patrick saw her book of sketches his eyes widened with pride and astonishment and he said: "These should be in a museum!" His own pictures started out strong and sure, but after a time he'd get frustrated and want to give up. Denise worked with him, coaxing him on, until first one, then two, then three pictures were finished. In a moment of optimism, they agreed that Denise would collect the pictures he drew every time he visited and make them into a book.

But Denise couldn't help worrying about Pat. Perhaps it was normal, she didn't know anything about eleven-year-old boys, but he seemed overly concerned about his weight. He'd put on a few pounds since moving to Maine, he said, and sometimes the kids' teasing got so bad that he'd throw up his meals in an attempt to slim down. Denise had done this all through high school herself, and it made her nervous to even imagine Patrick's self-esteem being as delicate as her own back then. And he was worried, almost obsessed with being popular in school. He kept saying, "Dad was popular, right? And you were popular . . ." All Denise could think of to say was that in fact she hadn't been that popular at all, and that neither were any of the best people she knew.

This brought him a bit of relief. She could tell because his body seemed to loosen just a touch and because he smiled then and told her there was a girl he liked in his class. A Spanish girl, he said, and then he pulled out a shiny new wallet to show her a picture. She was pretty, the girl, dark and long-haired and optimistic-looking, and Denise had been on the verge of saying something approving when Patrick flipped over the plastic casing to reveal an equally smiling photo of herself. Denise couldn't believe it. She'd sent him the picture two full years before, and he'd kept it all this time. It was heartbreaking, this eleven-year-old's wallet empty but for a picture of a girl and a picture of his mother. He showed it to everyone, he told her then, and trying desperately hard not to cry, she promised to send him a new one just as soon as she could.

DENISE DID HER best to keep busy with her horticulture classes after that visit. She was trying to get a step class going too, but she'd been waiting for the equipment for weeks now, so she spent most of her spare time down in the basement with the weight machines and walking around and around a path known as the loop, which was the only place women were allowed to take exercise. Denise didn't care much for it out there. All the women at Lancaster were men-crazy. It made her laugh. Locked up at Framingham, most of them turned quickly enough to one another for intimacy, but as soon as they got out of the van at Lancaster it was "men men men" again.

Contact between male and female inmates was strictly forbidden, of course, but the loop was right next to a path that the men used to get back to their house, and an elaborate system of sign language had long been established between the women and the men. Denise felt superior and isolated at the same time, walking around the track ignoring it all. She'd heard a rumor that Julie was coming to Lancaster soon, that threatening to spill the beans about Officer F. had gotten her on the list. Denise looked forward to seeing her. It was odd—despite the presence of men, the women at Lancaster tended to bond more. Perhaps because there were only thirty of them there at any given time. Or perhaps because there was so little to do, or because the presence of men reminded them just how much they needed each other. One way or another they stuck together more. Helped out more. Even Denise, who tended to steer clear of the desperate cases at Framingham, felt moved to action here. One woman, Maria-Cristina, returned her kindness by helping her out with preparations for the trailer visit.

Maria-Cristina struck me as very innocent and very sad—one of those women who seem to have been lonely all their lives. But it was amazing how she brightened when she talked of the "girls here at Lancaster." When she laughed, which she did a lot when she talked about them, the heaviness of her face vanished entirely. She looked almost beautiful then, vibrant, full of life, and it was in this capacity that she most helped Denise. The trailer was hard, Maria-Cristina knew. "Yes, yes," she'd say, in lilting Spanglish. "*Claro*—of course." But it could be wonderful too—you only had to prepare! "Food," she'd say. "Food!" Tomato sauce and cheese worked well for pasta and for pizza (the kids always love pizza); cocoa powder from Canteen was always good, and if you ordered early enough, you could get chicken—real chicken on the bone—and veggies too, she told Denise, eyebrows arching high now: broccoli. Carrots. Peas!

PAT ARRIVED FOR his first overnight visit early. Alan had put him on an earlier bus than expected, so he got to Lancaster at two-thirty instead of seven as he was supposed to. His clothes were dirty and torn, and he was wearing no socks, though Denise's mother had bought him a new bunch at the mall the last time she'd seen him. ("Dad took 'em," Patrick told her when Denise asked.) But he was doing well at school, she told herself as they got settled in. And her father had been able to take a look around the house up in Maine and told her it was clean. While Alan was in the bathroom, he'd stepped into the kitchen and looked in the fridge—it was full of food, he said, so things couldn't be all bad.

It was a lot to juggle, though, the past and the present, the memories and the up-to-date realities and the imagined scenes that leapt out at her sometimes, monstrously, as she struggled to read between the lines and through the silences in Pat's preadolescent speech. There were wonderful, heart-stopping moments, like when he picked a handful of tiny yellow weed-flowers from the grass outside and brought them inside to study, patiently taking stamen from petal, petal from stem, in an attempt to understand how such beauty was made.

But there were plenty of tricky moments too, like when he told her that they'd disappeared for a time before leaving Hawaii because Alan had been hospitalized. Patrick had spent a couple of months in a foster home, he said. But he didn't want to talk about it. Later he insisted on hearing accounts of Denise and Alan's relationship. He wanted the truth, he said, "Seriously." Denise did her best to dredge up some innocuous memories from when they'd all lived together in a little house in the woods up in New Hampshire. She remembered a time when they sat around the table together in front of the fire, but Patrick interrupted her with a "C'mon, Mom!" and asked for some of the real stories, like the one about the time his dad went into the strip club, he said, and gave her some money and asked her there, in front of everyone, "What you got for your husband?"

It was one of her most awful, darkest, and most secret memories, and to hear it now, coming out of Patrick's mouth, horrified her. She had been scared that long-ago night, and had gotten Alan thrown out of the club. She knew the bouncers had beaten him up on the street outside. Now Pat knew it too, it seemed. After a moment she asked Pat why he thought his father might have told him a story like that and was still more aghast when he answered with a wryness entirely unnatural to an eleven-year-old: "I think Dad wanted to *share.*"

SO THIS IS what it was to be in contact with your children. It was almost unbearable. With one fell swoop the barriers and dams she'd so painstakingly constructed were being blasted away. Yes, it felt great to spend time out in the trailer, to do laundry and cook and clean and make beds; incredible to be able to be a mom and pretend for a while that things were more or less normal. The problem was that it *was* pretend. Pat and Denise were slowly becoming real to each other again, but so was the horror of their separation, and the end of the visit was always calamitous. That first time, Pat woke up asking Denise to "please call the guards and get them to let me stay until one o'clock. Just until one o'clock—*please?*" Denise could do no such thing, of course, and when they were escorted out of the trailer at nine-thirty, it was hard for them to stop hugging each other.

The difficulties of keeping in touch by telephone made things even harder. Alan's money problems meant the phone wasn't always connected or that there was often a collect-call block on the line. Denise began to pop Sudafeds. "Just one a night," she told me. "But it's not because I need them. I don't have a cold. It's a comfort thing—in my head."

Her friend Claudia kept telling her that kids can survive all sorts of things as long as they have their mother to lean on. So from prison Denise wrote letters to Pat's school, informing them of her situation and requesting that they keep her abreast of his progress. She wrote the first letter to his teacher directly. When she received no reply, she wrote a second letter, this time to the principal, and almost immediately she got a letter back. It said that Patrick really was doing well at school, that he often talked about Denise and about her art, but that, truth be told, he was having a little trouble learning the states and their capitals.

Denise went straight to work. No one in the women's house knew the names of all the state capitals. But by being persistent she managed finally to cobble all fifty together. Then she created a game for Pat to play that involved filling in a blank map of the United States with matching names of the states and their capitals pulled from a pile at its center. They had a great time playing with it, and when Pat left it behind in the frenzy of leave-taking, Denise carefully wrapped it up and sent it to him. Pat wrote back thanking her but telling her apologetically that they had moved on now from states and their capitals to Canada and its provinces. If she wanted to make him a game for that, it would be great, he said.

Bit by bit they were developing a routine. Lancaster allowed one overnight visit every six weeks, more or less, and Pat came about half that often. He tended always to be tense and overly grown up when he first arrived. But he loosened up after playing a bit of ball outside, and once Denise realized that this loosening was generally accompanied by a bout of surliness, she found ways to work around it. Sending him to his room for a time worked if he got really awful—though she was completely shocked, initially, that he actually did what she told him. Often, as she sat on the couch blaming herself for her son's emotional turmoil, he would open the door and come out with something cute like "Ma, I'm nearly twelve. I'm going through puberty, and sometimes

I have a hard time with it, you know?" which would make her laugh and then she'd envelop him in her arms and tickle him until he begged her to stop.

He got to spend his twelfth birthday with her. She didn't have anything particularly great to give him (of course), but she bought him some personal-hygiene stuff from Canteen and wrapped each item in homemade wrapping paper. She made a nice dinner and a "jailhouse" cake out of Little Debbie cupcakes with Marshmallow Fluff for icing and M&Ms on top for added color. They weren't allowed candles, but he said he loved it anyway, and afterward, once they'd done the dishes together, they went out and sat on the back steps of the trailer at sunset with mugs of hot cocoa. They'd often drunk cocoa before she was sent away, during snowstorms, or while waiting for them to come. There was no snow this evening, but it was cold enough to make the hot chocolate special. Across the field was a one-lane country road. More fields on the other side. Somewhere a bird was calling. Denise began to unwind. Patrick mentioned that living with his dad made him nervous some of the time. He never knew what his mood would be when he came back from school, he said quietly, and he drank a lot, and that worried him too. Sometimes there were women around, and when that happened Alan made him go to his room and stay there.

"I think Daddy is a . . ." Pat wouldn't finish.

Denise said, "A what?"

"I can't say it—it's a swear."

"Well, you're twelve now. I'll give you permission this time."

"He's a slut," he said. "And he's absolutely not my role model." Anyway, he went on, he wasn't even around right then—he was serving ninety days for beating up one of his girlfriends.

Denise said nothing.

"He wasn't really going after her, Ma, don't worry," Pat added after a minute or two. "He was just trying to hurt *himself* with a knife."

Oh God. Denise was twenty-three years old when she first saw Alan do that. Afterward he'd do it all the time, corner Denise and threaten to kill himself. It was an awful, tormenting thing to witness. He would take a knife and hold it up to his wrist, or his neck, and shove his face next to Denise's and scream that he hoped she knew it was her fault, that she was driving him to this. If she left him, he would kill himself, he'd say, and she would have to watch him do it. "See, Denise? See? You want to hurt me?"

Of course Denise said anything she could think of to make him stop. She would tell him that she loved him, that she wouldn't leave, that she'd do whatever he wanted. Now Patrick was having to watch this too?

One afternoon, she remembered now, Alan had been so depressed that she finally agreed to meet him in a parking lot behind a restaurant. They were separated at the time, but Denise went and did her best to console him. Together they sat in his van, and when she left a half hour or so later she thought he was feeling a little better. Even then she didn't understand how bad things were in his head (what he called in his last letter his "head of horrors") because later she got a phone call from his grandfather. He had found Alan in his van in a pool of blood. His wrists were slit—deep this time. He almost didn't make it.

As she lay flat on the bunk above Patrick's in the trailer that evening, the memory undid her still. Mostly she felt rage. But underneath that she was shocked to discover deep sadness too—for herself. She should have managed the whole thing better. She should have left sooner, been cleaner about it, more decisive. But she was so young— how was a twenty-three-year-old girl who knew nothing about anything supposed to deal with a guy like Alan? She was still trying to make sense of it at thirty-four! How could Pat possibly manage alone? God help him. Dear God, please help him, she prayed.

TIME IN THE trailer was a source of conflict and shame for almost everyone who had access to it. But it was difficult to talk about. Most of the women at Lancaster had no access to their kids at all, and to be seen moping or, worse, complaining after a full twenty-four-hour visit was, quite simply, unacceptable. The only ones who understood were the ones who'd been through it, women like Maria-Cristina, who'd lost contact with her kids while she was over at Framingham. By the time she'd been classed to Lancaster, Maria-Cristina no longer had much of an idea who her kids had become or how to look after them. The little baby, almost two now, was the worst. He still couldn't talk, and he whined when he wanted something and then started to cry. It always took her forever to figure out what he needed to be soothed. Recently, communication with her nine-year-old daughter, Shayla, had also become difficult. Last time she visited she insisted on eating yellow rice with *sazón,* and when Maria-Cristina tried to explain that there was no *sazón* in prison, Shayla threw a fit. She stormed into the bedroom, slammed the door, and refused to come out. Remembering the parenting classes she'd been taking, Maria-Cristina spoke calmly through the door, encouraging her daughter to come talk about the frustrations she must be feeling, but nothing seemed to work. Shayla stayed in the bedroom, silent and alone, for hours.

DENISE AND PAT'S visits were never as bad as all that. Most of the time, in fact, they had something like fun. More than anything Denise was determined to provide a space where Patrick could at least sometimes be a kid. She kept him outside as much as she could, once even getting permission for him to join a volleyball game with the women, which he loved because they all so indulged him. They ate well and played word games and talked more and more. Over time they got into the habit of watching TV together in the evenings too. It felt like a waste of precious time at first, but it was pretty much the only way Pat allowed his mother any physical contact. There was something so intensely right about being curled up against the couch together, watching some dreadful show on TV.

One morning in early September, Denise got an emergency phone call from Alan's mother. It was a Sunday, midday.

"Denise?" she said. "Alan's hurt Pat." Denise's mind ran wild. "Denise? He's fine," her mother-in-law said. "I've got him here. But we've been talking, and I guess Alan's done stuff like this before."

Alan had lost control, that's all she knew, Denise's mother-in-law said. He'd been drinking, she was fairly certain, and then "something irritated him and he went off." He slammed Patrick's head against the couch over and over, and then he left—just up and left and Patrick had still been in the living room alone when his grandmother came to get him five or six hours later. He had bruises across his upper back, down his right arm and the right side of his back, along his collarbone and down near his spine on his lower left back as well. Denise wanted him out of there. She hung up the phone and called her friend Nicole, who agreed to drive up and get him. Alan's mother hadn't packed Pat a bag, hadn't even pulled a toothbrush and a change of clothes or underwear together, so there was just the kid, all beaten and bruised, to bring back to Massachusetts. Nicole took him to the hospital and, after getting the okay from doctors there, brought him to her mother's house for the night. A few hours later a friend of hers, a cop, came around and helped Patrick write up a report. He'd been reluctant but compliant and went straight to bed afterward.

The next day, when Patrick came to see Denise at Lancaster, his bruises for the most part were hidden by clothing and hair. Following his lead, Denise did her best to keep things on an even keel. She'd been given permission to have him there for three full days, and whenever she could she hauled him outside to hit baseballs and run around after a football. "I know you're madder than that, kick it harder—*harder!*" she'd say and even then was amazed by the force with which he'd kick the ball or swing the baseball bat through the air. Pat stayed angry even so. When Denise found him cooking himself a hot dog and tried to take over, for example, shooing him aside with a worried "I'll do that," he turned to her scornfully and said, "I've been doing this by myself for years, Mom. I've been looking after myself for years!"

Denise knew by then that Alan hit Patrick regularly. Patrick had told her once, more or less lightheartedly, that Alan didn't hit his butt anymore—he was too old for that now, so instead he hit him in the face or the head. She'd been so angry then. Fighting back tears, she told Patrick as firmly as she could that no one had a right to hit anyone, ever. "Oh, it's okay, Mom," Patrick had said. "My butt is really sensitive anyways." She'd wanted to explode.

It didn't help Patrick to see her furious like that, she knew, and if she'd said as much as a word about it to Alan, Patrick's life might have only grown worse. The Department of Social Services had still seemed out of the question—especially with Pat up in Maine. But not anymore. Someone from DSS had come to Lancaster to talk with Denise after the beating, and she'd agreed to sign voluntary placement papers for him. They'd find him a foster home in one or two days, they said. This was essential, as Denise was pressing charges against Alan this time. She remembered the way the cop had persuaded her to drop the charges years before, how he'd told her she'd be risking her own right to custody if she didn't. She knew that cop. He used to drop by the club to watch the girls dance. Sometimes she'd run into him in the parking lot outside her apartment, and he'd invariably ask her to set him up with some of her friends. The creep. But she wouldn't back down this time. Alan had done who knew how much damage to Pat since she'd been locked up in prison—and attacked a grown woman as well—and he was still free to do what he wanted. Yes, she said when someone from the hospital had called to ask, she did want to press charges, *Yes*.

Denise didn't talk much about any of this with Patrick. She kept him informed but only in the vaguest possible way, sketching out his new reality bit by bit. Mostly she wanted to reassure him, to let him know that the worst was past. She wanted him to know too that he'd done the right thing by writing the report on his dad. He was feeling guilty about it, and afraid, kept saying things like "Dad's going to kill me."

"We'll get through this," Denise told him. "Things will be better, Daddy will get help," she'd say over and over, like the soft and soothing refrain of a lullaby. And by the time DSS came to get him, she could almost persuade herself that Pat half believed the words he muttered, head down in her arms: "Yeah, Mom. I know. Dad's going to get some help."

TWO WEEKS LATER Patrick came back for a visit. He was furious. He hated his foster home and he hated MCI-Lancaster and he didn't want to be in either place, he said almost as soon as he arrived. Then he flung the trailer door open and stormed out to the far corner of the field where he knew Denise couldn't follow because it was off-limits to inmates.

It took Denise more than an hour to get him back inside. "What was I supposed to say? 'Get in here or *I'll* get in trouble'? That's hardly the point," she told me later. "He's as big as me, and stronger, so I can't exactly pick him up and haul him inside. I have no idea how to handle him. Should I call an officer? I don't know. I left him when he was nine. Now he's twelve. He's in the system and he's mad. I don't know anything about twelve-year-olds."

In the end she set the kitchen timer and told him he had ten minutes to get back inside or there would be consequences. It was a gamble. She knew she would have to call an officer if the bluff didn't work. Lucky for her, it did. Still furious, Patrick stamped his way back to the trailer and then slumped down on the couch in preparation for the talk Denise said they needed to have. That was when she let slip a derogatory remark about his father.

Pat exploded. Bursting into floods of tears, he sprung up from the sofa and slammed himself into the closet, where he stayed, sobbing, for ten, long minutes.

"Call an officer—I want to leave! Call a guard so I can get the hell out of here!" he kept saying, and Denise replied that she would of course call an officer if that was what he wanted, in just a minute, in just a minute . . .

"Send me back to the trash where I belong," Pat said when at last he stepped out of the closet. Then: "My dad did the best that he could."

"You're right," Denise said. "He did." Holding Patrick in her arms now, she did her best to let whatever he managed to say between sobs wash over her—a mess of Alan-sponsored lies about how it had been her affairs that had broken up the marriage, how she'd had three abortions and had never cared about Patrick but had only been a junkie and a whore. "You took me away from my father," he said then quietly, more sad than mad. "You'll never stay away from drugs."

"You're right," Denise replied. "I'll have to prove that to you."

"You won't be able to prove it to me," Pat retorted. "Because I'll be in military school. And then I'll be in the military. And then I'm going to crash into a building because I know that's how I'm going to die. I've had dreams about it."

Later that night, out of the silence, Pat said, "Mom. I feel so much better. I'm going to come over and do this all the time." And later still, after what felt like hours of wordless hugging, he quietly told her, "I have no tears left in my eyes. I have to go to sleep to get new ones." The next morning she thought it best to let him vegetate in front of the TV while she made an apple pie. Pat usually helped her cook, but he didn't seem up to much of anything now. He'd said sorry as soon as he'd woken up, and Denise felt it was best just to let him regroup.

Pat loved apple pie. As Denise cut the apples she told herself that everything would work out fine. She just had to keep strong; she just had to keep grounded. The bowl was almost full by then. As Denise fingered through the pile of moon-shaped apple slices, spreading sugar and cinnamon evenly, Patrick came up next to her, and Denise turned to him and smiled. Then Pat grabbed the knife from the counter and pressed its point into his neck.

Denise didn't know what to do.

Very carefully, painstakingly, she finished mixing the apples and the cinnamon as if nothing were happening. Then, still frantically ignoring her son, she began to roll out the dough, sprinkling the surface with flour front and back, until he finally relented, put the knife back on the counter, and ambled back to the living room to watch more TV.

APPETITES

CARMEN HADN'T HAD a visit from her family for eight months. She didn't like to ask her brother to come all the way out to Framingham because she preferred he spend the time with her kids, whom he looked after. She had three sisters, but they didn't get on. On the outside they'd lived with her for years, she said, not even trying to hide her bitterness. Now, because "I can't give them nothing, they don't come."

But a man does. A *moreno,* she said, a black man. He was a friend of the husband of a friend of hers, and it was good that he came, she told me, because after almost six years at Framingham she needed to speak to someone who listened to her troubles. Besides, she confessed, she was looking for someone to take care of her when she got out. She had lost her apartment, as well as her children, when she was incarcerated, and if she wanted to go straight when she got out, her former network of friends and family would be of little use. As a citizen of El Salvador, Carmen also faced probable deportation at the end of her fifteen-year sentence—a fate she could avoid most easily by marrying an American.

Carmen was very nervous the first time Henry Charles came to visit her. "So nervous I was going to die," she said. To begin with, they were awkward and formal with each other: lots of "Hello, how are you?" and "Very pleased to meet you" and not much else, as she speaks just a little English and he speaks no Spanish at all. By the end of the visit they were communicating better, though, and even at nine in the evening, after three hours in the visiting room, he didn't want to leave. How sad he was to leave her here, he said.

"Señor Henry has something," Carmen later told me in Spanish. "A very beautiful heart. He is an older man, sixty years old. But he looks good—you know, the black people don't age so badly—and he's a Christian man, so we have the same religion. God has a lot of power. For Him, nothing is impossible. I give thanks to Him, for example, that my daughters are good daughters even without me being around. No drugs, nothing. And now He sends me this man!

"Ay! But I suffered a lot with men," Carmen said then, changing tone. "Many beatings, many cheatings, and I don't want that. I want a gentle life, a peaceful life. This man is very sweet. He doesn't love women on the street—they think only of cigarettes and beer, he says. But with me he is happy. With me he has a happiness in his face that he didn't have before."

Henry visited Carmen regularly all through the summer and into the fall. He always deposited some money in her account, twenty dollars, occasionally forty, to keep her fed, he said, and beautiful. He stayed until the very last minute every time, and after several months, he finally leaned across the table and kissed her. Carmen remembered nothing about the quality of that kiss. She'd been too nervous to pay much attention. She did remember, however, every detail of his most recent visit. After greeting each other and buying the meal they would share—turkey-and-cheese subs, chips, animal crackers, and soda—they sat at one of the round tables, which he seemed to prefer. Then, before they even finished unwrapping their food, he asked: "Carmen, will we only be friends, or will we be more than friends?"

"I can be anything you want me to be," Carmen replied calmly. "Really," she said, pushing her sandwich slightly off to one side. "What do you want me to be? I don't have a husband. You are the first man to come visit me. I miss you when you are not here. I get crazy to see you. If it would please you, we could get married."

"Would that be possible?" he asked, openly eager now.

"*Sí,*" she said seriously. "*Sí.*"

Ecstatic, Carmen phoned her daughter, Carmencita, that night and told her, "Maybe I am going to marry!"

"But who with, Mami?" asked her daughter. "There are only women there, no? Are you going to get married with a woman?"

"*No, niña, con hombre*—with a man."

"*Bien.* It will be good if it is with a man," said Carmencita. "*Está bien.*"

Carmen laughed loudly as she told me this story. But her smile turned shy and proud when she told me that Henry had sent her a check for seventy dollars this month. "His parents are from Kansas," she said. "Kansas—*Imagínate*—a real *americano*! He's skinny, it's true, and he has bad hair, because he's a black man. But he has a house in Malden. He has money. I don't need to know any more. Now I will be . . . 'fat and happy'?" she said in English, still smiling but less certain now, shyly motioning toward herself with just the hint of a question: "Is that how you say it? *Gorda y feliz?*"

IT IS EXPENSIVE living in prison. Jobs in the flag factory at Framingham typically pay twenty dollars a week—ten to the inmate's cash account, ten to her savings. Cleaners and kitchen help make just five dollars, split the same way. Yet it cost $2.90 for a package of Ritz crackers from Canteen, $2.00 for a jar of peanut butter, and $2.36 for a tube of Crest toothpaste. To make matters worse, Canteen had recently been granted a monopoly over all clothes sold to the women. Now not only did your clothes have to be blue, black, or white, they had to be Canteen-selected brands of blue, black, or white. It is true that permitting clothes from the outside had created its own difficulties. Hierarchies express themselves through clothing as clearly in prison as out on the street, and before regulations were implemented, such competitiveness had run pretty much unchecked. Even a trip to the dining hall became a statement. According to Charlene, "Everything back then used to be brand-name—down to your Victoria's Secret underwear."

Now things were no better. Although fancy clothing brands were no longer allowed, Canteen sold Levi's and Nikes, and these almost always cost more than the brand-name knockoffs women's families used to send in. A pair of Levi's, for example, cost $43.69 from Canteen. A shirt, $26.88. The wealthier women in prison could still buy at least some new articles of clothing. But the poor, who could no longer receive generic or secondhand items from home, now had to do without altogether. What little money they managed to earn went almost exclusively to buying the basics: tampons, soap, and deodorant.

As in all U.S. prisons, a black-market economy is booming in Framingham. Unlike men, however, who are most interested in acquiring makeshift weapons and drugs, women in prison spend small fortunes on illegally procured underwear, food, and makeup. At MCI-Framingham all three rest in the hands of an inmate named Louise Cato.

Serving a three-year mandatory for trafficking three tenths of a gram over the limit for possession of cocaine, Louise is upbeat, smart, and engaging. It is a pleasure, always, to see her. She works a forty-eight-hour week as the head chef at Framingham and still finds time to take university-level classes on the side. She came to prison with almost forty college credits, which she had picked up here and there during her travels around the country, earning "a few credits at Hartford—not Harvard. I always say that—*Hart*ford, not Harvard!" She was now such a good student (3.38 average) that her math professor requested she be allowed to take an individual, directed study in physics.

In addition to her legitimate activities, however, Louise is the prison wheeler-dealer, the queen bee, the woman who makes whatever you want to happen, happen.

"I'm a major asset here," she told me matter-of-factly when I first met her. "Imagine there's something that you really want. Now imagine that you can't have it. Except if you get it through me."

With the help of a female officer, she smuggled makeup: lipstick (price varies, she takes specific brand and color requests) and eyeliner (Wet 'n' Wild), a half a stick of which she sold for ten dollars. Her best-sellers, currently, were tweezers, which fetched fifty dollars a pair—a massive amount in a prison economy.

"Fifty dollars!" I exclaimed. "What do people use them for?"

"For tweezing," she replied, like I was an idiot.

Louise smuggled drugs into Framingham when she first arrived. She'd been placed in Brewster One, the same large dormitory in which Denise spent her first few weeks. Louise had never been an addict herself, but when she saw all those "girls thirsty for dope," she hooked up with a CO whom she'd known on the street and started selling it big-time. The business came to an abrupt end when the CO was transferred for fooling around with an inmate. But Louise found it a relief to stop pushing the hard stuff, especially as dealing in makeup, and better still, her own artwork, was just as profitable.

These days women came to her for greeting cards instead of drugs, which she provided with message or without, depending on how much each customer could afford. More tantalizing still, she provided both inmates and COs with intricate and highly specialized designs for tat-toos. These she prepared meticulously, in ink, on a one-to-one basis. At least four Framingham COs actually went to a tattoo parlor to have these affixed permanently to their bodies: Officer S. has a cross made out of barbells in front of a globe all broken up and in flames. Officer D. has a combination moon and sun. Officer V. has two, both fairies; and Officer P. has an armband and tribal art on his back encircling his kids' names.

In addition to the makeup and cards and tattoos, Louise also ran a "food scam," which involved making made-to-order meal packets (veg-etables and rice; chicken and rice; cheese, peppers, and onions) for just sixteen dollars a week, and a "clothing racket," which, with the help of the property officer, provided access to a handful of real stores on the outside. Along with the Canteen company itself, Louise's clothing busi-ness was perhaps the only thing to have profited by the recent Canteen clampdown. She'd sold two shirts on the morning of our visit alone.

All this activity could have made Louise the wealthiest woman in Framingham. But that wasn't why she did it. She'd have had more than she could spend working just half of her scams. Instead, the furious and constant juggling kept her on her toes, she said, alert and alive and, most of all, dignified. Aside from the food, which she insisted be paid for in cash, she preferred to exchange the rest of her services for items direct from Canteen. "I'm a hoarder," she told me. Right then her locker contained ten cans of soda (Coke and Sprite), fifteen beef salamis, six bags of rice, a pile of M&Ms, a bag of bagels, three bottles of shampoo, three of conditioner, and three of hair gel.

"I'm a nut about the stuff, because I'm so afraid of not having," she said. "It's like an addiction. It comes from the street. You're always wor-ried about not having on the street."

Like many women at Framingham, Louise grew up without much

adult supervision. After running away from home, she took care of herself on the streets of Boston from the time she was thirteen. Unlike most women at Framingham, however, Louise found she was up to the task, at least financially. "I had my first apartment before I got my period," she told me. She started out running numbers with a Chinese man and soon graduated to selling crack, and then heroin, in a park on Green Street, where she was stabbed in the stomach at the age of fifteen. Later she went to New York and hung out with a group of Dominicans who moved her up a few rungs on the drug-business ladder. She told me that she has sold drugs to "judges, cops, lawyers, and selectmen." When I told her I didn't believe her, she named names: "It was mad shit!" she said. "My son's father, he's a crazy fucker. I was all happy selling my little drugs until I met him. I could tell you stories about robbing drug dealers for Ks of coke."

"Don't people kill you for doing things like that?" I asked.

"Yes," she said, straightforwardly. "I been robbed, raped, beaten. I seen my cousin get his head blown off. I've seen a lot of murder. A lot of shootings. A lot of fights—I seen a lot of bad shit, but I've seen a lot of beauty too. I been through almost all the states and have lived in a few too—mostly in Arizona and Virginia and Florida, though I dislike Florida. I also lived in the DR for eight months and in PR for a couple of months, and I've visited Sicily, where my father's family is from. And Jamaica. I often say that I've lived more and seen more in my short little life than most people have."

This was what seemed so different about Louise. After nearly two years of visiting women in prison, she was the first I'd met who embraced her choices, good and bad, as her own. The first who didn't seem at least partially defeated by the horror that ran through her life's center as a result. Claiming the chaos of her life by continuing, even at Framingham, to live on her own terms, she was able to fight despair effectively. As she said, "In here, it's who you know or who you blow. I might manipulate things, but I'm not going to kiss their ass, and I *can't* kick their ass. Dignity is a big thing in this place, and any tiny little way you can keep your dignity when you have to stand up and be counted every night like sheep is important."

Finally I'd found the woman I didn't even know I'd been looking for—the fearless, self-sufficient she-criminal: brazen, brash, and smarter than the men who ran things. She'd never done drugs, never been an addict or an adult victim of domestic abuse. She ran her own show, even here at Framingham. Most of all, she wasn't afraid.

"See, a lot of people have fear of repercussion in here. Me, on the other hand, I have nothing left to lose. Nothing. The way I see it, they can't take anything more away from me than the judge did the day he separated me from my daughter and sent me here. And then I got the gift of the gab too, you see," she told me. "Eighty percent of the time I can talk my way out of something. I hardly ever get in trouble. Even when I get caught red-handed I kid and joke and whine and play and I get out of it—never get a ticket, never get written up. Except for the bust that ended me up here, I was never busted, never once. I'm smart," she said, "I do things smart and I don't get caught."

It was almost time for count. The visiting room COs were already circling, asking if visitors would stay until after or leave now.

Exuberant, almost joyful, I asked Louise what she planned to do when she got out. I was expecting big ideas, elaborate plans of brazen criminality. Instead Louise turned away and said in a quiet voice I hadn't heard until then: "I don't know . . . I never had to work the legal hustle . . . It's my biggest fear. I'm afraid to leave here. I am. I have nobody out there no more. Nobody at all.

"You know, I weighed four hundred and forty-eight pounds when I came to Framingham," she told me after a pause. "That was why I had the gastric-bypass surgery. To reduce the size of my stomach, stop me from being able to eat so much." Louise is about five feet two. It is impossible to imagine her that size.

"Could you walk?" I asked stupidly.

"Yes," she said. She could walk. She'd sold drugs all over the Cape when she was that size. She'd gained the weight slowly. "I ate when I was happy. I ate when I was unhappy. And after my daughter, the weight just added on, and added on. It's the only thing I fear more than leaving," she said. "Getting big again. I still have about fifty extra pounds on me just from the skin. My own stretched-out skin. It's horrible. I feel like anyone who looks at me must get disgusted."

I looked more closely at Louise now, more gently. She was close to tears. The depth of female sadness never ends, I thought.

Because I couldn't think of anything else to say, I asked her then about the large tattoo that stuck half an inch out of her sleeve. She pulled up her shirt with a wry smile and stretched her arm toward me. But the drawing was intricate and difficult to make out.

"It's my cousin's face," she said. "His scream, when he got his head blown off."

"Why did you do *that*?" I asked, out of my depth again.

"Because I had nightmares about it every night, and it helped get it out of my system," she replied. Looking hard I saw it then—the wild and agonized distortion of a face at the moment of violent death. A perpetual, deafeningly silent scream.

THE DEPARTMENT OF Correction knew nothing about most of Louise's scams. In general they do everything they can to prevent this kind of stockpiling. While prisoners are allowed to buy as much food as they like from Canteen, strict limits are placed on personal-hygiene items. At any given time, each inmate is allowed fifteen. Depending on the officer, a piece of soap in a soap dish could count as one or two items; a toothbrush, toothpaste, and cup as one, two, or three. Closets can hold six hangers, three per inmate, which may hold two pairs of sweatpants, five pairs of pants, ten T-shirts (bras count as T-shirts too), five dress shirts, two pairs of pajamas, one dressing gown, and one pair of slippers. It is in order to maintain compliance with these regulations that groups of COs occasionally descend on a unit, forcibly evict the women from their rooms, and search them for "contraband": an extra pair of underwear or pillowcase, one bottle of shampoo too many, perhaps a sample packet of makeup pulled from a fashion magazine. The authorities don't even pretend to expect to find anything else. In the six years Deputy Superintendent Foley has been at Framingham, he confessed to having seen a weapon—a knife—only once.

"Bend-over-and-cough" inmate strip searches, both before and after a visit, form the frontline protection against incoming contraband. Inmates are not allowed to go to the bathroom during a visit at all. If they really must pee, the visit is terminated. Visitors are allowed to use the single-stall facility underneath the clock, but the door must be unlocked for them by a CO, and they are patted down both before and after the trip. Contraband does sometimes work its way in despite these precautions, and because of this, tables were recently pulled from the room altogether, replaced with row upon row of forward-facing chairs like those in a movie theater.

The inmate phone system has been set up to circumvent illegal activity at its source. AT&T and MCI have been competing fiercely for the market since the early 1990s, when the prison population first passed the one-million mark. In an attempt to secure primacy, both have developed a series of fraud-detection devices that monitor and control inmate access to the outside world. These include three-way-calling fraud prevention, caller-ID blocking, and on-site recording and compiling of calls. As well, televisions for the correctional market are built in transparent casings by KTV so that contraband cannot be hidden inside. Even Colgate is doing its part by marketing translucent toothpaste in a transparent tube: "Clear tube and clear cap help solve security issues in correctional facilities," its promotional literature proclaims. "Colgate is the only national brand with a CLEAR toothpaste and tube."

CORRECTIONS IS A huge business these days. With more than two million people behind bars the (literally captive) market is now bigger than major-league baseball. Bigger even than the pornography business. In addition to individual inmate spending, the government of Massachusetts spends more than $860 million every year on its prison system—and Massachusetts is relatively small. Larger states such as California and Texas spent $5.1 and $5.2 billion respectively in 2003. Contracts, then, can be worth millions. Private companies do all they can to give themselves the edge. And the place where a lot of the hardest selling is done is at the annual American Correctional Association Conference.

The conference is open to anyone willing to pay the $310 entrance fee. For the most part, it is attended by correction and state-government officials looking to make contacts and strike deals, as well as by representatives from more than 450 individual companies. The masthead on the conference's glossy brochure pretty much says it all. The thirty-six corporate conference sponsors include AT&T, Verizon, MCI, Bristol-Myers Squibb, Canteen, and Securicor.

In 2001 the huge exhibition hall was divided into corridors (euphemistically dubbed "avenues") lined with more than four hundred exhibitors, each in its own prefabricated display booth. Everything from new prison buildings, body armor, and detention equipment to dentistry products, fans, and eyeglasses was being sold. Toilets were also on sale, as well as uniforms, detergents, and videotaped, "in cell" educators. Each exhibitor had its team of salespeople in well-fitting suits, or skirts and scarves and high-heeled shoes, tempting possible customers to their stands just as they do at any corporate get-together where there is a lot of money being made. A sales conference is a sales conference, it seems, no matter what is being sold.

Not that some displays weren't particularly unsettling. The semi-automatic "Pepper Ball" machine-gun stand drew a huge crowd of people waiting for their chance to shoot at a three-dimensional dummy prisoner. But the chair-restraint salesman, the man whose company's tagline is "the CELL the size of a chair" and whose display featured an adaptive sheath for young children (juvenile accessory kit RC 1500), was only a little more off-putting than the Verizon Intellifraud salesman and his clean professionalism.

People selling "body bunkers" and ammunition and chains, people inventing new "spit guards" and 45,000-volt stun guns, which come with "complete legal service . . . in the event of litigation regarding product use and/or 'use of force' issues," mingled easily with well-dressed architects and lighting specialists and slick, twenty-first-century steel designers. They were there to make money, all of them, and were doing so well, apparently, that the premise behind their enthusiastic activity, the fact that the prison business was booming, had become an unquestioned cause for celebration.

Certainly the man selling the restraint chair felt no apparent self-consciousness about the feverish tone of his sales pitch. When I told him that the chair looked impressive, he said that yes, "it's been blamed for a lot of things—but it works."

When I asked what it had been blamed for, he whipped out a

sheath of papers and then flipped through them to a page labeled "Autopsy Report." The page was almost entirely covered by two bold diagrams of a woman's body, front and back. Drawn on these body shapes were representations of wound marks across the upper half of her skull, between her breasts, and across her ribs. The salesman told me with a disbelieving chuckle that this woman's lawyer was trying to prove that she had died as a result of the chair. "Ridiculous!" he said, rolling up the sheath of papers again and tossing them behind him on the shelf. "Ridiculous—but we have to pay attention to stuff like this!"

CANTEEN WAS ALSO well represented at the conference. Large advertising banners hung from the ceiling, and a slew of giveaways were handed out by roving representatives. The saleswoman staffing its main stand was particularly pleasant and well informed. She explained that Canteen was merely a subdivision of Compass, an eight-billion-dollar company based out of London. Outside the corrections field, it feeds 13 percent of the U.S. workforce every day, through cafeterias in companies like Microsoft, IBM, and American Express, she told me with the kind of professionally smiling pride most usually seen in flight attendants.

"Canteen has the purchasing power and flexibility to offer our customers competitive commissions while keeping the prices to the customer within market trends," she said. It has also become the largest correctional vending and food provider in the United States. In this country alone it feeds 150,000 inmates three times a day. Typically, she could tell me nothing about women in prison per se, or their dietary needs. But when I asked if they provide different menus for different states, she said that their menus were, in general, "all the same—the big difference is between county and state facilities."

In county jails, she went on to explain, they provided a caloric intake, per inmate, of between 2,800 and 3,000 a day, while in state prisons they provided between 3,000 and 3,600. When I asked if she knew what accounted for this difference, she smiled and leaned in toward me. "Inmates in county jails serve less time than those in state prisons," she said.

Confused, I asked if she meant there was a link between length of sentence and caloric intake. She nodded, as if pleased. "It's a management philosophy," she said conspiratorially. "You know, fat and happy."

DESPAIR

UNLIKE MANY OF the women at Framingham, Tanya Dermott has never put on weight in prison. She is short, maybe five-two, and trim, and has a smile that has gotten her both into and out of a lot of trouble. Tanya is a charmer—teeth so straight they look like a movie star's—and she is also mentally ill. A sociopath, doctors have called her. Also a paranoid schizophrenic.

The first time I met her, Tanya was upbeat and girlishly excited, so I didn't notice that she sometimes slurred her words. I did recognize that her attention wavered periodically, until there was no apparent congruity between what she was saying and her facial expressions, and this was disconcerting. So too was the scribble of bright, white scars that crisscrossed the pale skin of her neck and arms like the pattern left by ice skates on a frozen pond—some were thin and clean, some jagged, some curved. The longest one reached all the way from her wrist to her inner elbow. It was so straight and precise that I at first assumed it was surgical.

But it wasn't. Like the rest of them, the wound that had caused this scar was self-inflicted—this particular one in the shower stalls of Barton, the unit reserved for the seriously mentally ill at Framingham.

Like many residents of Barton, Tanya has been mentally ill since her teens. Not that it was ever discussed in these terms—or even really diagnosed before she entered Framingham. There had been little room for such attentiveness in her life, and even the clearest of symptoms were typically confused with antisocial proclivities. As a result she and her little sister, Chris, both dropped out of school and spent years trawling the streets of their western Massachusetts town, selling drugs, or their bodies, or whatever else they could find that might be of value to someone with cash.

Tanya and Chris were co-defendants in the assault trial that led to Tanya's seven-year sentence at Framingham—an assault that left an occasionally violent and elderly Portuguese man stabbed twenty-two times and close to death. The way Tanya tells it, the old man was pestering her for attention and, when she didn't respond immediately, he punched her in the face. Tanya was both high and drunk at the time, and "that punch in the face didn't really help me, you know?" Enraged, she found a knife in the kitchen, "not a butcher's knife but a steak knife about that long"—she spaced her hands almost a foot apart—"and I started to stab him with it in the back, in the stomach, in the face, over and over again. And then, when I was finished, there were twenty-two stabs."

Both Tanya and Chris must have gone into shock at the sight of the old man's wounds. Despite the fact that Tanya was covered in blood, the two of them waited politely at the bus stop after the stabbing, paying full fare for their ride to their motel, where they were arrested the next day. According to both Tanya and court records, however, Chris had nothing to do with the attack. She received just a one year's suspended sentence for being present at the scene of the crime and was only sent to Framingham later, after failing three consecutive, court-mandated urine tests.

Like many women with untreated mental illness, Chris had been addicted to illegally procured drugs for most of her adult life. She'd been in prison many times because of this—in Miami, and Ludlow, and Framingham—and though she'd also repeatedly tried to kill herself, no one ever paid much attention. Their mother, Marie, always thought of the cuttings as pleas for attention. So everyone, including, apparently, prison authorities, was surprised when Chris tried to kill herself by strangulation just a few weeks after arriving at Framingham.

It was easy enough to do, Chris found. She constructed a simple noose with a sheet in her room, but when she tried to strangle herself with it the knot slipped free and she fell to the ground, more or less unhurt.

She was sent to Tewksbury, a state psychiatric hospital, for evaluation but was soon back at Framingham. And though she was returned to the relative safety of Barton, she again tried to kill herself less than two months later, this time by swallowing four double-sided blades extracted from razors. Another inmate found her with blood pouring out of her mouth and called for help. Framingham's psychiatric team ordered that she be watched closely after that. For some reason, though, Chris was placed in a solitary cell at the end of a long corridor, where guards had to walk a distance to check on her. It was in this cell that she finally did manage to die just a few days later. Less than four months after another inmate, Rachel Day, strangled herself to death in the Awaiting Trial Unit, Chris buckled a belt around a pole in her cell's closet and hanged herself. She was thirty-one years old at the time, and the mother of two.

COMPRISING PREDOMINANTLY THE dispossessed and the dislocated, prison populations have always been more prone to suicide than most. In contemporary America the problem was seriously exacerbated in the 1970s when policies aimed at reintegrating the mentally ill with their communities closed many residential mental-health hospitals. Instead of reintegration, however, the result was criminalization of the mentally ill. Figures show that during the seventies and eighties the number of patients in residential facilities dropped by almost 70 percent and that the number of mentally ill inmates increased proportionally. In Massachusetts, many of the sickest men were ultimately transferred back to a secure ward in a state hospital where round-the-clock psychiatric care could be provided. There is, however, no such facility for convicted mentally ill women in the state.

Dr. Kenneth Appelbaum, the University of Massachusetts psychiatrist now in charge of mental health for the DOC, has acknowledged that about a third of women in prison in Massachusetts—as across America—are "seriously mentally ill." This figure is more than borne out by the more than 60 percent of women in Framingham currently on psychotropic drugs. Despite the prevalence of such medication, however, Dr. Appelbaum estimates that there are still three to four "serious suicide attempts" at the prison each month.

These figures do not include incidents of self-cutting like the ones that have so scarred Tanya Dermott. When I asked authorities about the frequency of these incidents at Framingham, I was told, "We do not compile them. Those numbers do not exist." The women themselves, however, tell me that these events punctuate life in Framingham frequently. I myself have heard several "Code 99" calls—the code for medical emergency or serious injury—screeching out over the intercom while I've been at Framingham.

There is something also in the tone the women use to speak about these incidents that lends their claims credibility. It's as if even the most serious attempts at suicide have become so routine that they now provoke a kind of worn-out irritation instead of sympathy. I've heard it time and again, this halfhearted talk of the selfishness of women who try to kill themselves. There's the blood someone else has to clean up, and the lockdowns everyone is subjected to, the trauma and the guilt. Worst of all, there is the impossibility of responding to another woman's crisis in any decent or proportional way. "Because I mean, what can we do?" Charlene asked a little defensively one afternoon. "You can't cry. You can't let yourself go, or *you* will fall. Everything you have built here will fall."

There are some funny stories too, of course. But not many. It's a stretch even for the darkness of prison humor to wrap a story around suicide, especially as almost every inmate I've met at Framingham has seriously considered killing herself there at one time or another. Julie swallowed pills. Charlene still talked about a longing to end it all, and, back when she'd first arrived, Carmen actually got so far as slinging a twisted sheet over the bar by her toilet and tying the ends around her neck. Her roommate had been sent to the Hole, so she didn't have to worry about being interrupted, and she stood there for a long time, she told me, listening as if from a great distance to two distinct voices in her head, one commanding her to "Do it! Do it!" the other saying "No!"

In the end, of course, she listened to that second voice, the voice she now called the voice of God, and ever since she'd been singing His praises every day as a member of what everyone at Framingham called the "Spanish Choir." Even for Carmen, though, the option has never entirely disappeared. Suicide continued to glint ominously somewhere along the horizon of her consciousness, a perpetual warning, I think, of the inevitable consequence of despair.

CONVICTED OF ATTEMPTED murder in the first degree, Tanya was housed in the Pioneer Unit back when her little sister killed herself in Barton. She was deemed disturbed enough herself to warrant heavy doses of psychotropic drugs, as well as a space in Barton before Chris arrived, but the authorities moved Tanya to the general population to keep the sisters apart. A couple of days before Chris hanged herself, however, there had been a walkathon, one of the few institution-wide activities still allowed at Framingham. Everyone was out in the yard walking for charity. Large barrels of water had been set up to keep the walkers hydrated, and a group of women ended up having a friendly water fight, throwing cold cups of water over one another in the yard. In the middle of this commotion, Chris abruptly sat down and went silent. Worried, Tanya asked what was wrong. "Nothing I can't handle," Chris replied.

Tanya had a bad feeling when she heard the "Code 99 in Barton" call coming in over the intercom a few days later. She knew that her sister had tried to kill herself twice since arriving at Framingham, and she wanted to make sure she was okay. But a Code 99 results in the suspension of movement around the prison, and like everyone else, Tanya was locked in her room until the emergency passed. Only then was she escorted to the Health Services Unit and told that her sister had died.

Tanya didn't believe it at first. She started screaming—her sister simply couldn't be dead! She'd just spoken to her the day before! The nurses were lying! That was when a group of officers in protective rubber gloves burst into the room. They grabbed Tanya, stripped her naked, and strapped her down, spread-eagled in four-point restraints, to a table-bed built for the purpose. Once she was secured, a doctor gave her a shot of something that made her sleep. After that, she was left draped in a flimsy paper-towel robe and locked in a solitary cell until she calmed down.

This is how they sometimes break news of bereavement in prison. Called "suicide prevention," it is why, Tanya told me later, "everyone who is really suicidal in Framingham knows not to say they are even depressed. If you do, they just send you to the room—to the solitary lockup in HSU. That's what they do, you know. They keep you there, all alone, with nothing but a paper johnny to wear until you don't feel suicidal no more."

ONE DAY, WAITING around as I often did for hours at a time to get in for a visit at Framingham, I met a woman named Lynn who'd been held for four days in one of these isolation cells after being arrested on a misdemeanor charge. She was brought to the prison, she told me, at about six-thirty on a Friday night two weeks earlier. They stripped her and searched her and made her take a shower to decontaminate her, as is customary. Then, after handing her a too large, gray DOC uniform, they took her photograph and a full set of fingerprints and asked if she was feeling sad or depressed. That was when Lynn started to cry. She had never been to prison before, she told them, and she was terrified. The nurse then asked if she was on any medications and if she'd ever attempted suicide.

Lynn answered yes, that she had once been suicidal, when a boyfriend had left her back in 1997. The next thing she knew she was stripped naked again, given a paper robe to put on, and locked up in an isolation cell on the Health Services Unit.

The HSU is really just a group of locked, cinder-block cells facing one another across a dimly lit corridor. There is no real nurse's station. No infirmary. No hospital beds. In the suicide-watch rooms there are no beds at all, in fact, or even mattresses, just four cinder-block walls, a dirty linoleum floor, and a toilet bowl without even a seat. Small, wire-mesh windows in the doors provide peepholes for suicide checks. Conditions here are so awful that Carmen quit not long after being assigned to clean the rooms in HSU, even though she needed the money. She couldn't cope with the screaming, or the smeared feces and urine that often coated the walls after women locked up there lost control.

A medical student who interned with Framingham's psychiatric department once confessed that the place "sometimes looked like something out of 1920s Bedlam." The first time she visited a patient there, the woman was raging around a completely empty room, naked save for her long, matted hair. In the next cell down, a woman who'd been banging her head against a door was being restrained by four guards.

"They only have one doctor, and he's only there part of the time," she told me. "The people who are there all the time are the guards, and no one can do very much in that setting. HSU is a blunt instrument, and it's a terrible place to be. But it's our only option when we feel any concern for anybody, which we do often."

The same was true when Lynn was there. Locked in an empty room, alone and with no explanation why, she was allowed out just once a day, in handcuffs, to walk across the corridor for a shower. Judged to be at too high a risk to have utensils, she was allowed only finger food, which was placed on a pop-out shelf in the door three times a day. Shouting coming from the other cells made her feel panicky and nauseous, so more often than not she left the food there, untouched. Soon she began to lose track of time. She developed headaches and grew increasingly scared. Despite frequently requesting medical attention, she didn't see medical personnel until the following Monday morning, when a therapist appeared on the other side of her door.

At first Lynn was confused when the food slot opened and no food appeared. Then she realized that this was how the therapist planned to speak with her. Out in the corridor, the counselor was sitting on a chair so that she could more readily talk through the six-inch-wide, stomach-height hole in the door. Because there was no furniture in Lynn's cell, she had to kneel on the ground to communicate.

By then a "Spanish" woman who cleaned the corridors over the weekend had told Lynn how things worked. "Don't tell them you feel like crying," she'd said. "To get out of here you have to tell them you are fine, that your sadness was just when you first come in." And this is just what Lynn did. When the counselor asked her how she was, she said she was feeling fine; that she'd just been a little bit in shock on Friday; that she was much better now. The therapist seemed nice, Lynn told me. She asked a few strange questions, like whether she knew who the president of the United States was, which didn't really seem relevant, but she was gentle and sympathetic too, so that kneeling down there on the floor, Lynn trusted her enough to chastise her a little. "When someone is depressed," she told her, "you shouldn't let them be by themselves. There's too much time in here. Too much time. Instead of making things better, you guys are making things worse. You guys really are going to make somebody think about killing themselves in here. I was very professional," she assured me. "I was furious, but I spoke to her in a very professional manner. They have lawsuits just waiting to happen."

IN FACT, NUMEROUS lawsuits are pending against both the Department of Correction and Correctional Medical Services, the private, for-profit health-care company that was responsible for Massachusetts inmates until 2003, around the issue of isolating suicidal inmates at Framingham. Both organizations, however, insist that they are just being careful. They have no way of knowing how serious a woman like Lynn is about taking her life, they say, and it is better to save their lives by isolating them than to ignore what might reasonably be interpreted as a call for help. The policy, though brutal, would be hard to argue with if it actually worked. It doesn't. Five women have killed themselves at Framingham since 1995. Of these, three were actually *in* isolation cells at the time of their death. A fourth had been moved out of isolation the day before she died.

In 1997 a twenty-eight-year-old woman named Cynthia Schiffgens managed to hang herself in a Health Services Unit suicide-prevention cell similar to the one Lynn was held in, despite the supposedly round-the-clock monitoring for which such cells were created. Schiffgens had been arrested in Lowell on nightwalking charges, and despite the supposedly continuous observation of the guards, she somehow managed to string a shredded piece of sheet through the air-conditioning vent and to hang herself with it there.

Two months later, another woman with a well-documented history of mental illness hanged herself with prison bedding in a solitary cell. Awaiting trial on charges of assault and shoplifting (and therefore, theoretically, still innocent), thirty-three-year-old Angela Arduini had attempted suicide twice before, once in a police station. After losing thirty pounds at Framingham, she was identified as being depressed and of "suicidal ideation." In a typical confusion between uncontrollable symptoms of mental illness and willful disruptiveness, correctional officers sent her to the Hole instead of seeking medical help when she displayed "disruptive" behavior. After just a few days there, she once again tried to kill herself. This time, by hanging herself with a tightly twisted sheet, she succeeded.

CHRIS AND TANYA'S Mother, Marie Griffith, still remembers finding out about Chris's death when she returned from a camping weekend. "She died on a Saturday," she told me. "I didn't know about it until Sunday night. I never even seen her in the hospital where she died, where she was pronounced. They claimed they tried to revive her, but she was gone. All I can visualize in my head, to this day, is the big mark she had around her neck where she hanged herself. It was obvious. She died very—not peacefully."

Each week Marie visits the small, treeless graveyard to replace the flowers and relight the candle she has set at the foot of Chris's headstone. She is a religious woman, and she took me there to pray in silence for a few minutes. The small graveyard was flanked on three sides by busy roads and was less than half full. Patches of it were bare and dusty, but Chris's section was well maintained—for just a little extra each month, someone came around and watered the grass regularly, Marie explained. In the year following Chris's death, Marie spent much of her time out there. She built a shrine to the Virgin Mary outside her small brown ranch house, surrounded it with azaleas and miniature statues of animals and kneeling shepherds, and when she doesn't have the energy to make it out to the graveyard, she spends time there instead. At night she sits in the La-Z-Boy in her living room and loses herself in the memorabilia she has collected in honor of her daughter.

At great expense she purchased a floor-to-ceiling cabinet specially to house it all. Its expansive, glass shelves are packed with neatly arranged photographs, ribbons, handwritten epitaphs, and conical red objects that pulse and flash in imitation of the eternal, beating heart of the departed. The tiny patch of floor between the sofa and the two stuffed rocking chairs is almost entirely filled with photographs and other artifacts as well, so that when you sit down you have to be careful where you put your feet.

"Last time I saw Chris before she died, she was in court downtown because she had assaulted me and my husband," Marie said out of the blue. "She went down and filed assault-and-battery charges on me. Then she filed the criminal charges on me, saying I hit her and all that stuff. But that wasn't Chris. That was the drugs. I really believe that if she found Mr. Right Guy and not someone from prison, she would really have had a good life for herself. But she never gave herself that chance. Maybe it was because she thought so low of herself. You know, when you do things with your life like prostitution or drugs or something like that, you have a low esteem of yourself. And I think that's what she felt.

"I took her death very hard, as you can see," she said a few minutes later. "I'll never get over her death, never."

Marie had clearly been undone by her daughter's death, and she had obviously poured herself into memorializing her in a manner befitting this love. But there was also something maudlin about her grief. She spoke endlessly about the bright, white coffin she'd bought for Chris's funeral, just like the one her boss had bought for his daughter when she died in a car accident, and about the special rosary she'd had made for the occasion. She told me of Chris's favorite song—"The Power of Love" by Céline Dion—and of the time Chris crashed her mother's motorbike the first time she rode it, and, years later, of the afternoon she pulled up in front of the house in a bright red convertible, her blond hair blowing in the wind, laughing.

Tanya, on the other hand, was barely mentioned. Referred to always as "the troublemaker," she seemed to exist only in the darkest corners of the darkest stories, and it soon became clear that Marie blamed her for Chris's decline. Tanya had been different from the beginning, Marie insisted, adding, with the kind of non sequitur that made it clear mental illness ran in the family, that it had always been this way. "The girl's own father was touching her ever since she was a child."

Tanya had made reference to these troubles with her father, and I knew that both she and her little brother had been used by him in this way. It hadn't been until Marie brutally reprimanded a six-year-old Tanya for "stealing" money from her purse, however, that the children were removed from the home. Marie told me this herself, though she insisted that she never touched Tanya that day. "Tanya made the marks on her body herself," she told me, still angry all these years later. "I don't know what she did to herself, but she made it look like I'd beat her up real bad." Watching Marie purse her lips again and then shake her head bitterly, I found it hard to know what to say.

Even Chris's funeral became complicated by tales of a family member stealing a rental car and driving off to Connecticut with it to buy drugs. Marie clearly has trouble negotiating the personal and emotional aspects of her life, and the effects of this, generationally, are clear to see. Aside from her trouble with Tanya and Chris, there have been drugs and prostitution and several babies adopted away; thefts and lawsuits and long, angry fistfights on the lawn that draw multiple calls to the police.

The family stories were so unremittingly dark, in fact, that I finally asked Tanya if she had any beautiful memories from her childhood, the kind she could sink into for refuge when she really felt blue. Tanya perked up at this. Sitting straight in her chair, she widened her eyes and said, as enthusiastically as a child being asked if she'd like an ice cream: "Oh yes! I have many! Many beautiful memories about my childhood!" She paused then, her face blank for a moment. "We grew up in River Run," she said, a smile tweaking the edges of her lips. "My mother's life was very hard. She had a very, very hard life. All I really remember was knives. Fighting and knives."

CORRECTIONAL OFFICERS ARE typically offered no training in recognizing symptoms of mental illness. The darker, more serpentine aspects of psychological confusion can be deeply unsettling to those unprepared to deal with its ramifications. Sometimes, in prison, even those who do have the training are intimidated. "Therapists?" Tanya said, sneering, when I asked. "In Framingham? I tell you one thing—they don't know how to treat a person. You tell them how you really feel and they get scared."

A little more than a year after I first met Tanya, I learned that she really had frightened staff in the psychiatric department. "They felt that she was a serious psychopath," the intern told me. "There were certain patients they were very frustrated with and another group who they were seriously frightened of, and she was at the top of that second list. They felt like she was a pure sociopath."

Certainly I was scared of Tanya sometimes. She could be so attractive, that was the thing—charming, and sparkingly rakish. And yet being that way, even as she described how she'd stabbed the old man twenty-two times with a knife, revealed a detachment from self so complete at times that it seemed like death. Worse, it felt as if her deadness might seep into me—madness as death by osmosis—because looking into her eyes sometimes was like looking into a vacuum. And a vacuum, like a black hole, sucks you in.

So in the end, I'm not entirely surprised that the mentally ill serve so much solitary time in prison. COs must find it frightening to deal with women whose responses are so unpredictable, and in the Hole, at least, they are out of the way. Of course, an environment where discipline trumps treatment every time is no place for the mentally ill.

It's not just a problem in Massachusetts. American women have been killing themselves in prison isolation units for decades. In 1997 and 1998, for example, nine women tried to kill themselves while being held in the isolation unit of the Jefferson Correctional Institute in Florida. Two finally managed to kill themselves there at the end of 1998, and six guards ended up facing charges related to their deaths. They were accused of, among other things, harassing the women by leaving them naked in their cells for extended periods and of failing to tell them they turned off the cell's water connection, making washing impossible.

In July 1998 a thirty-five-year-old woman facing charges for forgery and fraud smothered herself with a pillow in her solitary cell in Albuquerque. Less than an hour after being booked on drunk-driving charges, thirty-nine-year-old Sandra Harms hanged herself in her cell in Seattle. Amy Edgington also hanged herself there, less than two years before and just two days after being taken off suicide watch, and in 2001 Karan Wheeler, thirty-seven, hanged herself in an isolation cell where she was being held for "medical reasons." In an admittedly extreme incident, depressed female inmates in Georgia were stripped naked and left "hog-tied" in solitary cells after confessing to suicidal notions. Hog-tying, as the practice of binding an inmate's hands and feet together is known, was ordered stopped by a court order in November 1991. The practice continued, however, until a woman died as a result of the practice the following year.

Frequently the court's response to such untimely and unnecessary death is to insist on increased psychiatric care. As in the case of Angela Arduini, whose fatal stint in the Hole at Framingham had been authorized by the psychiatric team, the kind of intermittent, often substandard psychiatric care that is sometimes provided in prison has proven unequal to the task.

Ironically, the practice of hog-tying was itself instituted by a psychiatrist. Similarly, after two women, Linda Hogan, forty, and Bobbi-Jo Garcia, nineteen, killed themselves in 1999, it was discovered that mentally ill women in a Connecticut prison were being treated by being strapped to their beds for months and sedated with powerful psychiatric meds. And in New York, a seventeen-year-old girl named Nancy Blumenthal killed herself just a month after being incarcerated in 1996, when a prison psychiatrist discontinued the antidepressants she had been taking for more than a year. This same psychiatrist, Dr. Harvey Lothringer, had killed a woman in a botched abortion attempt back in 1964. Panicked by what he had done, he dismembered the patient's body with a hatchet and a scalpel and tried to flush the pieces of her body down the toilet. Despite this, Lothringer was hired by a for-profit health-care provider named Emergency Medical Services. They had known of his background, they said, but insisted he came "highly rec-' ommended."

As of 1998 almost a third of the estimated $3.75 billion a year spent on correctional health care nationwide goes to privately owned, for-profit companies like EMS. Industry and government officials insist that this system saves public money and improves health care for prisoners. Watchdog agencies, however, insist that many such providers exaggerate the amount of medical care they provide, fill positions with people only nominally qualified, or leave positions unfilled altogether in their attempts to save money. One of the least visible places to cut costs, of course, is in the anyway invisible realm of the mind.

Correctional Medical Services, or CMS, the company in charge of prison health care in Massachusetts until early 2003, is by far the biggest prison health-care provider in the nation. It controls roughly 45 percent of the market and, though now replaced by U Mass in Massachusetts, continues to be responsible for the prison health care in Alabama, Arkansas, Idaho, Michigan, Minnesota, Missouri, New Jersey, New Mexico, and Wyoming.

Over the past ten years, CMS has been accused of illegal cost cutting by the U.S. Department of Justice, and by judges and court-appointed monitors across the country. One million dollars in fines were levied against it by the Virginia government between 1999 and 2000 for, among other things, understaffing, lack of adequate training, and denial of medical treatment. A district-court judge in Idaho found that an inmate's care in prison there "more closely resemble[d] physical torture than incarceration." A federal judge in Michigan described CMS's follow-up care as "bureaucratic purgatory"; a court-appointed monitor in Georgia accused the company of establishing a "medical gulag" in its state's prisons, and, while CMS refuses to make available the names or records of its medical personnel, it has been revealed that several have been disciplined by state medical licensing boards, including two, Gail Williams, M.D., whose license was revoked for sexual battery, and Walter F. Mauney, M.D., who was found guilty of "crimes against nature" after confessing to three counts of sexually penetrating a sixteen-year-old "mentally defective" boy.

Not unsurprisingly, then, CMS care often leads to substandard treatment and even death. According to records, the company has settled more than twenty cases in which inmates died as a result of its alleged negligence, indifference, understaffing, or cost cutting. Four women were to die in MCI-Framingham in its first three years of stewardship alone.

A YEAR AFTER CMS took over at Framingham, an inmate named Joan Santos wrote to the father of her infant daughter:

> Hi Robert, How's the greatest dad in the world doing? Good I hope. Happy belated father's Day. I'm getting out early than expect. . . . Because of the condition of your truck you don't have to come to visit. Just be ready to come get me at or about July 19ᵗʰ OK? Lover, have a good time you deserve a break because you work during the week. I keep on forgetting. Thanks again for the pictures and letters. I'll call you Saturday afternoon.
>
> Love, Joan

A week later, Santos killed herself in solitary confinement.

In part because she spent so much time in solitary—both in the Hole and in the Health Services Unit—Joanie wrote literally hundreds of letters like this to Robert. As she said in one of them, "I have to write to you to keep from going stir crazy." And write she did, musings and ramblings mostly, sometimes about life in prison: "John's daughter Kayla does my hair everyday when I ask her. I wish my hair was long." Sometimes she is angry, sometimes delusional, and sometimes just plain nervous about the medication she was being given. ("They started the shots again. They are giving me a lot more—25 cc or something like that I had side effects for 2 days. I hope it was the right drug and not something else. Anyways, it scared the shit out of me because the whole needle was full and I only take not even a ¼ inch. I'm still alive and here in max so I guess I'll survive . . .")

Some of Joanie's letters go on for pages, some are short, and some, heartbreakingly, look like this:

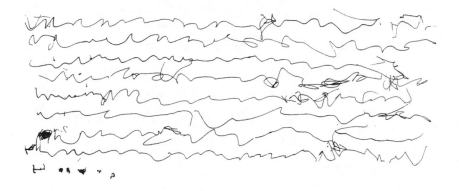

No one ever doubted that Joanie was mentally unstable. She was on hefty doses of the antipsychotic Prolixin at the time of her death, and even a passing glance at her files makes her history of mental illness abundantly clear. From about twenty on she was, according to her brother, in and out of both residential mental-health facilities and prison. This last time she was sentenced to Framingham for a parole violation and common nightwalking. Her mental health had so deteriorated by then that she logged an amazing *seventy-five* contacts with prison mental-health workers in the nine months leading up to her death. She'd also been admitted six times to the Health Services Unit because of psychotic behavior.

Nonetheless, when officers found a razor she'd been using to cut her neck and wrists in her cell, she was sentenced to thirty days in the Hole for breaking the rules prohibiting its possession. Isolated there for twenty-three hours a day, she grew delirious. After throwing her food tray at an officer and being caught trying to light a cigarette from an electrical outlet in her cell, she had her time in isolation increased to forty-five days. But it made no difference in the end. Joanie survived just twenty-nine days of solitary before threading a sheet through the same kind of ceiling ventilation grate as the one Arduini used, and hanging herself to death.

JOAN SANTOS WAS the fifth woman to die at Framingham in three and a half years. In part because of this, her death garnered uncharacteristically thorough coverage in the press. There was a hearing on Capitol Hill, and legislators became outraged that someone with such dramatically impaired mental health could be placed in isolation twenty-three hours a day. "She was being punished for having a mental disorder, that's the bottom line," one member of the committee, governor's councilor Dorothy Kelly Gay, said. "Instead of treatment she received punishment. I think it is time everybody realized that women who are going there [to Framingham] with psychiatric backgrounds are at great risk."

Kelly Gay was not alone in this opinion; committee chairwoman Barbara Gray, then democratic representative for the town of Framingham, concurred. "She should have been in a psychiatric hospital. She was obviously ill. She obviously had a long history of emotional and mental distress, including psychotic episodes . . . and yet it appeared they [prison officials] were surprised that she committed suicide."

Despite statements like these, both the DOC and CMS flatly denied any wrongdoing. Throughout the hearing they insisted that all rules and procedures had been followed correctly and that they had never had any evidence that Santos might become a danger to herself. The hearing committee had no power of subpoena. Citing a patient's right to privacy, both the DOC and CMS refused to voluntarily produce Santos's medical records, and without these, media interest dissipated. By way of apology, a spokesperson for CMS stated: "We are very sorry about her death but we don't feel CMS is in any way responsible." Framingham's superintendent at the time, now Commissioner Kathleen Dennehy, was reported as saying: "The reality is, people are going to die while in custody."

AS FAR AS Tanya was concerned, death was omnipresent at Framingham. She wasn't able to attend her sister's funeral. Though it is typically prison policy to grant furloughs for such occasions, Tanya was at the Worcester state mental hospital at the time, or possibly Tewksbury, and she still hadn't seen her sister's grave. Perhaps her death would seem more final if she had. As it was, she encountered Chris's ghost everywhere when authorities locked her up back in Barton, the very unit her sister had killed herself in just weeks before. She was being given hefty doses of Klonopin by then, but this didn't stop her from cutting herself more seriously than before. It was here that she sliced her arm from her wrist up to her elbow. Only after inmates twice found her collapsed and bleeding in the showers did the authorities think to move her elsewhere.

But Tanya never fully recovered. There was more space among the general population, and fewer ghosts, but she was still unable to access the sustained psychiatric care she so desperately needed. Her girlfriend

Giselle helped a little. She found time every day to take Tanya outside to the yard, and when Tanya didn't feel up to moving at all, Giselle brought food and hot drinks to her room. Most important, Giselle sat down and listened, even let Tanya dissolve into sobs in her arms if she needed to. But it wasn't enough. The following Palm Sunday Tanya threw herself out of a fourth-story window of the Catholic chapel.

The chapel was full, and Tanya hesitated for a moment on the ledge, but no one was able to stop her. Tanya herself doesn't remember much of the event at all. To this day all she is sure of is that she'd gone to church with Giselle, and that they'd sat together the way they did every Sunday since getting baptized there in silky white robes by Cardinal Law just the year before. Tanya credits Giselle with saving her life up until then. But something must have shifted that Sunday. Perhaps it was the pressure of keeping her feelings to herself—she'd been around long enough to know how to avoid isolation in the HSU. All she remembers now, though, is chatting quietly with Giselle during the mass, and then . . . well, nothing.

She has since been told by lawyers who have spoken to a number of women present at the time that she ran to the window and stood on the ledge for a while before jumping. One woman saw her "bounce off" the side of the building before hitting the ground. The fact that she didn't die on impact is generally regarded as a miracle. The constant rain of that spring had left the ground spongy and soft. Tanya did sustain broken ribs, a broken pelvis, and a broken spine. Her arm snapped, she punctured her lungs, bled from her brain, and ruptured her jaw. For a time, no one was certain that she would ever walk, or even talk, again. But she did mend, little by little. Now she's housed in another facility altogether, a jail, run independently of the DOC by a progressive county sheriff. Perhaps here she will at last receive the kind of care she needs.

PART

ESCAPES

THREE

SNOWSTORMS

"I LOVE IT here," Julie told me after we hugged each other hello in the rustic dining hall at MCI-Lancaster, where she had recently been transferred. "It's better than Framingham." Men, she said, were everywhere. Not guards in uniforms but inmates in jeans and sneakers and T-shirts. "They run around like they own the place, Tina—and they *all* have girlfriends. Guards even keep the peek for them. It's wicked cool. Wicked, wicked cool!"

Like Denise before her, Julie looked well here, refreshed. At the soda machine she went directly for a can of Cherry Coke, and by the time we sat down she was sparking with excitement. It hadn't always been this way, I knew. She arrived from Framingham depressed and disoriented. F. had been horrible when she first told him she was leaving. She sought him out as soon as she heard, and when she finally found him outside the Health Services Unit, all he said was, "I can't talk to you now."

"Don't you care that I'm leaving?" she asked.

"Not really, no," he said, then turned and walked away.

Julie was crushed. She'd been locked in her room on "Pending Investigation" status the whole week before, after F. threatened a rookie who'd spent a little too much time in her room and she'd again refused to cooperate when Inner Perimeter Security questioned her about him. She thought her loyalty should have been worth something. By the time Julie got back to her room, where she had to finish packing her things into a few cardboard boxes, she was "bawling," she told me only slightly ruefully now. "I didn't want to come over here—I didn't want to leave him!"

F. did say good-bye in the end. He came to her room, sat down behind the toilet partition where no one could see him from the corridor, and tried to reassure her that everything would work out. He even helped her pack. Still, she cried most of the way over here. The officer who first escorted her to her room in the women's house asked, "Did you fool around with that officer or not?" which only made her feel worse. Just a couple of days later she was escorted down to yet another IPS office, where she was told that Lancaster was too small for her to get away with things that might have been overlooked at Framingham. Nothing specific was mentioned. But everyone knew what they were talking about. They even said that they hoped she'd feel comfortable coming to them if any of their own COs made "inappropriate advances" toward her. She would have laughed had she not been feeling so vulnerable.

Her sadness lasted for days. Denise tried to snap her out of it, but nothing worked until she noticed a man named Peter in the men's dayroom, where she had been taken to wait for her ID photo to be taken. Peter was huge, six feet one, perhaps taller, biceps the size of grapefruits and a bald, shiny head just like Mr. Clean. Julie came instantly to life. She had dressed up as best she could for her photograph, but her eyes were still swollen from all the crying she'd been doing, and she'd had no time for makeup. As inconspicuously as she could, she released a strand of hair from her ponytail and let it dangle tantalizingly over one eye. Then she looked up at him with her own particular blend of brazen and coy, and smiled. COs were everywhere. One was sitting right next to her, waiting with her for the camera to arrive, so Peter's response was necessarily muted. But there was no doubt that he noticed her. When he paused for just a fraction of a second and looked right at her, Julie fell in love. "Oh my God, he's like all that and a bag of chips," she said. His nickname was Muscle, Julie quickly found out, and he was a flirt—as the second in command of the maintenance crew, he could afford to be, she was told.

It didn't take Julie long, even in her zombielike state, to figure out that none of the women much cared about the officers at Lancaster. One or two of them were fooling around, but there was a swagger to the male inmates, a strutting, manly quality that the officers could never match, even with their keys, their intercom radios, and their regular access to private rooms. White, brown, and black in about even numbers, most of the male inmates were young, and many were buff. But it was the men on the maintenance crew that really drew the crowds. Plumbers, electricians, and carpenters on the outside, they were essential to the smooth running of the facility. For meager prison wages they unblocked drains, fixed machines, corrected electrical problems, built walls, and shoveled snow. They had access to just about every place in the prison, and because they were good guys mostly, skilled and semi-skilled working men who'd made a wrong turn at some point in their lives, officers tended to befriend them—and let them spend a little time alone with their girlfriends whenever they could.

During the winter months, maintenance men were almost always somewhere around the women's house. It got to the point where a woman had to be careful walking back to her room from the shower because you could never be sure just who would be tinkering with a window lock or a clogged toilet down the other end of the corridor.

This suited Julie well. She was having a hard time with the women at Lancaster. It was great to see Denise again, of course. She loved Denise and spent an hour or two with her every day, talking and laughing about old times, mostly. But she rarely saw her more than that. Now that she was assigned to the highway-cleanup crew, her schedule didn't allow it. In fine weather, the eight women on the crew spent their days walking along the edge of the road with sticks picking up garbage. In bad weather they stayed inside a slowly moving DOC van, stopping only when they saw a large piece of refuse. Julie hated it. She loathed the orange jumpsuits they were made to wear, and eight hours was a long time to be stuck in a van with a group of women who disliked her.

They were jealous—that was what Denise said. Jealous of how young she was, and how pretty, and of the fact that Peter would inevitably fall for her if she kept after him the way she was, getting up early every morning and positioning herself casually outside of the house where he couldn't help but see her on his way to work. This rang true to Julie. Her quest for the much desired Peter drove the women crazy. One morning a "Spanish girl" told her she could dress up as much as she liked, she'd still look like a dog. This bothered Julie less when Peter actually whistled as he passed and said, "Looking good!"

"Did you hear that?" Julie asked no one in particular as she shimmied back into the house. "Did you hear Peter say I'm looking good?"

OFFICIALLY, THE MEN and women of Lancaster weren't even supposed to speak to one another. They lived in different buildings, worked in different locations, and their meal schedules were staggered in a further attempt to keep them separate. Ironically, the presence of men made the code of behavior for women even more rigid than it had been at Framingham. It was as if *everyone* reverted back to high school—not just the inmates but the administration too—so that gender once again became the defining determinant of what was acceptable and what was not. In numerous ways, men were silently encouraged to be dominant while women, for the most part, were expected to be submissive. This drove Denise crazy.

Men were allowed to come and go from the dining hall anytime they liked during the thirty minutes scheduled for chow, for example, while women had to walk back to their house in a group, escorted (for their own protection?) by at least one officer. While herded along the path, women were frequently greeted by catcalls from groups of male inmates hanging out on the benches to the right of the path, but Denise never heard a CO say anything about it. There were smirks, sometimes a little verbal jousting between the COs and the guys, but never anything like a serious reprimand.

The importance Julie and the other women gave to the men's every move also irritated Denise. Didn't anyone care that the maintenance-crew guys ran around the place more or less as they liked, and were paid for the privilege because they were classed as cadres, positions apparently unavailable to the women of Lancaster? Outside the prison most men earned fifteen to twenty dollars an hour at a cement plant named Wachusett Precast, while women had to make do with minimum wage at Burger King, or only slightly more for their overnight shifts at a factory called Injectronics, or their work at a nearby farmer's market.

Still, neither Denise's admonitions nor the potentially disastrous consequences of being caught did much to dissuade women from fooling around with the men of MCI-Lancaster. Rather than curtailing such activity, in fact, the risk lent a certain romantic charge to situations that might otherwise have run to the perfunctory.

Recently a woman named Tracey Howe had been caught kissing a male inmate by the Coke machine outside the dining hall. She was shipped back to Framingham, but before she left she told the administration everything she knew about who was with whom in the prison. It wasn't as if everyone didn't already know. Officers occasionally posted themselves as lookouts while inmates they liked enjoyed a few minutes of private time with their girlfriends, and it was common knowledge that the maintenance crew especially "got around." Formalizing the information this way, though, through an official inmate declaration, shifted the activity from the invisibly acceptable to the visibly unacceptable. Despite everyone's reluctance, some kind of investigation had to take place.

IPS summoned the officer in charge of the maintenance crew and asked all kinds of questions. But because the number of women at Lancaster was low at that time—just thirty-one at last count—they couldn't afford to ship many back to Framingham. Needing to keep the numbers steady, they brought the investigation to a close with a few hours of mandatory work service and a stern warning that any further contact between males and females would result in harsh punishment.

Romances continued, nonetheless. Even sad, doughy Maria-Cristina had her "crush"—a stocky, stubble-faced Dominican named Luís. "Oh my God, this is so embarrassing!" she squealed under her breath when he sauntered into the dual-capacity visiting/dining room to eat a late supper one evening with two of his friends. He paid her not the least bit of attention, yet she blushed the whole time and couldn't focus on our conversation. She kept asking me what he was doing. Was he looking at her? Was he smiling? And what was he doing now?

After he left, I asked Maria-Cristina how long they'd been together, and she blushed again before admitting that they hadn't actually spoken to each other yet. "We just look—well, *I* look," she corrected herself. "He is just so very, very *fine*!"

JULIE WAS SEEING Peter every day by then. She'd fixed his schedule in her head and made sure to be outside whenever he was due to pass by. He always acknowledged her with a smile and a wink, but she was ready for the next phase. She'd seen him clambering around the dividing wall between the kitchen and the dining room recently, fixing something, she supposed, and he'd looked so robustly agile up there that she'd nicknamed him Spiderman. That night, when she remembered that Spiderman's alter ego was actually named Peter Parker, she took it as a sign that they were meant to be together. Inspired, she wrote him a note:

Hey Sexy,

You know I been checking you out since I got here and even after I've seen all the other guys I still think you're the finest.

I told myself I wasn't going to get involved with anybody here but something in your eyes makes me think you're worth the risk. I swear I wait all day just to see you for five seconds and I'm driving my friend crazy talking about you. You have the most beautiful eyes . . . I'm leaving it on you—you know where I am.

For security reasons Julie couldn't sign her name to the letter, but she felt sure he'd know who she was. Brimming with confidence, she planted pink lipstick kisses at the top and bottom of the page, handed it over to a friend of his on the maintenance crew, then settled in to wait for his reply.

Love notes, passed surreptitiously this way through mediators, or sent through the three-way mail, were the real currency of relationships at Lancaster. While sustained conversation was hard to get away with, written communication offered, in its stead, the proof of lasting interest and burgeoning attachment that most women needed to proceed to the physical. The notes were strictly illegal. Discovery of even one meant an almost guaranteed trip back to Framingham. Delivery methods had been so smoothed by years of practice, however, that as long as no one was foolish enough to keep the notes lying around in their room—where they could easily be discovered in a raid—the actual risk involved was minimal.

Julie was shocked, then, to hear nothing back from Peter. Thinking he hadn't received the note, she wrote again, and when she again heard nothing, she sent him a letter through the three-way mail. When she received no reply even to this third missive, she stopped hanging out in front of the house. Then, just as she was beginning to consider looking around for someone else, he showed up in the women's house with only the flimsiest of excuses.

Julie had just stepped out of the shower when he came in. She had her hair in a towel and lotion on her face, and she nearly died with shame when she saw him there, all huge and shiny-headed, at the end of the corridor. Peter didn't seem to mind how she looked, however, and they ended up kissing in her room for ten whole minutes after that, with the door closed, his CO "keeping the peek" for them from the corridor outside.

Julie had persuaded a rookie officer named Tom to let her look at the inmate roster by then and had discovered, with the help of her dad, who'd run a background check, that Peter was serving time for armed robbery just like she was. "A match made in heaven!" she said. She asked him now if he'd been a dope fiend when he committed his crimes, the way she had been, and was taken aback for a moment when he said no.

"Why were you doing armed robberies, then?" she asked.

"Because there was a *lot* of money involved," he replied.

Julie was impressed.

"Yeah," he grinned. "Stick with me, kid, and you'll be all right."

. . .

FOR A TIME Julie was exultant. Peter was one of the best-looking guys at Lancaster. He was a big shot on the maintenance crew too—certain women she could name had been trying to snag him for months—and now he was hers. If she wanted to see him, all she had to do was stuff a wad of paper down one toilet or another and he'd be there, wrench in hand, to "fix it." Sometimes he'd surprise her by dropping in to check on the washing machines, or to fix a sticky hinge on one of the doors, and with the help of a friendly CO, they occasionally even crept down to the basement under the dining hall where they were more or less free to fool around in private.

They hadn't actually made love yet. The one time he'd suggested it ("Let's go over there and have sex"), she'd agreed ("Whatever, dude"), only to have him back down. It was hard to relax enough to let it happen, she concluded, and perhaps because of the tension that mounted as a result of this, she allowed him to grab her and pull her off to some corner to kiss and touch whenever he wanted.

The only problem was that he still hadn't written to her. It was easy to get a friend, or even a CO, to keep the peek for you for the five minutes or so it took to grab a hasty fondle someplace more or less private, but a note was something different. It was more intimate because of the time and emotional investment required, and every time you sent one off you were placing your fate in your lover's hands. In the end, it was an issue of trust, and he (or possibly she) was failing the test. Julie knew that the other girls had told him things about her—that she'd been with a guard at Framingham; that she'd been with a girl at Framingham; that her dad was a cop—and she knew it upset him because of the not-so-casual jokes he made about it occasionally between kisses. But if she was good enough to touch, wasn't she good enough for one lousy note?

It got to her. She was surprised at first, but it did. Somehow it eroded her sense of worth.

DENISE HAD TO admit that it was sometimes a relief to have Julie's agonies to worry over instead of constantly riding the waves with Pat. He'd been fairly settled for a couple of months by then. But foster care was difficult. However much Denise liked the sound of his foster father's voice over the phone and however pleasant it might be for her to imagine him coaching Pat and the other boys on his soccer team, there was no denying that Patrick was having a difficult time.

There were a lot of kids in the house, for one, and some stealing, which always created conflict. And Pat himself . . . well, he had issues. He'd threatened to kill himself again, though she didn't like to think of it. He'd been sent to a psychiatric hospital for two weeks, and while she remained convinced that he didn't actually want to die, that he'd simply learned to mimic what his dad had always done, she was relieved that he'd been placed on medication. He sounded better on the phone since he started taking it, she told herself. And the good news was that his foster dad still wanted to keep him in the house.

On the other hand, visits were almost impossible to organize, and Denise felt as out of touch with Pat now as she ever had when he was living with Alan. There was nothing at Lancaster to take her mind off it. At least at Framingham she'd managed to keep busy enough with her exercise classes to forget the worst of her fears. But here—men aside—there was nothing in the way of distraction. As a minimum-security facility, Lancaster had no traditional reason to offer programs on-site because most inmates spent their day working in the community. No one was quite sure why prisoners serving mandatory drug time were not allowed to participate in these work-release programs, or why it

made sense to have murderers and armed robbers, but not drug dealers, dole out burgers at Burger King. But the fact remained. And as a
result, an increasing number of inmates were having to stay at Lancaster all day long, with only one part-time horticulture program to
keep them engaged. A few parenting and antiviolence programs were
offered in the evening. And there was always kitchen work for those
who couldn't get out of it during the day. But apart from this, there was
literally nothing to keep inmates busy.

To be fair, in 2001 the DOC did eventually respond to the situation by opening an educational program specifically designed for the
women of Lancaster. Oddly though, it was a course in car maintenance
and repair. The program was said to be the commissioner's own "brain-
child." Perhaps this explains why it was greeted with such open-handed
enthusiasm by the department. No one ever did respond to my official
requests for exact figures, but a DOC employee told me unofficially
that the department had indeed had to pay for the tools and the car lift
as well as the cost of refurbishing the building and hiring a female me-
chanic as instructor.

There was even a media event to celebrate its opening. It was a
grand affair held under a huge tent with a podium as well as a couple
of long refreshment tables laden with bagels, coffee, and lemonade.
The inmates, both male and female, were locked in their rooms all day
(to make sure no one would trouble the commissioner, I was told), and
though almost seventy bigwigs from the DOC showed up for the cere-
mony, no one seemed concerned that enthusiasm for car maintenance
was so lacking among the women that only two inmates had actually
enrolled in the class.

The whole thing was surreal. Administrator after administrator
stood up in front of the shiny new garage to congratulate their co-
workers on a job well done. The commissioner spoke of the program as

an example of "thinking outside the box," of "taking chances" and "breaking ground" and being "nontraditional." After an hour or so, I began to wonder whether any of them knew that the program was so woefully underenrolled. Certainly Denise had no desire to learn how to fix cars. Maria-Cristina just laughed when I suggested she might like to try it. Even the two women who *were* in the class seemed a little bemused by it all. They were thrilled to be there, of course, in their very own garage, surrounded by state-of-the-art equipment. But they were as confused as everyone else as to why it had been given to them—and it had been a disappointment too to discover that the only certificate they could earn was for competence in car air-conditioning repair. Unfazed, however, officials from Central Office and from the Division of Inmate Training and the Access to Jobs Initiative gathered together by the garage to watch the commissioner hold a large pair of scissors aloft like a small-town mayor before ceremoniously cutting the plush red ribbon strung across its entrance.

Julie found the whole thing hilarious. It was just one more example of the DOC's cluelessness about the needs of female inmates, she thought. At least this one didn't seem to hurt anyone. She herself wouldn't consider enrolling in the class. Not in a million years, she said. Bad enough they made her dress up in an orange jumpsuit every day to pick up litter along the highway. Wild horses couldn't drag her into that garage. Besides, after months on the cleanup crew, she was finally being assigned to a real job behind the deli counter of a nearby farmer's market. In order to ensure "regular eyeball time" with Peter, she'd also agreed to take a job in the prison kitchen on weekends. In this way she was guaranteed at least one physical sighting of him each day. Because they were public, these meetings were silent, but they often managed to touch hands as Julie passed him his food. When he skipped a meal to watch a game on TV, she went ballistic.

She'd become increasingly engrossed with Spidey—was in love with him, she said, and intent on spending the rest of her life with him in a little cottage by the water someplace. But she remained also dissatisfied with his level of commitment. He wasn't as rigorous as he might have been about watching her from his window, and he sometimes forgot to pay enough attention when they were out walking, not together but simultaneously, she on the little loop and he on the path for the men. Most tellingly, and despite frequent promises to the contrary, he still refused to write her a letter.

"He isn't putting enough effort into it," she told me one afternoon. "Every time I see him I say, 'You gonna write to me?' He says, 'Yeah,' but he never does—I don't know, maybe I've grown up and I don't want people to see me for just my body. I'm getting tired of that. It's getting old. I love Spiderman, I really do, but with him there's no, 'Hi, how you doing?' It's just like, 'Come in your room, let's have sex!' "

Things got so bad that during the last snowstorm she refused even to ask permission to "go shovel around the house" the way the women always did when they wanted to kiss their boyfriends on the work crew outside. It was a huge storm, and the maintenance men were "all over our house like fucking ninjas! They were all over the fire escapes. All their girlfriends were out there kissing, and I stayed in my room," she told me. This was extreme behavior, she knew. A snowstorm in the dark before count didn't happen very often, and Peter was sure to be furious at being stood up. Sure enough, other men's girlfriends kept sneaking back into the house to tell her that Peter was asking for her, saying he had better things to do than to actually shovel the snow on a night like this. She should go down, they said. He was getting mad.

"Yeah? Get him to write me a letter about it," Julie spat out from under her covers where she'd retreated in tears. Secretly, of course, she was hoping he'd climb up the fire escape to talk to her himself, but the entire maintenance crew left the house just before count. By nine-thirty, when count was finally completed and the women who had gone downstairs were out in the corridor again, comparing their escapades, Julie was filled with regret. In fact, she was crying when she heard a tinny *ding-ding-ding* on the fire escape by her room just before ten. It was Peter. Julie rushed to get Denise to keep the peek and then let him in. Filled with the romance of mutual forgiveness, they stayed in her room, alone, for almost forty-five minutes—an extraordinarily long time in the scale of prison life.

DENISE DIDN'T MIND keeping the peek for Julie and Peter. She'd done it for her friend Erica when she'd dated another man on the maintenance crew, and she was used to hanging out in the corridor as if she were daydreaming, keeping an eye out for officers who might be feeling officious. If she were honest, she might even acknowledge it as a way to enter the thrill of the situation without actually risking anything. After more than three years in prison she'd have liked a man as much as anyone. But she'd worked too long and hard to risk it all now for a con with muscles. Trailer visits alone were enough to make her stick to the rules. She hadn't seen Pat for months, but knowing that she *could,* some weekend when it worked out with his foster dad and with her mother and with the prison itself, went a long way toward keeping her sane.

Besides, she already knew that men were not the answer. Look at Alan! He was out again, she'd heard. After just a couple of months in prison he was free. Thank God he'd gone to Alabama or Louisiana or someplace to "get close to Jesus" and was leaving Pat alone. Meanwhile she . . . well, she kept to her books, to her ever-growing piles of nutritional, low-fat recipes, and so managed, aside from occasionally keeping the peek, to remain resolutely aloof from the eddying excitements that punctuated life at Lancaster as regularly as count.

. . .

I WAS ASTONISHED, then, when Denise called one evening to let me know she'd begun to "enjoy the snowstorms" herself.

It all started with the season's second blizzard, she told me the next day when I went down to visit. The inmate in charge of the maintenance crew, a man named Chuck whom she knew a little from when he'd dated her friend Erica, had tapped on her window from the fire escape. It made sense that Chuck, as the head of the maintenance crew, would be out shoveling on a night like that. And he'd made his seeing her through the window that night seem so casual, so coincidental, that it felt normal to chat for a while through the screen.

Chuck was too cool to wear the bright orange snowsuit the rest of the guys wore when they shoveled snow. For some reason he was wearing a crisp white T-shirt instead, and he never once shivered, Denise noticed, despite the cold. He seemed oblivious to every kind of discomfort, in fact, crouching out there on the tiny patch of black metal grating. Though when Denise decided to answer his questions honestly and reveal that Erica had started partying again, just a few weeks after being released, she could tell he was upset. It was snowing so hard that Denise could barely see his face through the increasingly snow-draped screen, but she decided not to tell him about the guy Erica had started to see.

Instead they talked about life in general, regular stuff. As the snow continued to fall they discovered that they'd grown up in neighboring towns and knew a lot of the same people. At one point Chuck had even lived on the same block as Pat's day-care provider. During the same years too. It was strangely comforting to think they might have run into each other back then, when they'd both had whole vistas of options to choose from. He was thirty-seven, two years older than she. He had no kids, she knew, but he told her now he wanted them. When he asked, she told him just a little about Pat.

The snow was falling in fuller, broader flakes now. Heavy with barely frozen moisture, it piled up on the screen until she could see only one small bit of him at a time: his ear, an eye, a corner of his smiling mouth. It was romantic in an odd way, talking to a sympathetic, deep-voiced man whose face she could barely make out through the snow. Like talking to a priest through the grid of a confessional—only not.

Chuck showed up twice in the women's house the next day. First in the laundry room ("Things have been conveniently breaking all around us"), then later in the weight room, where Denise had started to work out every day. They talked for almost an hour again. Denise shared some of the ways she'd devised to eat well with ingredients from Canteen. Chuck discussed his struggles in trying to teach GED work to some of the men in his house, and suddenly, as she sat there in her workout gear, it struck Denise that for the first time in her life she was talking honestly with a man without having had sex with him first. "Which was weird for me," she said. "Really weird, 'cause we're sober, remember?"

When the prison moved the maintenance crew over to a new building, Putnam, so they could come and go during snowstorms without disturbing the rest of the men, Chuck's window ended up being directly opposite Julie's. During the next snowstorm he waved at Denise from up there, all lit up against the dark, snowy night, then pointed over to the women's house. Denise decided it was too soon to meet him outside, and she didn't speak to him again until the following Wednesday, when he came into the weight room with a big tool in his hand and told her with a smile: "Hey, go to your room." For some reason she complied. Heart beating, palms sweating, she walked upstairs to the end of the corridor where her room was nestled in the corner. She knew what would happen up there, and a part of her was astonished to find herself sitting on the bed, waiting for it. Then Chuck was suddenly up there too, closing the door and pouncing on her, kissing and touching her all over until Denise got mad and told him to cut it out.

It wasn't that she didn't like him. It was just too much, too fast. ("Don't sleep with the ones you like, I know, I remember," she told me later.) Happily, Chuck seemed to understand this. She was in the dayroom having coffee the next day when Julie came to tell her Chuck was in the house. Denise ran to her room "like a coward," she said. Chuck followed, but this time he left the door open, kept his hands to himself, and, after one gentle kiss, gave her a note.

> Hi cutie,
>
> I'm sorry for yesterday. I'm really not like that and I know you're not either. We have a lot of time to get to know each other and we'll take it slow . . . Everything's totally up to you. Tell me if anything ever bothers you at all . . . I'll be honest with you and totally respectful. I just ask that you be totally honest with me . . . I'm being sincere with you. I wish I could stop this life we both are stuck in and get us a new life, one that contains you and me and of course your son . . . I love the way you make me feel and hope and pray it's not only a one sided feeling. . . .

The note ended with a PS: "You know what to do with the letter." She did. She tore it up into hundreds of tiny pieces and threw it away in a girlfriend's garbage pail.

Denise was giddy and girlish for months after that. The next time I saw her she was all dressed up in an immaculately pressed jean jacket, matching blue jeans, and a new pair of Timberland work boots. She was even wearing eyeliner, mascara, and lipstick, and her hair was tied softly up on top of her head, a few loose strands framing her face.

"I didn't do this for you," she told me first thing, then settled in to explain in a whisper that Chuck usually stood in his window when she walked past. He was there every time she walked to dinner, she told me, and tonight, if he was listening for it, he might have heard "visit for Russell" over a CO's intercom and gone to his window to watch her walk by.

"That's the big thing here, standing in his window!" she said after we'd bought some chips and a couple of diet sodas and sat at the table in the corner farthest from the visiting-room officer.

"I'm like, my God! I'm getting like one of them!" Denise added, catching herself. "I've been making fun of these girls for a year, and now I'm just like them! I walk the gerbil treadmill, and he walks in the area the guys can walk on just so we can see each other! It's really stupid, but it helps get me through the weekend! He'll raise his Walkman to wave suddenly, and my heart pounds, even seeing him far away. It's amazing how after two and a half years of completely shutting that part of your life off, it can mess you up when it gets turned on again! Blows my mind! All I know is I'm happy all the time. Well, most of the time. Every day we talk—on paper mostly. One day he writes me, the next I write back, and so on."

The letters were always sealed in stamped envelopes addressed to an attorney, which made the opening of them by anyone in the DOC illegal, even if they were to be found and confiscated. Sometimes as long as fifteen pages each, they were delivered back and forth by Jane, a friend of Denise's who passed the maintenance guys every morning on her way to the warehouse where she worked. In this way they got to know each other. In one of these letters Denise even told him about her past. It had taken her a while to let him know the truth of it—especially the dancing and the drugs. But he'd written back saying, "I'm just proud of you for looking after your kid," and that was it. No questions, no chastisement, only a gentle "Perhaps you'll do a lap dance for me one day," and the matter was closed.

He understood women. He'd grown up with four sisters, all of whom were married now and had kids, and all he'd ever wanted, he said, was a family of his own to look after. He was gently romantic too, even under prison conditions. Every time they met in private he held her face between his palms and told her that he'd missed her. Most recently they'd shared ten minutes alone in the laundry room, and he'd tilted her head back, looked right into her eyes, and said, "I'm not going anywhere. I'm not going to hurt you."

"That cut right through my soul," Denise told me. "Okay, that's a little dramatic, but . . . it really caught my attention!"

Just the week before they had made love. The conditions had been perfect. Not a single guard had been on Denise's floor, and with her next-door neighbor keeping the peek, they managed to share twenty minutes together on Denise's bed.

"It was short but . . . do not worry!" she interrupted herself when she saw my face. "It's *very* safe. He's the head of the maintenance crew, remember? No one's going to let anything happen to him! Oh, and I had Julie's dad check his record. None! Prior to this. No domestics either. No restraining orders or assault and batteries. I don't meet too many people like that!"

CIRCUS

THE TRAPEZE FEELS highest when you stand right on top of it. From the ground, gazed at through the gauze of the crosshatched safety net, it looks relatively low, and it seems eminently possible to jump off the narrow, wooden platform right up there next to it and fly, in great looping arcs, from one end of the circus tent to the other. Certainly this is what Carmen's daughter, Carmencita, thought as she stood under the net for a moment's instruction.

At thirteen, Carmencita exudes the kind of brash confidence that often leads to trouble in a dark-skinned girl. Tall and lanky, and dressed fashionably in oversized black clothes, she is all sound. All mouth.

"Morning!" she'd said loudly but reluctantly as she got into the creaky old van the Girl Scouts used to gather up the troop of incarcerated women's daughters for their annual trip to the circus. And then, "Yeah-yeah-yeah!" when the volunteer troop leader, Erin, asked if she remembered to have her guardian sign the oft forgotten permission slip. Half a second later Carmencita was slumped in the all-the-way-back seat, staring out the window, arms crossed tightly across her chest, silent.

Helena, the second girl in, retreated to a seat in the van's middle row and then sank into an almost invisible quietness. Like most members of the Girl Scouts Beyond Bars program, Helena has never told anyone outside this van that her mother is in prison. For a long time no one mentioned such things even here. It took weeks for one of the girls to cautiously venture, "I haven't seen my mom in two years, what about you?" and for the reply to come back, "Grandma tells me never to talk about it."

Jessica, the third girl to be picked up that morning, and the newest to the group, dealt with the situation by responding to the slightest attention with a cloud of needy sweetness; her cousin, Kara, would also lean in toward you like a tender young plant, ready to give you her heart after three or four minutes of conversation. Some, the lucky ones with feisty and doting grandmothers, like the twins Angelique and Sam, managed to exude a more settled kind of energy. Sometimes they slept a lot the day after visiting the prison, or their sleep was interrupted those nights by fretful, unwanted tears so that the next day, Monday, would be spent in a haze of head-on-forearms absence at the back of the class at school. But for the most part they approach the world with the same sturdy resiliency as most ten-year-olds. The Girl Scouts Beyond Bars program, or GSBB as it is known, works hard to build on such solid ground.

As the only program that guarantees regular biweekly visits between Framingham mothers and their daughters, GSBB provides a small but convincing escape route from the estrangement that eats away at most mothers in prison. Every two weeks, no matter the weather, a volunteer makes the long trek around Boston's four innermost neighborhoods—Dorchester, Roxbury, Jamaica Plain, and Mattapan—collecting the girls so that they might spend a couple of hours with their mothers at Framingham.

The mothers themselves have to surmount a slew of hurdles in order to have these visits. Their crimes have to be nonviolent and their records at MCI-Framingham clean—a single disciplinary report is enough to get you kicked out of the program. Elements of the Girl Scout ethic were sometimes difficult for them to swallow too: even during the mothers-only meetings, women were asked to gather in a circle and recite the Girl Scout promise, the three fingers of their right hands raised in neat little spires beside their heads as if they were children themselves. Louise Cato, the prison wheeler-dealer, could never get through this without laughing. "Can you imagine it?" she asked me once. "I mean, can you? A bunch of criminal women, promising to do their duty to God and country? Every time I do it I feel like I'm joining the army!"

Nonetheless, in prison, regular visits from your children were like treasure. It was good also to have the time structured; a relief not to be stuck with your preteen daughter in the semiformal setting of the visiting room with nothing to do but eke out conversation about school and friends and family. Whatever it took, then—that was Louise's attitude. If they wanted her to make Girl Scout promises, she'd make Girl Scout promises. And if they wanted her to cut out little rectangles of paper and then cross the visiting room by jumping from one to the next like a frog, she'd do that too. It usually ended up being fun, anyway. No matter how foolish, team-building exercises like that one almost always got them going. It was even hard, sometimes, to stop laughing when it was all over; a strain to remember they were supposed to be preparing to lead meetings, not to goof around the place like hormone-rattled preteens themselves.

CHARLENE GRIMACED. SHE was the one who'd first told me about the GSBB program, and she was increasingly upset that her mother wouldn't allow Trinnie to join. Every other Wednesday, two of

Charlene's best friends trooped off to the visiting room for the mothers-only meetings and came back giggling like fools. It made her mad. She didn't want it to, but it did. She slept every night with a photograph of her daughter under her pillow just like they did. Her half of the wall space was crowded with Trinnie photos, drawings, and elementary-school certificates. She wrote all the time. She called. But Charlene saw her so seldom! She knew it was hard for her mother to get down to Framingham—a bus, then a train, and a taxi ride after a full day of work. But the Girl Scouts got around all of that with their van. Several times now she'd sent Anna-May the paperwork and begged her to consider enrolling. But her mother remained reluctant. She didn't want Trinnie to be out of her sight that way, she said. At six she seemed too small to be going so far on her own. Anna never said that she didn't like the idea of Trinada spending Saturday mornings with other little girls whose mothers were in prison, but Charlene knew that was how she felt. Anna liked large, conservative organizations. She'd never be so standoffish with a regular Girl Scout troop.

It was particularly hard, Charlene said softly now, every other Saturday when the girls actually came to the prison. She saw the way her friends acted before the children arrived: the care with which they did their hair and chose their clothes, the smiles, the energy, the actual, physical flush that pervaded their rooms. It hurt to know that Trinnie could be there too, if Anna would only allow it. But Anna was adamant. Charlene might still be Trinnie's mother, but Anna was in charge, and nothing Charlene could say would make any difference. The Girl Scouts program was just one more thing over which she had no control.

This was a problem the Girl Scouts often encountered. More than half of the GSBB girls lived with their grandmothers, most of whom were reluctant to join at first. Taking care of grandchildren while daughters were away was a massive undertaking, physically, emotionally, and financially, and the last thing they needed was another group of official-looking people coming by, knocking on their doors, peering around their latches, to see what they could see.

It was hard too for these already overburdened women to cater to the constant demands their incarcerated daughters often unwittingly placed upon them. Harder still to keep summoning the generosity and the grace to respond in the affirmative. Requests for sneakers, for money, and for meetings with privately hired lawyers everyone knew they couldn't really afford became heartbreakingly irritating after a couple of years. Even worse were the interminable requests to see their kids in that dreadful visiting room where who knew what kind of behavior they might be exposed to. Most mothers of mothers in prison couldn't sustain the energy for a regular visiting schedule. Some grew to resent their daughters' constant demands for one. A few were not even sure they wanted the children to maintain relations with their mothers at all, and a handful of the girls in the program hadn't seen their moms since they'd first been sent away.

It had taken time, then, and a lot of organizing for the GSBB program to get off the ground. It was one reason why Erin made the long van trek around the low-rise projects every other week. No one showed up when they'd asked the girls to gather at a more central location for collection, so they chartered this old van with its even older driver and set up door-to-door service. This helped with enrollment. But no one was ever ready on time, and they ended up waiting at each apartment.

On Circus Day, it took close to three hours to pick up all nine girls. Two were still asleep when the van arrived, so Erin barged right into their room, hauled them out of bed, pulled some warm-enough clothes on them, and then dragged them into the van, bringing a brush and a handful of twisties to do their hair on the way. Some boy-cousin was watching them, she said tersely as she tugged at bunches of sleep-tousled hair. No one had gone to bed until three. "He wanted to let them sleep," she told me. "But that isn't fair. Why should they miss going to circus camp because *he* messed up in that way?"

The Girl Scouts' big top was no ordinary circus tent. It was a place not for watching but for doing. Every year they hired an organization named Over the Big Top to teach the girls the basic circus arts: juggling, clowning, acrobatics, even trapezing. Unfortunately, the day we attended, everyone had to be out of the tent by noon, for a corporate fund-raiser, which left the GSBB troop just an hour and fifteen minutes to participate. The big top was so beautiful, though, that this didn't much matter. From inside, it was yellow, striped with red and blue. Yellow and white juggling pins sparkled above purple and silver-glitter costumes. Red-cloth-covered tables dotted with white, green, and orange balloons were laid out with theatrical makeup and bits of cloth for costumes. Circus performers, some on stilts, strolled from one table to another helping groups of excited Girl Scouts complete whatever task they were currently absorbed by, and right in the middle, strung from highest point to highest point, impossibly high, floated the trapeze. Who cared that they wouldn't learn how to paint their faces like clowns when the GSBB girls had been promised a turn on this? Even Carmencita and her diminutive ten-year-old-sidekick, Latiffa, were stunned, the song they'd sung over and over in the van forgotten now in the face of such extraordinary promise. Looking up through the safety net, Carmencita watched a lithe girl with long, blond hair twist and soar from the plush velvet trapeze. "I could do that, I will," she said almost under her breath. "Just watch. Watch me do that!"

CARMENCITA AND HER little sister, Alina, lived with their uncle and aunt on the top floor of a green three-family on Centre Street, just up from the high school in Jamaica Plain. Their uncle Pedro, their mother's brother, had never been drawn to the fast life. Instead he cleaned schools during the day, subway stations at night. His wife also worked two jobs, and though they remained precariously poor, they'd been happy to take in Carmencita and Alina when their mother was sent away for ten years, mandatory, for drugs.

Mami Carmen had been in Framingham for five and a half years since then. She'd been in the Girl Scouts program since it first came to the prison and remembered when girls were allowed to bring home-cooked food in for snack. Every other Saturday they had arrived with great steaming plates of foil-wrapped *arroz con pollo, picadillo,* or *ropa vieja* with rice and beans. Now only cookies, fruit, and chips were allowed. Life both inside prison and out had become increasingly difficult.

Mami Carmen had been head of the household before she went away. First in her family to arrive from El Salvador, she had been the one who'd provided an apartment and connections for jobs, both legal and illegal, for the rest of her siblings as they arrived. Since she'd been incarcerated, however, this earlier beneficence seemed forgotten. Not one of her sisters had visited her since she was sent to prison. Only her brother, Pedro, kept in regular contact. And it had been he who'd taken over her role as family support system. Within a month or two his small, clean apartment had become filled with an ever-rotating selection of cousins, second and third and fourth. Its well-kept solidity provided a springboard to the promise of America, just as Carmen's had before it.

The girls, then, were luckier than most. They lived surrounded by family in an apartment that felt like home. There were no cabinets in the kitchen, but there was always a clean oilcloth draped over the wobbly round table, and the appliances functioned. Despite the fact that someone or other was usually asleep in it, the bright blue living room was kept impeccably clean. And during the day at least, when most of the adults were out, each girl had the use of her very own room. The girls even had decorating rights: Carmencita's looked like a boudoir. Windows were darkened with scarlet blinds and drapes of black lace. Faux leopard skin covered the double bed. The only clue to her age lay in the Pooh Bear dolls scattered about. Alina's room, by contrast, was painted the same bright blue as the living room and decorated with cuddly toys, each hung from its own nail on the wall. A black-and-white TV and a bare, striped mattress were the only other objects in the room. This was where the girls slept at night, Alina told me. "It's the biggest room in the house," she added with her usual, uncertain eagerness. And when I asked how come they, the littlest ones, got the biggest room, she matter-of-factly replied, "'Cause no one else wants to sleep with the rats."

"CARMENCITA! CARMENCITA AIN'T scared of nothing!" one of the younger girls answered when a circus performer asked who would like to try the trapeze first. Elbowing her way to the front, Carmencita smiled and said that it was true, she wasn't scared, she *wanted* to go up there and fly. The narrow, aluminum ladder that led up to the platform, however, felt more dangerous than she'd expected. Twice she had to stop, and turn, and look down at the increasingly distant floor behind her.

"I am not scared. Don't be looking at me like I was scared," Latiffa said, though Carmencita hadn't been looking at her at all. "Don't you be looking at me when I do it neither," she said again, to no one in particular. "Just pretend I'm not there."

Carmencita struggled up onto the platform from which she was supposed to launch herself. She took a step toward the trapeze and then froze. There was a thick length of rope that stretched from the platform to a series of hooks and pulleys above, and when she passed it she grabbed on with both hands and refused to let go. Three times she managed to stretch out a hand toward the trapeze, but she never came close to reaching it. Five minutes later she agreed, in tears, to climb back down the ladder.

The next four GSBB girls all had to climb back down the ladder the same way. Carmencita was visibly relieved. "I know *she's* coming right back down," she said as Latiffa reached for the uppermost rung.

On the other side of the tent, girls from another troop were jumping off the platform and onto a sister trapeze as if it were nothing. Little white girls, brimming with confidence and privilege, they flew across the ring, backs arched, straight hair flying one after the other. As Latiffa hesitated, the GSBB girls started to chant, "Go, Latiffa! Go, Latiffa! Go, Latiffa!" But it was no good. Even their brazen little mascot couldn't make herself jump. She climbed, she looked out, she concluded that she didn't want to do it, and then she came back down the ladder still strutting.

"I am never doing that again," she said. "I was scared. I don't care—I do not care what anybody says. I ain't never going to do nothing like that again!"

Vanessa, the next girl up, managed to make the jump. She played sports after school and looked every inch the young, limber enthusiast she was as she flew down-down-down, then up-up-up; down-down-down/up-up-up in perfect, silent arcs until she let herself fall the way we'd been shown, and landed bouncily on the safety net below. "I did it!" she said with a broad, gummy smile as she was helped back down to the ground. "I can't believe I actually did it!"

"It's scary going up the ladder though, ain't it?" Carmencita asked, groping for some kind of mutuality. She needn't have worried, though.

Every other girl in her troop, save, inexplicably, the impossibly shy Angelique, had had to retreat back down to the ground the same way that she had. She was shaken, nonetheless. Showing fear—*feeling* fear—wasn't what Carmencita Ramirez was usually about, and she was uncertain, now, how best to reclaim her identity.

Over by the exit, one of the GSBB girls who hadn't even tried climbing up to the trapeze was clinging desperately to Erin's forearm. Her name was Sianna, and she was a relative newcomer to the group—her mother had been gone for less than a year. As she approached, Carmencita heard the girl begging: "But Erin, my house is awful. I hate it there. Please please please can I come live with you, Erin? Pleeeaase?" The shameful display gave Carmencita the confidence she'd been looking for. She snorted derisively as she stepped through the tent flap, back into the real world.

I'D BEEN PLAYING cat and mouse with the DOC over access to these kids and their mothers for months by then. The Girl Scout program was small—tiny if you looked at it statistically. There have never been more than twelve women enrolled at one time, and there are usually fewer. But it held such promise that I was determined to see how it worked, both inside the prison and out.

Despite warnings to the contrary, I felt confident that the authorities would allow me in because successes like these are rare in prison. But when I asked if I could attend a Saturday troop meeting, deputy superintendent Bob Waitkevich responded with an unequivocal no. I sued for access for a second time, and this time the DOC refused to back down. We attended hearings presided over by three different superior-court judges and spent months trading affidavits and briefs. In court the DOC suggested I might aid in drug deals, exploit children, and unwittingly feed weapons to the inmates at MCI-Framingham. They even compared my effect on the prison population to pornography.

Perhaps it was just a coincidence, but it even became difficult to get into Framingham for my regular afternoon visits during this time. Mami Carmen had written to say that she needed to speak with me urgently, but I was refused entrance when I arrived at the prison to meet with her. My official, Central Office–embossed, DOC permission letter had been removed from its habitual spot just above the desk in the guard's bubble, the officer on duty informed me. Without it, I couldn't go in. Infuriated, I insisted he call Deputy Waitkevich. When the CO finally did so, and then told me with a smile that I wasn't to be allowed in unless I had the inmate's original, signed permission slip, I lost it. Just as I'd seen other people do when they were arbitrarily refused entrance, I began to shout at the uniformed man in front of me, ratcheting up my outrage in an exact and inverse proportion to my behavior's effectiveness. It was the first and only time I lost my composure in prison, and after five minutes of it I stormed out, desperate for air.

The feeling had not entirely left me the next day when I returned with Carmen's original permission slip. An addict with stringy hair and a blotchy sweatshirt was meandering around the waiting room, smiling vacantly. A twenty-month-old child was running between the chairs, playing peekaboo with her mother's driver's license. Three older men, all dressed up as if for the promise of sex, were sitting upright and nervous at the back; and over in the corner, on the dirty, tiled floor, a grandmother was angrily struggling to diaper her two-and-a-half-year-old grandson who had wet himself despite, apparently, having made numerous promises to do no such thing ever again.

By the time I was finally allowed into the visiting room I was ready to snap. It was a relief to see Carmen stride into the room, red lips freshly painted, hair bunched up behind her, hips swaying. She lingered a while by the vending machines, though she wanted only a soda, and made her usual funny small talk about the other women in the room. It wasn't until we sat down at the table, her can of Diet Pepsi perched neatly as it always was on a small, perfectly straight pile of untreated paper towels, that she let her voice drop a little and said she had something difficult she needed to talk about. She glanced around, then leaned in toward me. Her daughter, she whispered, the big one, thirteen-year-old Carmencita, was pregnant.

I tried hard not to flinch.

"Yes," she said. "Carmencita is pregnant. She had the heart to tell her mother to her face last Saturday. Pregnant," Carmen said again. "Four months. Yes."

At the beginning of every Girl Scout meeting there is a ten-minute period where mothers and daughters are allowed to settle into quiet corners of the visiting room to meet privately with each other. It had been then, Carmen told me, that her daughter had broken the news. "Ay, it was dreadful," Mami Carmen told me now. She'd had no idea, she said. Hadn't even thought that her daughter was "with boys." But there she was, little Carmencita, saying that she was too afraid to tell her uncle, that she was sure that if she did he would throw her onto the street. Carmencita had started to cry then. This wasn't like her. When she noticed she was frightening her mother, she dried her tears and quickly reharnessed her anger. She needed her mother home, she said curtly. Her stomach hurt a lot, she knew nothing about babies, and there was no one home to help her with anything. She needed her mother, she said again as if such desperately cool insistence could actually make her mother free. "*Pero ahora, Mamà*—now!"

ALINA HAD JUST turned three when her mother went to prison. Carmencita was eight. Even before then, though, they'd often been left to fend for themselves. Carmencita fed, changed, and diapered Alina and carried her on her hip when she went out to play. If Alina did something wrong, it was most often Carmencita who got the blame. Not much had changed now that their mother was at Framingham. Pedro and Melissa were kind. But because of their work schedule it still pretty much fell to Carmencita to take care of Alina. Perhaps because she was thirteen, she did this roughly, and with only the smallest modicum of patience. Mostly she snarled. Sometimes she hit. Often she ignored Alina altogether.

The first time I'd gone to visit, Alina quietly came out of her room and politely asked her big sister's permission to take a plastic tube of bright blue "juice" from the refrigerator. Without even turning to look at her, Carmencita replied, "No, you fucking can't!" leaving eight-year-old Alina to decide whether she meant it or not. After a moment, she decided that she didn't. With a self-mocking shrug she took her juice from the fridge anyway and then tiptoed off back to her room. This was how it was between them: Carmencita as temperamental mother, Alina as trepidatious child. Perhaps I shouldn't have been surprised, then, by Carmencita's response when I asked if she was excited about having a baby.

"Nah," she said, more like a worn-out fifty-year-old than the child that she actually was. "It feels like I already had a baby. I feel the same way about this one as I did about that."

Neither girl left the house much. The world was too dangerous, their uncle and aunt believed, for them to be safe outside the apartment. It would be different if they were boys, but as girls they were required to stay in. Aside from the stoop, on which the two of them sometimes sat on warm summer evenings, watching the traffic pass by, this was where the sisters spent most of their days. It was ironic, then, that of all people in her class it was Carmencita who managed to get pregnant. She'd met Paco on the street across from her school, and they'd hit it off immediately. This had been at her old school, back on Centre Street, before she'd had to transfer to the middle school for pregnant girls that she attended now. Carmencita was a sixth-grader. Paco was twenty. But he looked sixteen, and with her makeup, her woman's body, and her well-honed, bad-girl style, it was entirely believable that he'd at least at first assumed she was much older than she actually was. More than once, in fact, it seemed as if Paco was afraid of Carmencita, and they both insisted that the pregnancy was a result of her desire, not his.

It certainly wasn't an accident. Someone who volunteered with the Girl Scouts had accompanied Carmencita to a clinic for a pregnancy test a year or so before. Carmencita had been disappointed when it came back negative, and told the doctor that next time she would be sure to be pregnant. Would-be mentors, both professional and volunteer, had tried to steer her away from this path ever since—to no avail.

Despite her determination, however, Carmencita knew nothing about being pregnant. She had had no prenatal classes, and though her stomach was large and round from the fourth month on, she had no maternity clothes either, just a big, man-sized T-shirt and a pair of shorts undone at the zip. She knew she needed more information, but she paced herself carefully, asking only as much as could be contained by her veneer of disdain.

"You ever got these?" she asked, casually lifting her T-shirt to reveal a slew of broad red stretch marks that extended from one side of her belly to the other. I said no, that I had been lucky, but that she could minimize their effect by slathering herself with moisturizer. "And how you knew when you went into labor?" she asked then, as if to test the validity of this suggestion.

"Because it started to hurt more than I could bear."

"Oh," she said, trying hard to sound nonplussed. "And is it true that your belly button comes out with the baby? Tha's what I heard, that your belly button comes out in a big slimy string." At this Alina grimaced and laughed and said "Eeeeww!" prompting Carmencita to attempt a withering look that she couldn't quite pull off.

"*Imbécil*," she said, sneering.

Paco patted Carmencita reassuringly on the shoulder and tried to smile, though it was clear that all this was more than he had bargained for. It was one of several occasions that he actually looked younger than Carmencita, and even more out of his depth.

MAMI CARMEN'S FRAMINGHAM friends were scandalized when they first heard about Carmencita. They advised her to have Paco arrested for what he had done—little Carmencita was a baby herself! There were laws in this country against behaviors like this! She should make out a report, have him sent off to prison or shipped back to Guatemala where he belonged! Carmen considered this for a time but rejected the idea because, truth be told, she wanted him dead, not deported. Later, after speaking to her daughter, her brother, and his wife, she decided against it for more practical reasons too.

The other women looked down on her for this, she knew. But just how would it help her daughter to have Paco in prison? Carmen asked me, drawing herself up tall and straight now. How could he support her from there? Carmencita was still a child. What good could she do on her own? The Lord knew that her brother and his poor childless wife were stretched further than they could manage already. No! Paco must work, she told me then. He must know that she could have him arrested whenever she wanted, but that as long as he took care of her daughter, she would not trouble him in that way.

Besides, she added, softening a little, Paco was respectful. He'd sent her a letter addressed to Doña Carmen, very formal, very nice, and in it he had apologized and told her that he would of course do everything to help with the child; that he loved her daughter and intended to behave honorably. It was her own brother who worried her more, Carmen confessed. He'd been good to take her children in, but news like this was difficult for him to accept. Out of respect, Carmen pretended that she'd known nothing when her brother came to tell her the news. But when he spoke of his worries about what *la gente*—people—might say, Carmen blew a fuse.

"*La gente? LA GENTE?*" she raged. "And who is *la gente?* Certainly we are not *la gente! La gente* do not look after you! *La gente* do not help you out when times are bad. If you are going to pack her clothes and put her on the street, '*mano,* tell me now. It will hurt me, that's my blood, and what you do to her you do to me. But I have to know what you are going to do, because even from here, even though I'm in here, I will find her a program, I will find her some place to go that is safe."

Intimidated and chastened as he had been by his sister so often in his life, Pedro demurred. Of course Carmencita could stay, he said. And of course, *of course* Mami Meli would be with her in the hospital. They would treat the baby as their own. It would be the child they'd never had.

MIRIAM VAN WATERS

THE ABORTIONIST'S GRAY, marble headstone stands at the very edge of the untended cemetery where prisoners who died in Framingham during the first half of the twentieth century lie buried. Her name was Dr. Caroline Tinning, and she'd stayed in the reformatory voluntarily for years after her sentence expired because she had no place else to go.

The prison superintendent of the time, Dr. Miriam Van Waters, allowed many women to do this. Maintaining ties with former inmates, both inside and out of Framingham, was one of the cornerstones of her approach. Of all her charges, however, perhaps none grew closer to her than Caroline Tinning. Born in 1866 in Staffordshire, England, to a father whom prison records describe as "a man of adequate means and some education," Tinning displayed intelligence early on. She was educated, on scholarships, at local private schools, studied nursing in London, and ultimately immigrated to Boston, where she enrolled in the Boston School of Medicine in the hope of becoming a doctor. Tinning was an excellent student, consistently one of the best in her class, and shortly after graduating, she opened her own practice.

As was the case with most female doctors of the time, however, her practice soon floundered. People didn't trust women to be their doctors, and Tinning quickly discovered that the only way she could earn a reliable living was by performing abortions. The result was her first arrest in 1911. Though the procedures themselves were of course illegal at the time, there was never any intimation of medical wrongdoing on her part. Her operations were sanitary in nature and humane in their intent. She herself rationalized her actions by insisting that she had "sufficient medical knowledge to prevent the women who come to me from suffering any serious physical harm." But the arrests continued apace with her work, and in 1923 she was finally committed to Framingham. There, despite having her medical license revoked, she assisted in the infirmary. Miriam Van Waters was so impressed by her there that she recorded the following description of her in her diary in 1932: "She is quite immovable during the post mortem, never taking her eyes from the baby. Her lips are gray colored, full, tightly compressed. There is no trace of life, or thought, or feeling in her face—but something formidable. She is a study in sculpture. She has been cast and the pressure of the material into which she has been formed (if ever she was fluid) is all about her firm wrinkled flesh."

When Caroline was released, then rearrested for continuing to perform abortions, prison records note that her "behavior was as far from reproach during her second commitment as it had been during her first." Now she gave English lessons to foreign-born inmates, and provided classes in painting and history to whoever was interested.

After four years she was granted parole. But, like many elderly inmates, she had nowhere to go. Van Waters hired her to care for her own ailing father, and after his death, Dr. Tinning returned to the prison, where she was granted free room and board in exchange for office work.

"Caroline's natural dignity made an arrangement which might easily have proved difficult, very successful," prison records tell.

"She . . . is saving money so that when she is too old to work she may still be able to provide for herself here." The friendship between Van Waters and Tinning deepened as months of voluntary residence at Framingham turned to years. They corresponded copiously, and it seems likely that when Caroline finally died, free and from natural causes at the age of eighty-six, it was Van Waters herself who paid for the doctor's grave.

It is a simple memorial. In the tight, still-semicleared space that serves as the graveyard's center, a large boulder glistens. IN MEMOR it reads. Behind it, half buried under rotten leaves, is the doctor's grave. Standing just six inches tall, the polished tablet reads: CAROLINE K. TINNING M.D. 1866–1952.

IT WAS 1932 when Dr. Miriam Van Waters first took control of what then was called the Women's Reformatory at Sherborn. "Bars off . . . curtains in . . . Will bring the outside world in," she wrote in a letter to her parents. "I have to go slow inside. Staff thinks I'm crazy to be crazy about pictures, colors, curtains, flowers and not morals!"

Despite her determination to "go slow," Van Waters's first three months at the prison were a whirlwind of activity. She spent the first two weeks meeting, individually, with every woman incarcerated in the facility and insisted on calling them students instead of inmates. Then, just as Eliza Farnham had done almost one hundred years before in Mount Pleasant, New York, she set about improving the physical appearance of the place. She had curtains hung on the windows and repainted the walls. She allowed women to decorate their rooms as they liked, to choose from a variety of printed cloths for their dresses, and to wear their hair as they pleased. Letter-writing privileges were instituted, and free use of the library was encouraged. Movement between one area of the facility and another was allowed to proceed more or less unimpeded.

Above all, Van Waters insisted on the primacy of education and training at Framingham. Always a great believer in the reformatory strength of education, Dr. Van Waters had created one of the first schools for delinquent girls run by student self-government and was a recognized leader in the field by the time she took over at Framingham. Rigorously educated and a dedicated professional social worker, she stressed hard work, personal responsibility, and the importance of psychological insight to the women in her care. As the eldest of five surviving children of an Episcopalian minister, Van Waters also saw the reformation of women and girls as her "ministry," and it was her dedication to a Christian-based notion of unconditional love that lay at the heart of her work. Believing every inmate was as capable of learning and emotional growth as herself, she refused, ever, to subscribe to the notion of the incurable, "fallen" woman.

By the time she took over Framingham, in fact, and despite her measured public stance, her private opinions had become almost radical. "The institution is old and still terrible," she wrote candidly to a friend soon after her arrival. "In saying this I should explain that I am not one who believes there are good and bad prisons. I think all prisons bad. But I think they can be vanquished from within at the same time we are transforming people's ideas about human bondage in community life."

Declaring Framingham a "child-centered institution," she was determined to create adequate facilities for mothers and their children. Shocked by conditions in the nursery when she first arrived, she applied for and won (despite the Depression) funds to build a separate residence for the young mothers in her care. Wilson Cottage, as it came to be known, stood about a quarter of a mile away from the main prison building and possessed not a single locked door or barred window. Between twenty-five and thirty mothers lived there with their children as well as ten officers and several volunteer child-care interns. When a reporter for a local newspaper, the *Worcester Telegram,* paid a visit, she noted, in an article entitled "Babies Are Babies, Even in Prison," that "there are no restrictions within the building, no sense of imprisonment . . . for the children there were remarkable play areas such as are available only in some of the more progressive schools and wealthier homes."

Women without small children also benefited from Van Waters's approach. Drawing on her large circle of friends and acquaintances, the superintendent was able to gather a hitherto unimaginably large group of teachers and staff, both professional and volunteer, with which to develop a range of extracurricular clubs and activities for the women. A newspaper was started, as well as a racially and politically focused theatrical troupe, a gymnastics club, a public-speaking quorum, a choir, an occupational-therapy department, and even something called "the Happy Circle" for women who were shy or depressed. Intended to increase women's professional and emotional skills alike, these activities were combined with complementary classes. There were classes in singing, parenting, physical education, poetry, literature, playwriting, English as a second language, cooking, dressmaking, handicrafts, sketching, and painting. In 1936 a course on current events was offered. Also, woodcarving, hiking, and rug making. For those who were able, Van Waters also made college-level courses available, taught, via correspondence, through the university extension system. By 1944, 178 women—more than half the prison population—were enrolled in this program alone.

Many of these activities would take years to become fully established at Framingham. As early as Easter of 1932, however, just three months after Van Waters took control, the reformatory was already being transformed. Women were leaving the prison sober and, in most cases, employed. Attempts at escape had been reduced to "practically zero." As well, production of sewn garments and farm produce had been increased by 6 percent, despite the fact that the workday had been shortened by two hours in order to allow time for classes and other activities. In addition, the prison's solitary-confinement holes, or "dungeons" as they were then called, were no longer used, and the length of time spent in general punitive confinement had been reduced by 90 percent. Within a year, Framingham had once again moved to the forefront of progressive political reform, becoming, in the words of one of Van Waters's contemporaries, "an admired showpiece in the eyes of modern penologists."

Van Waters could never have effected this transformation without support. Her predecessor, Jessie Hodder, had already begun the process of converting the prison from the increasingly discipline-oriented institution of the bronze-medal-winning Ellen Cheney Johnson to a more holistic place of reform. One of Hodder's first acts as superintendent had been to strike the word *prison* from the name of the institution. She also broadened the professional training available at the reformatory, extended the school, and built a gym.

In addition, Van Waters was in a position to access help, both political and financial, from her wide circle of powerful and influential friends. Both money and manpower flowed to Framingham as a result of these connections. As a woman held to great account in the public sphere, she had a social status that protected her, to a degree, from political attack, and for a time she was able to enjoy a level of autonomy unimaginable in the Department of Correction today. Ironically, it was the blurring, not the heightening, of such social distinctions that lay at the heart of her work.

Throughout her tenure, celebrities were continually invited to visit the institution. When Robert Frost gave a reading at Harvard, for example, Van Waters sent him an invitation signed by every one of her students, and he visited the prison to give a reading the very next day. More frequently, however, it was the women themselves who visited the superintendent, unescorted, for dinner, lunch, or tea. Parties were thrown at the reformatory and attended by all. Parades were organized, concerts performed, and great celebratory picnics held out on the lawn—all, Van Waters maintained, with a mind to get the women of Framingham in touch with their own valuable humanity. This was what rested at the heart of her approach: belief that every woman sent to her was a full, potentially viable human being. As she so often said: "Every child is a child of God."

That many inmates internalized Van Waters's message is clear. One wrote "Dr. Van Waters is our saver" in pebbles on the lawn outside the reformatory, and many stayed in touch with her long after they had been released.

"Some day I hope to have the opportunity to talk to the student body," wrote one ex-student. "I would like to tell them, en masse, what Framingham means to me and why I insist that it spells opportunity to anyone who goes there for any cause whatsoever. I would like to tell them how I found *freedom* while imprisoned and how real freedom and real imprisonment are conditions within our self and not a matter of locks and keys."

Women inside the facility also wrote to Van Waters frequently. One addressed her—in a neat, pencil-written note—as "Mom" ("I don't like being mush, but I do believe in letting a person know I like them and appreciate them and I do you. I love you like I love my mother."). On another scrap of paper, no more than two inches square, another student wrote: "Doctor Van Waters, I want you known [*sic*] my birthday on July 4th. Will be 50 year old and I will dance—I may be dead by next fourth anyhow. Want to known [*sic*] I love you."

Improbably, many of these notes from prisoner to warden read like love letters. In fact, their tone is often so intimate that at first I assumed that that is what they must have been. But there are too many of them for that. In the Schlesinger, a library dedicated to women's history in Cambridge, there are literally thousands of them—boxes and boxes of carefully filed notes and postcards and envelopes that stretch on, page after page, stack after stack, for a period of twenty-five years or more. Each reads as if the author's relationship with Van Waters was an exception, but I came to see that they were in fact the rule. Somehow Miriam Van Waters had the ability to connect and, through that connection, to redeem.

One ex-student wrote:

December 25, 1945. Dear Doctor, Christmas night,

Tonight I am very humble in the face of your unfailing kindness and thoughtfulness. The sweater—yours—will do for me physically what you have done for me spiritually—the warmth of understanding and guiding sympathy. . . . You have given me so much—so many, many things. You have given me—Cordelia—the girl I might have been, the girl I might still be. You have given back the faith I had as a little child, the cloak of faith that was torn from me and trampled in the mud by a man that didn't know nor care what it was. . . . You have given me protection and security. Courage to face the future—not with the courage I would have had—the doing it because it had to be done—but the triumphant march of faith, belief that I was right with my world . . .

Not all of the women who passed through Van Waters's Framingham became so fully reformed, of course. Though many ex-students did go on to live engaged and productive lives, the world remained rife with difficulty for the poor, often single women who came out of Framingham in the 1930s and '40s. Many faltered. On January 22, 1944, one drug-addicted ex-student, Lucy Rutherford, wrote:

Dear Dr. Van Waters, . . . I am in my dear, clean cozy little room as you described it. It is high up isn't it? Near the sky. I can reach out almost and take in a cloud—then I am sure it would elude my grasp. How sad, we never can hold beauty so fragile long, sometimes never, but some are always on the watch for it and one does find it in the strangest places. . . . Your visit was a happy memory—kind lady—knowing all your work and responsibilities. I am honored and hope you can manage another. . . . As you say I do not need "medicine." It is an escape, I guess—and a little part of me dies each time I realize I have been weak enough to take any. Do not trouble about my loneliness—it is a natural part of me—a deep thing—more of a longing than anything for things beyond my reach. . . . Thank you again for your visit and encouragement. . . . I shall be all right and you must be too.

Ever Lucy

Prior to receiving this letter, Van Waters had sent Lucy a winter jacket. Two weeks later, when things were still not going well, she asked her secretary to send Lucy ten dollars. As she did with so many others, Van Waters also kept in close contact with Lucy's parole officer and quietly sent letters to her doctors requesting that they send bills for their services directly to Framingham. "I have a small fund which can be dipped into for such purposes from time to time," she wrote.

Despite these interventions, however, Lucy continued to struggle.

Sliding in and out of a series of depressions, she voluntarily admitted herself to the New York House of Detention for their forty-day detoxification program or "cure" ("It was forty days of horror suffering and filth . . . I left there deeply wounded, spiritually, mentally and physically") and ultimately checked herself into Bellevue. Tellingly, Lucy gave Miriam Van Waters as the name of her nearest relative or friend on the intake form there. Writing to thank her for the "lovely daffodil and narcissus card," she told Van Waters that she'd been diagnosed as suffering from emotional fatigue and psychosis. Nonetheless, she had "been taking nothing in the drug line except those little sedative pills," she wrote. Her letter ends: "I need you more than ever. Pray for me. Ever Lucy."

EVERYTHING, OF COURSE, was not perfect at Framingham. When Van Waters first arrived, almost 40 percent of the women incarcerated there were serving time for crimes that would never have led to prison for men. By the end of the 1930s, almost every woman sent to her—over 90 percent—had been sentenced for nonviolent "crimes against the public order." As a pivotal figure on Harvard's ambitious National Crime Survey of 1928, Van Waters was well aware of how arbitrarily certain gender-specific behaviors had become criminalized for women. Worse, many of her charges were serving lengthy, "indeterminate" sentences for these behaviors. Reserved exclusively for women, indeterminate sentences were based on the idea that there was no telling just how long it would take to reform a female convict. In part because of Ellen Cheney Johnson's passionate requests for longer sentences, these were, often, outrageously long. Their "up to" format allowed, however, for the possibility of parole well before the maximum time had elapsed. In this way, women serving "up to two years" for drunkenness could be paroled after eleven months, and those serving "up to five years" for adultery could be paroled after fourteen months.

Under her predecessor, Jessie Hodder, parole had been recommended only rarely. Like Johnson before her, Hodder believed that true reform required substantial time in a reformatory. Van Waters, in contrast, proposed parole as frequently as possible, far exceeding the willingness of the parole board to grant early release. As she recorded in her journal after one such parole-board hearing in October 1935, "6 out of 45 get it. I take a beating and am wretched."

Despite the increasingly blurred distinctions between the incarcerated and the free, the institution at Framingham was still a prison, of course. No matter how enlightened, it had certain fundamental rules that could not be overlooked, and throughout Van Waters's tenure there were women who chafed at the restrictions. Prisoners acted up. They broke the rules, got drunk, started fights. Once, after the transfer of fifty women from a state hospital made Framingham seriously overcrowded, Van Waters was confronted by a near-riotous mob demanding better food. Even then, however, she refused to fall back on coercion. After suggesting that they all gather in the chapel, she listened closely to their complaints and then created a new committee to handle further grievances, selecting one of the ringleaders to become chairperson. The crisis dissolved without further incident.

DESPITE HER UNRIVALED success at reform (or perhaps because of it), Van Waters always sparked her fair share of controversy. As early as 1932 she made headlines for taking members of the newly formed parole club downtown ("Women prisoners let out to do Xmas shopping," one newspaper exclaimed). Large groups of students often accompanied her to church in town, and Van Waters also sent them—in an early experiment with what came to be known as modern-day furloughs—on unaccompanied visits with their families. This disturbed even the most liberal penologists of the time, especially when, in later years, staff began to escort students to the movies.

The truth was that Van Waters always cared more about the women in her care than the rules that were supposed to govern them. Throughout her tenure she overlooked regulations forbidding released inmates from visiting those still incarcerated, encouraged released mothers to visit whenever they needed medical or psychiatric help for their children, and in an attempt to maintain open communication between women still incarcerated and those released to the community, she threw annual parties for released women and their families on prison grounds. Believing that "only delinquents can solve the problems of delinquents," she also hired released inmates to work in the prison as therapists, educators, and members of her administration. Alongside Dr. Caroline Tinning, she appointed a former larcenist to be the choir director, and even her deputy superintendent, Peg O'Keefe, had been a juvenile offender.

It was the process of indenture, or professional work outside the prison, however, that caused most outrage in the community at large. The system had always been controversial. Unions complained about the sudden availability of an uncompetitive labor force, and, as still happens today, students occasionally abused their newfound freedoms. The sudden need for labor prompted by the outbreak of World War II, however, enabled Van Waters to dramatically enlarge the program. Now she was able to send Framingham students to work in restaurants and factories as well as in private homes. Believing the experience to be essential to her students, Van Waters insisted on publicizing the program's benefits. Despite mounting political pressure, she was also able to maintain the commissioner's support with a constant reiteration of the facts: 97 percent of the 120 indentured women between 1932 and 1935 had remained self-supporting upon release from Framingham.

Still the practice rankled. When a change of personnel at the Department of Correction brought Eliot McDowell, a conservative former woodworker, to the commissionership, it was used as an excuse to investigate the institution as a whole. Fundamentally opposed to Van Waters's independent and reform-minded practices, McDowell resented the autonomy she had always enjoyed. His ensuing report, a 364-page document compiled by his assistant, Frank Dwyer, clearly revealed this antipathy. In it, everything from the indenture system to the sense of community at Framingham was criticized. The flexibility of the treatment programs, the fact that former inmates were allowed to visit and were hired as staff, as well as the cleanliness of the kitchen, the state of the filing system, and the policing of the grounds, were all catalogued. Most damaging, however, were Dwyer's allegations that homosexual activity—"the doll racket," he called it—ran rampant at the prison. Unsupported by witnesses (despite the fact that Dwyer visited both jails and mental asylums seeking women to support his claims), complaints of this kind took up a full half of the report. When the report was leaked to the press, it was, needless to say, these allegations that the tabloids ran with.

As they had done in Eliza Farnham's New York almost one hundred years before, the tabloids spun a series of front-page sensations on the alleged misconduct in Van Waters's institution. Criticism of the superintendent grew increasingly personal. Within weeks reporters were erecting ladders against the side of her house in an attempt to see into her bedroom. In the first week of January 1949, Commissioner McDowell summarily fired Van Waters. She had been superintendent of the prison for seventeen years and was seventy years old at the time.

It seemed as if another period of reform was being brought to an end. Unlike Eliza Farnham in New York, however, Van Waters refused to leave without a fight. She challenged her dismissal and insisted on a public hearing to clear her name. Chaired by the commissioner himself, the hearing lasted eighteen days.

Six days into the hearing, Dwyer questioned the legitimacy of addressing Van Waters's charges as "students" instead of "prisoners." "I find that . . . the statement 'Here you are a student, not a prisoner' is a misstatement of facts," he had written in his report. "The legal status of a person sentenced by the courts of the Commonwealth is that of prisoner."

By way of rebuttal, Van Waters read from the handbook she herself had written for the use of reformatory newcomers. "To you it may seem a tough break and Framingham nothing but a lockup. However you have it in your power to build your own future both here and in the world to which you will return. Nothing you have done in the past will determine your future here. We hold no prejudices. . . . It is true the court punished you when you were sent here but that is in the past. . . . What matters now is education for the future. Here you are a student not a prisoner. If you will, you can help make this a better place. In making your contribution to help others who are sharing this experience with you, you will find this time worthwhile."

To the commissioner's dismay, the passage was greeted with long applause. Newspapers began coming out in favor of Van Waters, many of them conceding that the letter of the law might have been broken by the superintendent. "However, in our view," they wrote: "The offenses in this realm were so strongly overbalanced by the general good which was achieved by . . . Dr. Van Waters's rehabilitation work that the idea of their being the mainstay of a removal proceeding is ludicrous. The more serious charges of undue perversion running unchecked through the reformatory have been so discredited that we wonder how they gained credence in the beginning."

Ultimately, Van Waters would win the legal battle as decisively as she had the public relations one, though it would take several months and a second hearing to do so. Upon her return to the reformatory, more than four hundred women voluntarily gathered in the chapel to celebrate, and according to newspaper reports, ecstatic inmates greeted her with "a sustained ringing of the institution bells and with wild and uncontrolled cheering." As a member of her administration pinned an orchid on Van Waters's lapel, one of the inmates, aged and hunch-backed, ran up and embraced her. More than half the women were cry-ing by the time they "knelt to offer thanksgiving to God, who has sent us back our angel." They then sang the national anthem and listened, in thanks, to their own choir perform the *Te Deum.*

"Each one of you knows," Van Waters said after the impromptu concert, "what it's like to have to be alone and face a judge." "You ain't kidding!" an inmate cried out. "I thought of that, too [during the hear-ing]," Van Waters continued. "I thought of you, often friendless and alone in a strange city and place. The knowledge that after that experi-ence you could come here and face life all over again and be cheerful and kind to one another, and come to church to sing and pray, gave me a great deal of courage."

VAN WATERS CONTINUED to run Framingham until 1957, when she finally retired after twenty-five years of service. During that time Framingham grew in strength, and her opinions with it. Two years be-fore she left she spoke in a radio broadcast entitled "Should All Penal Systems Be Abolished?" Van Waters was of the opinion that they should be. When asked to clarify her position, she explained simply: "My state-ment that prisons must go applies to all penal institutions. They are as obsolete as the 'Pest House.' "

By 1957, however, such opinions were no longer in sync with the times. Headlines reminiscent of those ten years earlier were appearing in the press after an escaped inmate tried to fight her return to Framingham by declaring that the institution's "low moral standards" frightened her. Van Waters had always suspected that her work would not be sustained after her departure. Now her political enemies had an excuse to move in. Almost as soon as she left, an investigative committee comprising mostly police and FBI was sent into Framingham. Their report, made public the following year, produced fourteen recommendations for change. Many, including the recommendation to isolate "aggressive homosexuals and belligerent non-conformists," were effected immediately. Others, like the creation of a punitive maximum-security program, and the removal of children from the prison "as soon as possible," would be implemented over the next few years.

Having suffered both a brain aneurysm and a stroke, Van Waters was less and less able to communicate effectively. She had moved to the town of Framingham, where she lived with two ex-students in a semi-detached house near the church. Despite her attempts to keep working to "do away with public apathy and indifference as to the fate of those in captivity," more "reforms" soon added barbed wire to the tops of Framingham's walls, shut down the farm, and closed most of her cherished educational classes and activity groups. Friendships between inmates and staff, as well as those between inmates still in the facility and those in the community, were made illegal. Social gatherings such as picnics and barbecues were banned, and outside visits from volunteers reduced. In this way, politicians argued, Framingham would once again return to the disciplinary norms of the state correctional system. Once again, an era of openness, and of hope, had been brought to an end.

ESCAPES

"I HAVE TO get out of here!" Denise wrote in June. "Pat's back in the mental hospital. He admitted himself this time because as he put it he had anger-management issues. He was feeling angry and felt he would explode, he said. And you know they only take them if they're suicidal or homicidal."

The foster-care system, it seemed, just wasn't working out. Pat, now thirteen, had been moved from his placement with Dave the soccer coach back in March. There was reason to suspect drug dealing in the home, Denise was told, a full two weeks after the fact. Shortly after that he was uprooted again, taken away from his second family because of suspected child abuse. He ran away from the third—there were too many kids, he said, sometimes five in the small ranch house in Hingham, and the place felt hectic and unsafe enough to persuade him to try his luck on the streets. Later that same day, he was picked up at the bus station and taken back to the Department of Social Services. One of the problems with DSS is that behavior that might warrant punishment in a family becomes criminalized when you are a ward of the state. Instead of being grounded for running away, Pat found himself placed on probation by a judge. One more slip, he was told, and he'd be sent to a "lockdown" facility.

His most recent "home" (Denise couldn't help but sneer when she used this word) was in the town of Lancaster itself, perhaps a half mile from the prison. Denise could have jogged there if she were allowed. As it was, it took a month to discover where he was. That's another problem with DSS—too many kids, too few social workers, and a messy chain of command that often leaves parents entirely out of the loop. Over and over they'd assured her, promised her—and once even *guaranteed* her—a monthly visit from Patrick—but regular contact still hadn't been established. And if it was hard for Denise to establish a rapport with each new foster family, what must it be like for Patrick? Think of it: thirteen years old and a new home, new family, new town, and new school every month and never, anywhere, a place to unwind.

Denise was beginning to worry that she'd been wrong to take him away from his father. During the evenings she went through the box she kept stuffed with Pat's papers, and they made her feel terrible. He'd been doing so well back then: there was an honor-roll certificate, sweet letters from the teachers, wonderful, almost-happy letters from Pat. And then it all stopped. Since he'd arrived at DSS she'd gotten just one letter from him; he was being suspended from school nearly every week, and she'd hadn't received a response from any of his teachers. The latest school had been particularly rough. It even made the six o'clock news when two twelve-year-old kids brought guns into the building.

So when someone from DSS did finally visit and inform Denise that Alan's mother wanted to take Pat in, once he was released from the hospital, she thought, at first, that she might push for the idea. The old lady wouldn't be an ideal guardian, of course, but at least Pat would have a home again. "And she wants him badly, they said," Denise told me, rigid with anxiety. "Alan's enrolled in some crazy Christian program in Alabama—he'll come back worse than ever, but at least he'll be gone for a while."

The next time I saw her, Denise seemed to have changed her mind. Placing Pat back in his father's realm felt dangerous, and she couldn't imagine relinquishing responsibility for him in that way. But then there was the school, he'd loved that school, and the feeling of belonging. She spent days going back and forth and came no closer to a decision. After three and a half years in prison, it was as if she'd reached her limit, hit the dead end of her decision-making processes. She needed to be home, that's all she really knew. And she wouldn't be for another one and a half years.

SPRINGTIME ALSO FOUND Julie depressed. "This birthday is killing me," she told me one balmy afternoon in May. "I'm going to be twenty-four in eleven days, and I feel like I've wasted my best years. I've wasted them in jail. I feel like shit. I feel stupid. I feel like I got played like a sucker by the fucking police." Nothing particular had made her feel this way, she said. Work at the farmer's market was going well—she enjoyed preparing the food and flirting with the customers—but the better it went at the store, the worse it felt to return every evening to the cramped confines of MCI-Lancaster. She had a parole hearing coming up soon, and a good chance of making it, she'd been told, but even this failed to cheer her. If she was going to be honest about it, the idea that she might soon be released only made things worse.

She could not imagine life after prison. She had almost four thousand dollars saved from her job, which was more than she'd ever had before. But other than moving back to her father's house, she had no idea what she might do. Her co-defendant was still in jail. She didn't trust her friends and hadn't seen any of them since she'd been in prison anyway. If she made parole, her only plan was to have her stepmother pick her up and take her directly to Wachusett Precast so she could go "make love to Spidey in the bathroom." Spiderman, of course, was pleased by this, but when Julie asked him if he wanted her to bring something special for the occasion, he said only: "Nah. Nothing. Just bring a towel."

Lucky he wasn't the only man around. Just the other day a new officer approached her in the gym. "Did you used to dance?" he asked, eyeing her from the door.

"Yeah."

"You took it all off?"

"Yeah."

"Nice," he said, then left.

Moments like this still made Julie happy. It was as if all the man's strength and certainty poured out of himself and into her. She knew who she was then, knew her power. At the farmer's market, the high school boys who worked the registers fell completely under her sway. In three months she'd made her way through all of them, one by puppyish one, in the bathroom or stretched out across the backseats of their cars during breaks. She did the same with the customers. A handful of men came back to see her day after day. She particularly liked a man named John or Joel "or something," who had a "wicked Mohawk" and a motorbike and who'd begun writing to her at Lancaster after she fooled around with him a couple of times during lunch. Even Tom, the nerdy young CO who'd let her look through the inmate roster when she wanted to check Peter's background, began to "drop by" her room occasionally—once, he confessed, when she was asleep. She'd never considered Tom lover material, so it surprised me to hear her whisper, "I slept with him the other day," as he loped past us that sunny afternoon, shoulders hunched, hands thrust deep into his pockets like a high school kid on his way to have a surreptitious cigarette during recess.

"Yeah, with Tom," Julie said again, flatly, when I registered surprise. "Well, not really slept with him but fooled around, you know, did things I probably shouldn't have done. But he's scared now, he says. Won't come near me. Feeling guilty, he says."

JULIE SEEMED TO be regressing. In the face of her possible and impending return to freedom it was as if she was determined to do something, anything, that might keep her back. She was scared, she said, mostly of the drugs. Self-obliteration was how she'd always coped with stress, and soon she'd be out there again with no COs, or rules, or strip searches to prevent her from doing whatever she wanted. She knew well by then where that journey ended. After a couple of years at Framingham, she was quick to recognize the ingratiating self-deprecation of women returning to prison after a few short months spent high on the street. She'd watched too as this shame and self-doubt solidified into a more impervious defiance that clamped itself like armor over their too thin bodies. At twenty-four, Julie was no longer young enough to have an excuse.

"When I get out I want to have a baby right away," she told me firmly one afternoon, soon after being told about the possibility of parole. "I think that will help me with my recovery. Help me stay focused. I'm excited and all, but I'm scared too, I guess. I think about getting high every day. Shooting up, shooting two bags . . . I don't know . . . I feel like I'm going to have a panic attack, I really do." Then, without missing a beat, she added: "But oh my God I had such an exciting day last week! I met a guy at an AA meeting in town. His name's Jake, and after the meeting he came straight over to me and said, 'So you in jail, huh? I just got out myself.' Oh my God he's so fine! He has beautiful green eyes, a tattoo that says IRISH on one arm and a gun on the other— and he's still sober after nine months of freedom!"

"So does this AA stuff really work for you?" she had asked him.

"Yes, it does," he had replied, all manly and serious.

"And you, Julie?" I interjected. "Do you think the program could help keep you clean as well?"

"Nah," Julie said, shrugging, kicking the table leg a couple of times. "Nah, I don't think so. 'S too boring!" she replied with a grin.

THE MOOD SWINGS had begun to exhaust Denise. Julie was one of a kind—wild and funny and generous—and in Framingham, where there were clear limits to the trouble she could cause, it had been fun to have her around. Here at Lancaster, though, it was becoming demoralizing. The dramas Julie created piled up and up until all she could do was bounce from one to the other like a hard rubber ball, as if the endless motion itself would provide a solution.

"She keeps telling me all the things she's been doing lately, with the guys at work and the guys here and the customers, and she's upset with me because I haven't been giving her advice," Denise told me one afternoon. "But I can't be responsible for her anymore. I can't be her mom—I don't have the time. She says I have a holier-than-thou attitude, and I know what she's saying. But she has it all confused. She put *me* on a pedestal and treated me as someone who has it all together. *I* never put myself there, at least I don't think I did . . . I'm human just like everyone else! I mean, how am I supposed to resist someone as awesome as Chuck?"

Awesome was never a word I'd associated with Denise. But she'd used it to describe Chuck more than once in her letters to me recently. "He's just so awesome!" her last one read. "So far every 'red flag' that's come up I've talked to him about and it goes away. I'm being so careful I'm almost a paranoid schizophrenic! I cannot take another heartache and to be honest, I don't really want a man—it's not worth the risk, being shipped, caught, trailer visits, everything. I wouldn't risk it all for some flight with a dingbat or moron. But he's not and I feel like it's worth it."

For the first time in more than three years, Denise was feeling like a person again, like a teenager almost: the excited, unsure knot in her stomach, the one-track mind. Like a teenager too she was losing interest in the rest of the world. Certainly the political scene no longer held much fascination, nor did the status of the DOC budget. Even the sudden demise of the shiny new automotive-repair program after just two months of operation warranted little interest. If it bothered her at all, it was only because she'd sometimes been able to chat with Chuck outside the garage there, on the pretext of watering the potted flowers left over from the opening gala.

After so many years of prohibition, it was as if the experience of real and immediate emotion now left no room for anything else. Gone was her obsessive need for order, gone the segregation of herself into neat, self-contained compartments. Instead she wanted, simply, to be. Just the other morning she'd been transfixed by a hawk that settled on a tree branch by her window. He was beautiful, she said, breathtaking: piercing eyes, lethal beak, feathers a deep range of gold and black. She sat there watching him for a full twenty minutes before he finally flew away. The rest of the day she felt liberated and open, as if the hawk really had been the sign of God Chuck said it was often thought to be.

Chuck was full of good information like this. He knew about hawks and beaches, knot tying and investing. And he knew a lot about kids too. He could make her feel better with a well-timed comment or a soothing response, even when Pat was at his worst. Denise knew by then that he'd treated his ex-girlfriend's two children so like his own that they'd long called him Daddy. He was the favorite of his nieces and nephews too—every weekend someone from his family came to visit and they always brought cards and notes from the little ones. In prison, this kind of sustained, familial care spoke volumes about the kind of man he was. It gave Denise hope.

They'd figured out how to see each other privately three times a week by this time. They exchanged letters daily, and shared five or six silent seconds during lunch, which she'd started to serve for this purpose. They'd even decided to have a baby, once they were married, and that they'd live in a house on "a lot of land"—a house big enough for Pat to come join them in. Chuck had it all figured out. He'd be working prerelease soon, he said, and even if he didn't make parole until 2004, by the time he got out he'd have plenty saved for a down payment on a house. "See, I don't want us to have to stress over money," he wrote in one of his daily, ten-page letters. "I want to be able to concentrate on you, me (us) and Patrick."

"I've never had a guy say anything remotely close to that," Denise told me, wide-eyed again. "I always had either a bum or a spendthrift. Alan hardly ever worked. Dave knew I would take care of myself and bail us out of money problems if we got too deep—even if I had to 'go out to dinner' with Chinese men to get it! As for Joel? Spend anything on a good time, but rent, phone bills, car payments? Yeah, sure! Chuck seems so responsible, so grown-up, oh my God, could it be—is he an adult? A man?"

JULIE HAD PREDICTED that Denise and Chuck would get together long before Denise ever acknowledged the possibility. She'd bet Denise forty dollars over it, and Denise had accepted, promising to do Julie's laundry for a month if she lost, as she'd had no money coming in at all back then. So Julie had been doubly pleased when they first paired up. "Oh no!" she laughed when Denise first told her. "The two of you are going to educate the whole prison!"

But things hadn't worked out quite as she planned. Julie had imagined Denise and Chuck forming some sort of secret club with her and Peter. But Denise's involvement with Chuck meant that she had less, not more, time for Julie. Now, instead of sitting cross-legged on the bed sharing intimacies with her, Denise spent her evenings hunched over cheap, yellow legal pads, writing interminable letters to Chuck.

Julie found it difficult not to resent Chuck's intrusion, but she did everything she could to help the two of them along. One afternoon, for example, Denise blocked up a downstairs toilet by stuffing it with paper towels so that Chuck would have to come by and "fix it." But when he did arrive, an hour or so later, Tom the CO was there and wouldn't leave them alone. It wasn't until Julie passed by and hauled him away that Tom realized what had been going on. "Oh, those two are together?" he said with a gasp. "I'm sorry. I woulda let Chuck get some. I like Chuck." But even after this, Julie felt dismissed by her one-time best friend. Denise neither thanked her, nor giggled with her about the absurdity of it all the way she'd always done before. It was as if none of that had ever happened.

The truth was that since hooking up with Chuck, Denise no longer seemed to care about Julie much at all. For years Julie had relied on her to act as her anchor and guide, and Julie had grown used to the freedom such careful tethering allowed. Now, no matter how recklessly Julie behaved, she always got the same response: indifference, in the guise of a blank-faced shrug. Also, there was something jarringly superior about Denise and Chuck as a couple. They plugged up toilets and jammed washing machines the same as the rest of them, but they acted as if they were different from everyone else, as if they'd never even committed the crimes that got them there in the first place.

Julie knew this tendency bothered Spidey too, though he so revered Chuck it was hard to get him to acknowledge it with more than a shrug. Besides, words weren't exactly his strong suit. Nor, of late, were they

Julie's. The possibility that she might soon be released was making it increasingly hard to unravel a single, coherent narrative from the impossibly tangled ball of them in her head. She hated prison; she needed prison. She feared punishment; she craved restraint.

She tried keeping busy—even apart from the sex: worked overtime at the farmer's market whenever she could; served food in the kitchen on weekends; even became a regular at the AA meetings in town. But without Denise to talk to there was no way to release the pressure. Like trailer visits with your kids, freedom was something you were supposed to quietly and gracefully celebrate, not bemoan. Hurt and humiliated, Julie began to get angry, pointedly going quiet and glaring when Denise passed by. As tension between them grew, so too did Julie's wildness. She started sneaking away with Peter for five minutes in the middle of lunch when she was supposed to be serving, or slipping off for a quickie with him after count. She sashayed past Tom in front of his colleagues and flaunted the illegal food items she brought back to the prison from the farmer's market. When Denise still didn't react, Julie started to spend time with a young outcast named Edith who'd just been shipped over from Framingham. Edith was cute, and it was good to share intimacies with a woman again. But she wasn't Denise. Edith was a kid. Denise had been a mother. There was, in the end, no comparison.

"Denise's changed," Julie told me over the phone one night, almost in tears. "She's gotten so stuck up—everyone says so—the girls, the officers, everyone. It's Chuck who's done it to her, you know. He's an asshole. A freaking dumb-fuck asshole."

JULIE HAD SUSPECTED all along that Denise was complaining about her in her letters to Chuck. What else did she have to talk about? But one afternoon, when Peter asked her if it was true that she was two-timing him with Edith, she finally exploded. The information itself wasn't particularly difficult to negotiate—every man Julie had ever met had been turned on by her bisexuality, and she found it easy to summon her old dominatrix superciliousness and reply: "Yeah, it's true. So what? You got a problem with that?"

Appropriately chastened, Peter replied, "No," and started grinning like a kid. This was satisfying, in a way, but not the point. The point was that Denise had betrayed her—consciously betrayed her over a man.

That afternoon, on her way to dinner, hurt and rage still scouring her insides, Julie shouted up to Chuck's window: "Yeah, I'm fucking her! I'm fucking her and he's dying to watch!" The shift commander was right behind her, but she couldn't have cared less. For a moment, she managed to still look brazen while telling me this. Then she started to cry. She hated Chuck, she said. Hated him so much that last time she passed him on the way to the dining hall she couldn't stop herself from snarling: "I hope you kill someone else when you get out."

"DUMMY!" DENISE SAID. "She really overreacted. I'm the one who should be mad. And she keeps making it worse! Five people have come up to me to tell me she's talking all kinds of shit! I'm not sure what to do. Usually I would say, Okay, let's just forget it, but I'm not going to do that this time. I'm not going to be a fool. She's been causing problems for too long now with her attitude and anger. No more! I always stick up for her and give her the benefit of the doubt, but this time she went too far."

Close friendships between women in prison often ended like this, frequently just before one of them was released. The presence of male inmates at Lancaster, however, made this quarrel particularly dangerous. Between them, Denise and Julie knew just about all there was to know about sex in the facility. The circle of physical contact touched almost everyone, and as Denise and Julie formed one of its axes, the tension between them was beginning to taint everything. When a note was found naming women in relationships with men in the prison, many concluded it was Julie who'd written it. The list was found under the stairs by an inmate on cleanup duty and was quickly destroyed. But there was something about the way Julie responded to its discovery—with false, eyebrow-arching surprise instead of panic—that seemed odd to Denise.

In July, Denise refused to let Julie know the date of my next visit. She couldn't, she said. They no longer spoke to each other. For weeks, no matter the question, the answer always circled back to the tension between them. Each blamed the other, of course, for getting Inner Perimeter Security involved in the feud. Julie insisted it had been Denise who first approached IPS, when she'd grown scared that Pat's upcoming visit might be canceled. Denise denied this absolutely, though she agreed that Pat's visit—and Julie's intimation that she might spill the beans about Chuck in order to prevent it—raised the stakes to an entirely different level. Pat was in worse trouble than ever before, and the thought that Julie might do something to hurt him made Denise loathe her. "Just hearing that girl's name makes me want to puke," she said.

There was, to Denise's mind, no question as to what had imperiled Pat's visit. The superintendent's "right hand" called her into her office one morning and told her that they'd been hearing rumors about her and Chuck, specifically about certain plans to bring Chuck to the trailer to meet Pat. "We really like you here," the superintendent's assistant told Denise. "We don't want to see you make any mistakes. The pitter-patter will go away, but don't risk it. You are being *very* watched."

Denise mentioned Julie and the fact that the two of them had been having "some problems."

"Yes, I know," the administrator replied. "Women can be very catty and very jealous." Her enigmatic smile seemed proof enough that Julie had spilled the beans. Certainly someone had tipped off the administration about the letter-delivery system Denise and Chuck had set up through the warehouse—a friendly CO told the woman who exchanged letters for them to stop before she was busted. This was little more than an inconvenience. Denise left her letters to Chuck under an exercise mat in the gym instead, placing her tea mug on the windowsill as a sign that she'd done so. More difficult to circumvent, however, was the new policy—could it possibly be a coincidence?—of banishing women to their rooms whenever a member of the maintenance crew entered the house. The fact that Julie was as adversely affected by this as anyone seemed irrelevant. The way she'd been acting recently, publicly venting her fury without bothering to check who might be listening, made her the number-one candidate for blame. By August, the underground life of the place was on the verge of collapse—and almost everyone held Julie accountable.

"No one trusts Julie anymore," Denise confirmed. "No one. The guys all call her 'Four O'Clock'—for the 'Four O'Clock News.' That's how good she is at spreading information around."

JULIE'S PAROLE HEARING was set for Friday. She took the day off work, got herself ready, and then sat around outside the room used for these hearings in the men's building and bit her nails and played with her hair and tried to distract herself by catching eyes with guys as they passed. The actual hearing lasted less than five minutes. The three-person board asked if she acknowledged that her crimes had victims. She said that of course she did. They said, "Okay. Would you mind waiting outside?" And that was it. When they called her back in, the board's smiles turned to chastising frowns when they told her: "If you mess up, you'll be coming right back and serving every day of your time!" But she'd made parole. She'd be home within a couple of weeks.

Sitting in the courtyard of the farmer's market, chain-smoking Newports and scanning the customers as she *tap-tap-tapped* her foot against the bench, Julie burst into tears when she told me this. The rest of her life was about to start, she said, and she hadn't a clue how to do it—not a clue! She loved her dog and she loved her nephew, and it would be good to be able to come and go as she pleased and eat what she wanted, but what was she supposed to do after that? As far as she could remember, her life had been a blur of heroin and men and dominatrix work, and how did any of that help now?

It wasn't only she who feared for her future, she said. Almost everyone at Lancaster thought she'd be back in Framingham "right away." COs, women, they all taunted her with it, and it made her feel crazy because they were right, she said. Her father's town was tiny. It would take her about three and a half minutes to get her hands on some dope, and she'd never been there for long without doing just that. She gave herself six weeks. Six weeks—and then back to Framingham.

The stress of her impending release made Julie testy and wired and a little more frazzled each day. Still not on speaking terms with Denise, or with most of the other women, she smoked more, and slept around more, and in between, when she wasn't in the store or behind the kitchen counter silently serving food to the men of Lancaster, she began to drop hints about some impending disaster—something she knew about but couldn't share—to anyone foolish enough to listen.

Denise knew it was paranoid, but she couldn't help worrying about Pat when she heard about these threats. Julie was a cop's kid. She had connections. Who knew what she'd be able to do on the outside? But it turned out Julie had smaller things in mind. One afternoon, when passing Chuck on the way to the dining hall, she hissed: "As soon as I leave here your fun will be over." She said the same to Denise: "When I get out I'm going to tell them everything. Every fucking last thing." And: "When I'm outta here, I swear the game's gonna be over." Julie wanted a reaction. These threats, however, failed to move Denise much. "Hmnnf!" she said with a snort. "What can she tell that she hasn't already?"

ON THE MORNING of her release, Julie packed her bags, went down to try to make amends with Denise, was rebuffed, and then walked alone to her stepmother's waiting car sometime around ten. Surprisingly, the women of Lancaster actually followed through on their promise of a party to celebrate her departure. Almost every woman in the prison brought something from their Canteen stash down to the dayroom, where they played music and cheered until they were told to disperse a few minutes later.

Rumors were circulating by then that, in an attempt to save money, the DOC was going to shut the prison at Lancaster down. The men would be scattered to various facilities across the state, while the women, so the story went, would be moved to a worn old place just the other side of a country lane from MCI-Framingham. There were no hard facts yet, nothing on the news, but just the possibility made everyone tense. The COs, suddenly anxious about their career prospects, felt the need to clamp down on behaviors long ignored. Clothing sweeps were instituted, as well as room searches and strict new oversight of all incoming inmate mail.

Though no one could be quite sure whether Julie had followed through on her promise to "reveal all," everyone was tense, especially Denise. Pat was back in the same foster home he'd been in before he committed himself, and she felt the need to go home with a force that was almost physical. Only Chuck's presence helped. Despite the COs' new officiousness, Chuck still managed, through the three-way mail, to get letters to Denise almost daily, and cards too, real store-bought ones with beautifully written messages inside. One in particular made her laugh with its elaborate descriptions of the luxury cruises he would take her on. It was funny; just the night before she received it, she'd had a dream about being on such a cruise with him. Coincidences like this happened all the time.

But not even the black ribbed sweater, wrapped and delivered by Chuck to her door, could distract her when Patrick got arrested. He had two charges against him, she was told. "One for pushing his foster mother and one for stealing batteries—that's right, stealing batteries, not assault and battery," she told me, bitterly. He'd never liked this placement—the school had been intimidating and the house crowded and he'd been convinced from the start that it was some kind of setup. He'd been begging to leave for weeks but was told by his social worker that a kid did not leave a foster home just because somehow the place felt wrong. Something concrete had to happen. So Pat pushed his foster mother. Then, just to make sure that everyone knew something concrete had happened, he stormed over to a BJ's outlet and stole a large pile of batteries.

To Denise, that push and those batteries seemed like such clear and desperate calls for help. The social worker shrugged. While perhaps a good mother's response, Denise was told, such sentiments hold little water in the system. The same afternoon that Patrick owned up to pushing his foster mother, he was sent to a lockdown evaluation facility for sixty days. "When they find out what his needs are they'll try to place him elsewhere," Denise said sarcastically. "In the meantime he gets zero visits and no incoming calls."

Denise stopped being able to sleep after that. When she'd first left for Framingham, Pat had been obsessed with Beanie Babies. Now he was in prison himself. There was no way to speak to him for days. Just as in an adult prison, residents of Patrick's facility were only allowed to place outgoing collect calls. Lancaster did finally arrange for her to receive ten-minute calls from him once a week, but she found, in the end, that this was worse than not hearing from him at all. There's a limit to how much you should know when there's nothing you can do. They were medicating him heavily, she could tell. He sounded dopey all the time, sloppy-tongued. Otherwise, Denise found out nothing at all about how he was being treated. Left to imagine the worst, she panicked. "I know way too much about prison to have Pat in there," she said.

THE NEXT TIME I saw Denise I barely recognized her. I had heard she was having trouble getting out of bed in the mornings, that she didn't want to talk to friends, or to exercise, or even write to Chuck. She looked exhausted. Gone was the starry-eyed, love-struck woman; gone the furiously feuding ex-friend of Julie; gone even the sad but intelligently restrained and increasingly politically savvy woman that I'd known from pre-Chuck days. Instead Denise sat, heavy and lifeless, at the table, hunched over a couple of Twix bars and a package of strawberry licorice. Life was too much, she said. And then, as if I didn't know, "Patrick is in prison."

Denise was one of the few women at Lancaster whom almost everyone respected. Both COs and inmates had grown used to her reliable and upbeat energy, and now that it was gone, they went out of their way to help her regain it. After a few weeks, a CO she'd befriended named Rankin brought her to the Health Services Unit for an appointment with the psychiatrist. The acting nurse there let Denise use the phone in her office to make direct, noncollect calls to whomever she needed to speak to at Department of Youth Services. But Denise only rarely took her up on the offer. She no longer had the energy, she said. And anyway, there was nothing she could do—look at her! She was an inmate herself! What could she possibly do to make a difference in a world where Pat was suffering nightly lockdowns, and bend-over-and-cough strip searches at the age of thirteen?

The shrink gave her Prozac. Denise liked him—he worked over at Framingham as well as at Lancaster, and she told me he gave her whatever she asked for. He didn't have many answers, though, and even the Prozac didn't seem to help. Meanwhile, Pat was beginning to sound like a miniature criminal on the phone. He used phrases like "Don't worry, Mom, I'm gonna beat this rap," and it was frightening to hear him sound like such a very young boy when he did. After one grueling talk, during which he told Denise that he was again being restrained, she took to bed for days. Friends came by with hot soups and sandwiches. Others dropped off magazines and made offers of prayer. When she still didn't rouse herself, CO Rankin finally relented and brought Chuck over to the house for a visit. After summoning him on the pretext of "stabilizing the water heater in the basement," Rankin fetched Denise down from her room.

Denise had no idea what was going on and was irritated to be forced out of bed. She followed Rankin down to the basement in her pajamas and slippers, hair uncombed, teeth unbrushed, to find Chuck there, standing awkwardly next to the boiler: "You've got fifteen minutes," Rankin said, and left.

Stunned as much by Rankin's magnanimity as by her depression, Denise leaned rigidly up against Chuck. "Denise, I love you," he murmured, stroking her hair. "I want to take you home just like this."

CONTACT

SUPERIOR COURT JUSTICE Janet Sanders's ruling about the Girl Scouts case came in April 2002. It was unequivocal. Almost eighteen months after first requesting access to the program, I was granted the right to observe Girl Scouts Beyond Bars both in and out of prison. "Given the history of this litigation," she wrote, "this court concludes that it is because of who Rathbone is and what she may write about that forms the true basis for prison officials' decision. Such decisions cannot withstand constitutional scrutiny."

Once again, however, the Department of Correction prevaricated—this time by requesting that a new set of official-looking media-access forms be filled out by each of the program's participants. It took a month and several visits to Framingham to gather these, and it wasn't until the end of the summer that I was finally able to attend a meeting in the prison.

Heidi, the troop's new volunteer facilitator, gathered the girls in the same old rickety van, circling around Boston's innermost neighborhoods just as Erin had done before. This time the girls were ready for her, all freshly washed and nicely dressed to visit their mothers in prison. Carmencita Ramirez wasn't part of the group anymore. Her baby, a girl, had been born a couple of months earlier, and there was no provision for grandchildren in the program. But her kid sister, Alina, was there, in a pleated skirt and shiny open-toed pumps, and she had with her the latest batch of baby photos to share with her mother.

It took less than an hour to drive down the highway from Boston to Framingham. Heidi had brought along construction-paper journals with plain cardboard covers for the girls to use as they wished, and she handed these out now, along with lengths of brightly colored wool to sew them together. For later, she kept next to her on the floor a white plastic bag filled with peanut M&Ms and bags of chips. It was easier to harness the girls' excitement on the way to the visit than it was to bring them out of themselves on the way home. The candy, she found, came in most useful then.

Sitting close to the front, Alina sat with her neatly tied journal on her lap, in silence. Behind her sat Latiffa, rowdy as ever in matching shorts, shirt, and vest. Hair newly braided with beads that cascaded down to the base of her neck, she beat out rhythms on the back of her journal while Angelique and Sam (in identical pink pants and pink cup-sleeved T-shirts) made up lyrics that didn't really rhyme. Vanessa, one of the two girls who'd managed to jump onto the trapeze and fly across the big top almost a year before, was already writing in her journal, occasionally stopping to straighten a fold in her brightly flowered dress, or to pull a corner of her white stockings free from her brand-new black patent-leather strapped sandals. Only Tiffany, who at eight was the youngest in the program, was wearing everyday clothes. She looked cute in her simple blue shorts and fresh white T-shirt, but she drew stares the minute she sat down. "You better be dressed like a girl next time I see you, or else!" Latiffa teased.

The girls knew the prison-entrance routine well. They took off their jewelry in the van and gave it to Heidi to store in a pouch, which she locked in one of the waiting room lockers. Most brought nothing in their pockets, and the two wearing sneakers unlaced them well before the magnetically locked door that would take them to their mothers popped open. So well dressed were the girls that even their laces looked ironed. When a CO finally opened the door, the girls all turned their pockets inside out and removed their shoes. Those who wore belts removed them too, and then all the girls walked through the metal detector as if it were the most normal thing in the world.

Every other Saturday morning the visiting room was reserved for the Girl Scouts, so aside from one correctional officer and a couple of administrators, there was no one else in the room. Eight girls had shown up today—nowhere near enough to fill the space. They became anxious as they sat in a line against the wall and, in an attempt to hide this, focused intently on last-minute beauty checks. "I'm mad ashy—I don't know why—I put mad lotion on," Latiffa mumbled to herself.

When the door leading from the prison itself finally popped open, all but the oldest girls ran to their mothers. Mami Carmen was the first one out, then Louise Cato, then Sidharra, Latiffa's mom. They'd all been strip-searched before being let in, and some were still tucking in shirts as they reached for their daughters. But the hugs that followed seemed to stop time. Even the bigger girls were in their mothers' arms now, and a floating, weightless ease filled the room as they rocked together. There was a sense, for once, of naturalness in this most unnatural of places. The volunteers and I stood back as each mother walked with her daughter to a place in the room away from the rest, then crouched or sat down to talk. "Happiness and talk," my notes say. Each mother-daughter pair like its own solar system, alone together, wrapped not in separation but in intimacy.

ALINA WAS SITTING quietly on her mother's ample lap, their legs resting entwined on the edge of the chair next to them. She hummed as

Carmen played with her braids. The past few months had been hard for the Ramirez family. Not being with Carmencita during the birth had been more difficult for Carmen than it had been for her daughter—in part because she was still battling the disrespectful opinions of the other "Spanish" women at Framingham. According to them, children were a treasure, but not when they had children themselves. When Carmen heard that little Rosa had been born, that she was healthy and weighed almost eight pounds, she had to celebrate on her own. First she nearly fainted. Then she praised God and cried in her room for hours. It wasn't until she received photographs a couple of weeks later that even the most judgmental women came around to her side. Here, truly, was new life, they now said. Not death but hope.

Carmencita had wanted a boy, Mami Carmen knew, but daughters were the ones that counted in the end. Look at her: Rosita. Little Rose. Leaning over Alina's shoulder, she asked now if the baby was eating well. "*Sí, Mami.*" And was she sleeping? "*Sí.*" Was Carmencita taking care of her the way that she should? "*Sí, sí,*" Alina said, increasingly relaxed—as long as she was in her mother's arms, she didn't seem to mind not talking about herself.

All around the room, conversations were settling into this new kind of seriousness. Over in one corner, Latiffa and her mother were sharing a tiny, hard candy, passing it from mouth to mouth as they discussed, in hushed tones, the Six Flags trip Latiffa had not been able to attend. Her mother nodded, quietly sucking on the candy before offering advice, which for some reason made Latiffa kick, kick, kick her foot against the chair in embarrassment. Across the room, the only man, a skinny, shorn-headed white CO, seemed abashed by all this femininity and hid behind his hands at the desk.

The whole meeting felt like an excuse for these ten minutes of intimacy at the beginning and the additional ten minutes at the end. But everyone knew that the more official Girl Scout meeting had to happen in the middle. Before anyone was ready it was time for circle. Gathered together again, the women stood next to their daughters, raised the middle three fingers of their right hands, and first in English and then, more desultorily, in Spanish, they recited the Girl Scout Law:

> *I will do my best to be*
>> *honest and fair,*
>> *friendly and helpful,*
>> *considerate and caring,*
>> *courageous and strong, and*
>> *responsible for what I say and do,*
> *and to*
>> *respect myself and others,*
>> *respect authority,*
>> *use resources wisely,*
>> *make the world a better place, and*
>> *be a sister to every Girl Scout.*

I remembered Louise Cato telling me about how foolish it felt reciting this promise in the company of so many female felons, but, the line about respecting authority aside, I thought it just about as good a rule to live by as any I'd heard. Of course, in a prison, respecting authority is the bottom line, and fittingly, one of the volunteers, a pleasant-looking, pale-faced woman from Springfield, started right in then with a reminder about the rules. The Girl Scouts had been off for a month, she said, and she thought it was best to run through them quickly. No jewelry was allowed, of course. No running, no taking off your shoes—"And no cartwheeling!" interceded Latiffa.

We went around the circle next, listening as each girl offered a "special thing" she'd done since the troop had last met (movies, visits with cousins, barbecues, school shopping, school shopping, school shopping), and in the minute or so it took for everyone to settle down on the floor afterward, the daughter of the woman on my right said: "Grandma bought me a new jacket for school. Is that okay, Mami?"

"I think it is good," her mother said, smiling broadly, and then asked if I agreed.

"I think it's very good," I said, and before I could add anything more, the pale-faced CO tapped me on the shoulder. "Ms. Rathbone. Could I talk to you for a moment in private?"

Standing up, I followed him all the way across the visiting room and then around the corner to the door. "I feel like I'm being taken to the principal," I said, both because I wanted to break the ice and because it was true. But the CO didn't smile. Instead he settled his feet about two feet part as though preparing for a blow and said that the terms of our agreement allowed me to observe, but not to participate in, the Girl Scouts meeting. I did not have permission for interviews, he said. I replied, calmly, that I hadn't been interviewing anyone.

"Talking, interviewing. Interviewing, talking. It's the same thing," he said. "One more time and I'll have to ask you to leave."

Speechless, I returned to the circle, allowed myself a muted "I'm not allowed to talk to you here, I'm sorry" to my neighbor, and then fumed.

Just two months earlier, between the time Judge Sanders wrote her opinion and the time that the DOC allowed me, finally, to observe this unremarkable meeting, the Massachusetts DOC had rewritten the policy pertaining to media access to its facilities. Titled 103 CMR, the new regulation was a clear step away from its previously professed openness toward the media. Gone now were the statements "Conditions in a state correctional institution are a matter of interest to the general public" and "The department has a proactive posture when communicating with the news media." In their stead would be five new stipulations, which, if passed, would make it virtually impossible for journalists to cover state prisons at all. Under the new guidelines, all media interviews of prisoners would have to be "conducted in the presence of, and under the supervision of, a correctional employee." The use of cameras and tape recorders at all but seven of the state's twenty-two correctional facilities would be prohibited, and contact with prisoners housed in segregation units or solitary confinement precluded altogether. More alarming still, "the maintenance of . . . legitimate penological interests" had been added to the list of criteria that the DOC could weigh when evaluating a media request. Most chillingly, the DOC would be allowed to decline requests for access after considering "whether such access would result in significant benefit to law enforcement agencies."

Insisting they were only keeping apace with "industry trends," the DOC denied it was making these changes in response to any particular situation or person. It was mandated to hold a public hearing on the matter, but as current commissioner Kathleen Dennehy later confessed, it was not mandated to pay attention to anything anyone might say there. Shortly after the hearing, 103 CMR was sent over to the Administration and Finance Department in the State House, where, as always, it was approved without question or change. The regulations became effective later that summer. Since then no one has been able to interview a state inmate in Massachusetts without the presence of a correctional officer—no one except, because the law is not retroactive, me. Just the fact that I was there at all, in the prison visiting room, on a Saturday morning, must have been irksome in the extreme for the DOC.

THE MEETING HAD officially begun. Chante, Vanessa's mother, was troop leader today. Working toward the "becoming a teenager" badge was the overarching theme, and "hygiene" the topic for the day. The supporting materials the Girl Scouts had brought in were not needed. Personal maintenance is a passion among women in prison, and Chante needed no help. More time, perhaps, but no help.

"Hygiene is something that is very dear to women," she started. "Men? They don't care about hygiene much, but it's very dear to women. You have to groom yourselves, and looking around, I see that you do. That y'all do groom yourselves, and that's nice. That's right. That's good.

"Now, it might seem like y'all a little young, but, you know," she went on, "how many of you floss?"

"I toothpaste!" said Dominique.

"I hope we all toothpaste," Chante said. "But I want to tell y'all something else here. You also need to floss. My mother uses floss sticks, and if you smell the stuff that those catch between your teeth, you'll see it smells like sewage!" At this, the entire circle, both mothers and daughters, collapsed in a cloud of grossed-out giggles.

Unfazed, Chante continued: "And don't pay no attention to the manufacturer's instructions to brush twice a day. Do it five times or more. And besides brushing your teeth, you also gotta brush your tongue," she said, sticking her own out and demonstrating the best way to cleanse it of "fluff."

Meanwhile, Carmen and Alina quietly left the circle to set up snack. Over in the corner they draped grapes delicately across the corners of cheese slices and piled up pyramids of crackers on thin paper plates until the offerings looked like still lifes in a painting by Velázquez.

". . . clean your ears, the insides of your ears, 'cause wax builds up inside there every single day, and also clean your nose up inside, and wash inside your belly button," Chante was saying now. "Sweating is natural. Don't worry about sweating, but you do need to take care of your feet." When she added, out of the blue: "I don't know how many of you have your period," every one of the girls fell silent, listening now almost as hard as they pretended they weren't.

"My mother never talked to me about my period, and y'all's mothers is incarcerated, so I wanted to let you know all about it *today*," she said. "Now, on the box it says change it every six hours, but I say do it every two, or every time you go to the bathroom."

"Don't be afraid," Latiffa's mother interjected. "Don't panic if you get cramps and if you go to the bathroom and see a little blood there—don't panic! Don't be running around the house all scared, because I know I did—Latiffa, be quiet, or I'll hit you—Go talk to the guardian that's there and tell them what's happening."

"And don't be afraid to talk to your mothers," added Louise Cato. "Don't be afraid to write us a letter. We like getting mail, good or bad. Periods. Boys. We want to know about your lives—and you'll get an answer too. It might take a couple of days, but you'll get an answer—an honest one. Your period can start as early as eight or as late as sixteen." She combed her daughter's perfectly ridged cornrows with the very tips of her fingernails as she spoke. "I know I was a late comer. I was a later bloomer. But I got it. You will *all* get it—and don't forget, for the older girls they have the special teenage tampons—"

"No!" interrupted Chante urgently. "These girls should use pads! They don't know about insertion . . ."

"Umm-hmm," agreed Latiffa's mom. "Until someone can show you how to use them the right way. And God willing, we'll be home for that. We will be home."

EPILOGUE

IT WAS A beautiful day in February 2004, clear, crisp, not too cold, when I finally interviewed the Massachusetts commissioner of Corrections. I'd been trying to get this interview for years, but it had never panned out. This was typical DOC: an hour or so before the appointed time, someone would call and, very politely, cancel. It wasn't until Commissioner Michael Malone was forced from office after a scandal involving the murder of a pedophile priest in a maximum-security cell that I was finally able to meet with the titular head of the department. The scandal uncovered a slew of unsavory correctional practices, including a propensity to place disliked inmates in harm's way. The appointment of then deputy commissioner Kathleen Dennehy to the commissionership was hailed by the department and press alike as a clear move away from business as usual.

"Kathy has proven over the last twenty-seven years that she is ready and able to begin the long arduous task of reforming the Department of Correction," Public Safety secretary Edward Flynn was reported as saying on the day of her appointment. "These are exceptional times at the department that require exceptional leadership."

Initially this struck me as odd. More than four years before, it had been Dennehy who'd so adamantly rejected my request for access to the women of MCI-Framingham. After months of prevarication, I'd been told that it was she who finally came up with the "offensive to victims" excuse, yet she refused to meet or even speak with me, despite my numerous letters, phone calls, and faxes. She had been the superintendent at Framingham before being promoted to Central Office, and I'd always assumed this was why she'd been so reluctant to let me in. When I finally met her that bright February day, however, she insisted she'd had little to do with the decision and had known even less.

"When I read some of the history of your case I was just furious!" she said in the conference room where we now met. This seemed so incompatible with the Kathleen Dennehy I'd experienced before that I nearly laughed. But she went on, clearly angry now, at the memory. "It infuriates me how many people didn't do their job, or did it out-and-out horribly! It is exactly, precisely the type of document that I want to take to superintendent's meetings, and to command-staff meetings, because people need to see that there are real consequences to their actions or, more often than not, their *inaction*. Because this doesn't just happen with the media! This can happen with volunteers, it can happen with religious groups, it can happen with any outsider. It's a big piece of our culture, and it's a big piece of what needs to be changed."

MUCH HAS HAPPENED in corrections since I first tried to gain access to the women of MCI-Framingham. In an era of reduced state budgets and soaring fiscal deficits, the financial cost of tough-on-crime policies is becoming prohibitive. There are today more than 2.1 million people behind bars in this country. It costs an average of $38,000 a year to house each one. Because of this, twenty-five states have recently changed their sentencing and correctional policies in attempts to save money. Seventeen, including Michigan, Louisiana, Washington, Texas,

Kansas, and Mississippi, have rolled back elements of their mandatory-sentence structure. Sixteen, including Colorado, Kentucky, and Ohio, have reduced prison populations by shortening time served; and eleven, including California, Florida, Georgia, Utah, and Virginia, have closed entire prisons.

In another attempt to scale back costs, California recently nominated a female reformer to run its Department of Correction, the third largest in the nation. Her approach is straight out of the history books. Like Eliza Farnham and Miriam Van Waters before her, Jeanne Woodford gathered huge numbers of volunteers to provide extracurricular activities at the maximum-security prison she ran before being promoted. A gospel choir, group therapies, sports, art, and comparative-literature classes were all instituted. She also expanded the college program, reinstated the inmate-run advisory council, and spent much of her time, day to day, speaking with inmates individually, listening to their grievances, and trying to help. In a department that expunged the word *rehabilitation* from its mission statement in 1976, these were dramatic changes indeed—and Woodford has her share of detractors. Unlike Farnham and Van Waters, however, Woodford has seen her determination to rehabilitate inmates resonate in a state with huge budget deficits and an annual prison tab of close to six billion dollars. Significantly, California suffers from the highest rate of reincarceration in the nation. Woodford's notion that "there are no irredeemable souls" is all well and good. The reason she was tapped to take over the system, however, is that rehabilitation ultimately costs less than reincarceration. "She addressed substance abuse, mental illness, lack of education, and other factors that drive criminality," *The New York Times* quoted the state's secretary overseeing corrections as explaining. "And she did it without cost to the state."

In Massachusetts too, budget shortfalls have forced a correctional reshuffling. MCI-Lancaster was finally closed as a cost-cutting measure in 2003. As planned, the women were moved to an old prerelease facility just the other side of a small country lane from Framingham; the men went to various facilities across the state. It has been the question of integrity, however, that most urgently drives the engines of change here, and in our meeting, Dennehy spoke repeatedly about the need for reform.

"I'll say it boldly," she said. "The phenomenon that has most impacted corrections in the last ten years is that innovation and creativity have been beaten out of any administrator willing to take the risk, to step up out of the bunker and say, 'You know, we need to try this differently.' "

Dennehy is a history buff, I knew, and given the access she enjoyed to documents most of the rest of us could only dream about, she knew as much about the history of Framingham as anyone—maybe more. She certainly knew that the consequences of reform had always been disastrous for the reformer. Was she willing now to take that kind of risk herself?

"I think I'm already beginning to," Dennehy replied with a laugh. And then: "There is a big difference between being number one and being number two. Number one gets to drive the bus, number two is the passenger—and often isn't given a map. I can't do everything at once—I'm up to my tush in alligators—but I'm trying to impact the organization by removing people that I believe need to be removed, promoting people who I believe need to be promoted, and at the same time responding to what I see as four or five huge systems failures. We need to address the classification issue head-on, somehow or other try to figure out the dollar piece so that we address the critical needs of education—and we don't do enough with families of inmates. Also we have to be much more open to the community coming in—to the whole notion of inreach. Reentry doesn't work if you set an arbitrary barrier at the door. It needs to be—it's an overused term but it really does need to be—a seamless continuum."

I'd been prepared for anything but this. Four years of constant antagonism from the DOC had left me skeptical, and Dennehy's posture was, frankly, hard to believe. Much had happened in the two years she'd run MCI-Framingham. A private health-care company took over at the same time, more or less, and two women died at Framingham in the next six months. Controversy swirled around both deaths, but as superintendent, Dennehy remained, publicly at least, squarely within the party line. It is true that she facilitated improvements in the method and quality of health-care provision over the next few months: a mental-health unit was established, as were health screenings, physicals within twenty-four hours of arrival, new sick-call procedures, and improved medication tracking. It is hard to know now, however, whether these were political moves designed to appease or acts of genuine goodwill. Though the entire Health Services Unit was renovated after a woman named Robin Peeler died there, for example, the process of pulling up dirty linoleum and tearing down floor-to-ceiling fencelike partitions from the psych cells began the day after her death—and before investigators were allowed onto the scene.

The more I looked into it, though, the more I heard other reports of Dennehy as superintendent—glowing reports from people not generally partial to the DOC. She'd always been a clear proponent of treatment and education, had convened regionwide conferences on medical treatment and pre- and postnatal care, and backed up embattled social workers and teachers at the prison, earning their unwavering support.

Certainly since becoming commissioner Dennehy has been zealous in redefining the department's mission. She created the new post of associate commissioner in charge of reentry and reintegration—and appointed another female reformer to fill it. With the help of representatives from all levels of the department, she also rewrote the DOC vision statement. It now reads: "We are professionals committed to an open and respectful organization dedicated to public safety through the safe, secure, humane confinement and successful re-entry of our offender population." In April 2004 she promptly fired one supervising CO and demoted five others when it was revealed that they used excessive force on a male inmate and then lied about it to investigators. This action so outraged the correctional officers union that it spurred threats of a strike, and prompted letters like the following in the local press: "Kathleen Dennehy is nothing but a social worker. Why don't they just hire a couple of daycare workers and start taking these inmates out on field trips?"

She has not yet rescinded the new regulation barring the media from anything like free access to her prisons. She insists, however, that it is only a matter of time. She did rescind a similar policy that prevented law students from representing inmates. And when I asked for her opinion on mandatory minimum drug sentences, she was as clear as she had been about anything. First she smiled, caught a little off guard. Then she sat up straight in her chair and, every inch the new commissioner, said evenly: "Many practitioners would *really* question their efficacy—myself included."

Of course Dennehy doesn't have the power to reshape sentencing laws on her own. But even her willingness to speak so clearly about their flaws lends hope to women like Charlene, who still struggles under the weight of her fifteen-year sentence. The last time I saw Charlene she'd been in a state mental hospital, where she'd been transferred after refusing to eat at Framingham. Remembering this took some of the shine off Dennehy's grand political talk. It had been Christmastime, and for Charlene the secure ward represented a kind of vacation getaway from the crushing sameness of life in prison—an impossibly dark vision, as the hospital was of the kind conjured up in childhood nightmares: huge, brick, Victorian, with row upon row of small, barred windows. It was a change for Charlene at least—the first in more than five years—and the staff were nurses instead of COs, which helped. As well, visiting regulations were less strict, so she could see her little girl, Trinnie, more easily.

It's a cliché, but true nonetheless, to mention here that the amount of money spent on keeping Charlene in Framingham could cover an all-expenses-paid undergraduate degree at Harvard. As it is, she will likely leave the system with no more demonstrable skills than she had when she entered. Denise certainly did—unless an attitude of resilient acceptance counts as a skill. But this Denise earned on her own. Despite, not because of, prison policies and programming.

Patrick was still in lockdown the day Denise was finally released, five years after leaving him with a new TV and a collection of Beanie Babies at her mother-in-law's. It would be another six weeks before he'd be able to join her, she was told, and Denise convinced herself that even this was a good thing. She was luckier than most, she knew. Her mother had spent months preparing a room for her: fresh lilac paint, new clothes in the closet, even a childhood doll on the bed. But adjusting to life on the outside would take time. Perhaps it was best she and Patrick didn't do it together.

Julie certainly found life on the outside difficult at first, even without a child. Her dad's house felt cramped and confining. It wasn't until she moved in with Joel, the farmer's market customer with the Mohawk and motorbike, that she began to unwind. Joel neither drank nor smoked, and the fact that Julie was still clean six months after her release continued to astonish her. Sitting cross-legged in their unheated wood cabin on the edge of a lake, she gushed with the astonished air of a lottery winner about Joel's bike and his friends and the snowmobile he'd recently bought her. His friends called her "the Bandit," she said, giggling. "They treat me real well." It wasn't until I got ready to leave that she grew somber: "Is Denise okay?" she asked, sounding suddenly close to tears. "I think about her all the time, you know. I guess I must miss her. Will you tell her I say hi?"

Denise hadn't been much interested when I passed on Julie's message. I wondered if she thought of her now, on the day of her own release. She said nothing if she did. In a daze she finished loading her stuff into the back of her friend Nicole's pickup truck: a few cardboard boxes; a couple of black plastic garbage bags, and a small, prison-issue, transparent-walled TV. As most women do, she'd given the rest of her stuff to the women she was leaving behind.

A couple of COs gathered to wave her off. One said: "It was a pleasure working with you here, Denise." Then Nicole turned the car on and headed out of the parking lot. Denise found it unnerving, almost frightening, to be back in a car again. Oncoming traffic looked as if it would crush her; curves were impossibly sharp. She clutched the handle above the window and tried to laugh about this. She was free. And she was terrified.

After months of planning, Denise decided to stop first at a once favorite seafood restaurant on the bay near where she used to live, and then to visit a farmer's market where she'd be able to buy the kinds of fresh fruit and vegetables she'd been dreaming of for years. The restaurant went fine, though she was unnerved by the waitress's attentiveness ("What's *her* problem?" she asked, after the young woman stopped by to check that everything was all right). The farmer's market, on the other hand, proved to be too much. Entranced, she wandered down the aisles touching things lightly with the tips of her fingers: plums, grapes, peaches, pears. She picked up an orange, then put it back. A few minutes later she placed two round and perfectly shiny eggplants in a small plastic bag, but then she started to cry and said she had to leave—such abundance was making her panic. Outside she relaxed a little. Or pretended to. The store kept a herd of buffalo in the field next door, and their long black tongues made her laugh. "I used to bring Patrick here," she said. "Before." Then again she started to cry.

It was hard to keep scenes like this front and center as I listened to Dennehy talk enthusiastically about classification and "best practice" and revamped management systems. Hard not to forget it all came back down to women like Denise in the end. It was what Jeanne Woodford most worried about when she was asked to take over California's system. She was excited by the power she would wield as the head of the department, but "I don't want to forget that this is about people," she said. "About humanity."

It's too soon to say how Dennehy's period in office will affect the lives of women at MCI-Framingham. Perhaps the combination of a reform-minded commissioner, department scandal, and budget shortfalls might really come to affect the day-to-day life of women like Charlene and Carmen. As far as Denise is concerned, though, it's no longer relevant. The damage has already been done. It's time now for her to start picking up the pieces. In the pickup truck that day, Nicole slowed down as a light turned from green to orange to red. As the truck came to halt, a man in the next car grinned at Denise, who was back to smiling madly at everything, perpetually astonished. "Hello," he said, friendly enough. "You look happy."

"Yeah!" Denise agreed cheerfully. "Happy enough to have just got out of jail?"

"Yeah!" the man said. And then more tentatively added, "Did you? . . . Just get out of jail, I mean?"

"Yup! I sure did!" Denise said, and she and Nicole burst out laughing and drove away, past the green light on the way to the ocean.

Acknowledgments

I would like to thank the Open Society Institute, the Fund for Investigative Journalism, and Radcliffe Institute's Bunting Fellowship, which provided me with much needed time, money, and support during the writing of this book. My agent, Barney Karpfinger, and editor, Ileene Smith, were both courageous supporters from the beginning—and it would literally never have begun without John Reinstein and Mark Batten, whose legal acumen gained me access to MCI-Framingham in the first place. The powerful work of Estelle Freedman opened similar doors into Framingham's history.

The real truth, though, is that this book should be listed as written by Cristina Rathbone and friends. Leah Cohen, Annie Rogers, and Ide O'Carroll all guided me through the dark panic of early drafts with patience and care. Michael Attias brought me with inspired generosity to its close. I could not have written this book without them. Jane O'Connor, Cameron MacDonald, Lisa Osborn, Nina Calabresi and Bob Oldshoe, Lori Taylor, John Moukad, Sue Singer, Jonathan Maury, and my mother, Margarita Sanchez, all provided love and care when I needed it most. Impossible not to thank Meg Turner here too, and Margaret Bullitt-Jonas, whose passions for life—real life—have so helped me to deepen my own. My deepest gratitude, of course, goes to the women of MCI-Framingham, especially "Denise," "Julie," "Charlene," and "Carmen." Their courage, humor, and grace I have only managed to approximate here—even with as much help as all this.

ABOUT THE AUTHOR

CRISTINA RATHBONE has written for numerous magazines and newspapers, including the New York *Daily News* and *The Miami Herald*. Her last book, *On the Outside Looking In: A Year in an Inner-City High School*, was a finalist for the *Los Angeles Times* Book Prize and was selected as one of the best books of the year by the New York Public Library. She lives in Jamaica Plain, Massachusetts, with her two young children.

ABOUT THE TYPE

This book was set in Plantin. A Classic roman typeface named after the famous sixteenth-century printer, Plantin was designed in 1913 by Robert Granjon for the monotype system. Its even strokes and lack of contrast make it a highly legible face. It was, later, the typeface from which Times New Roman was modeled.

WITHDRAWN